B/T

Rainbow Bridge
to Monument Valley

Rainbow Bridge to Monument Valley

Making the Modern Old West

Thomas J. Harvey

University of Oklahoma Press : Norman

Also by Thomas J. Harvey
(co-ed.) *Imagining the Big Open: Nature, Identity, and Play
in the New West* (Salt Lake City, 2003)

Library of Congress Cataloging-in-Publication Data

Harvey, Thomas J., 1955–
    Rainbow Bridge to Monument Valley : making the modern Old West /
Thomas J. Harvey.
        p.   cm.
    Includes bibliographical references and index.
    ISBN 978-0-8061-4190-9 (hardcover : alk. paper)   1. Colorado Plateau—
History.   2. Landscapes—Colorado Plateau.   3. Navajo Indians—Colorado
Plateau.   4. West (U.S.)—In popular culture.   5. West (U.S.)—Civilization.
6. Rainbow Bridge National Monument (Utah)—History.   7. Monument Val-
ley (Ariz. and Utah)—History.   I. Title.
    F788.H37 2011
    979.1'3—dc22

                                                                    2011013166

The paper in this book meets the guidelines for permanence and durability of
the Committee on Production Guidelines for Book Longevity of the Council
on Library Resources, Inc. ∞

Copyright © 2011 by Thomas J. Harvey. Published by the University of Oklahoma Press, Norman, Publishing Division of the University. Manufactured in
the U.S.A.

1 2 3 4 5 6 7 8 9 10

This desert solitude was the storehouse of unlived years, the hush of the world at the hour of its creation.

Zane Grey, *Captives of the Desert*

Contents

Illustrations

Acknowledgments

For making this book possible, I wish first of all to thank the members of my graduate committee at the University of Utah. Mentor and friend Bob Goldberg, who chaired the committee, provided insights and kept me on track to complete my dissertation, which turned out to be a good first draft of this book thanks to his patient but firm hand. Rebecca Horn, Eric Hinderaker, J. C. Mutchler, and Steve Tatum, the other members, all guided my development as a historian and the thinking that is behind this book. Dorothee Kocks's class and ideas also were an important contribution. My fellow classmates and friends Liza Nicholas and Elaine Bapis brought me new ways of thinking about history and helped walk me through the thicket of theory that informs it. Archivists of the collections I cite were without exception efficient and helpful in providing me materials. Ann Poore read a draft thoroughly and offered important suggestions on writing, style, and grammar. Editor Matt Bokovoy in the beginning and then Jay Dew of the University of Oklahoma Press expressed enthusiasm and unwavering support for this book. The readers for the press, Andrew Gulliford of Fort Lewis College and Carter Jones Meyer of Ramapo College of New Jersey, were gentle with their criticisms and insightful in their suggested changes, which only made the final manuscript better. I honor the continued presence of my father in this book even though he left the world too soon to see it. My mother continues with the steadying force of her love and influence. My brothers and sister also are foundations of love and strength. My daughter, Donna, came late on the scene but provides daily laughter and reminds me how much fun life can be. My wife, Joanie, nurtured me through this with advice, encouragement, love, and financial help. To her I owe the biggest thanks of all.

UTAH

● Kanab

Glen Canyon Dam

ARIZONA

● Fredonia

Paria R.

Lee's Ferry

Kanab Ck.

Snake Gulch

Colorado River

Thunder River

GRAND CANYON

Little Colorado

to Flagstaff

0   50 miles

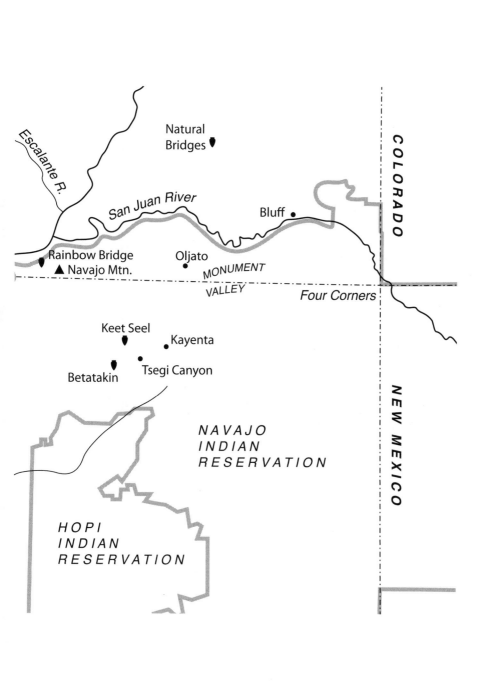

Rainbow Bridge
to Monument Valley

Introduction

An American Occidentalism: The Archaeology of a Space

In 1922, after he left Princeton at age seventeen because of ill health, Clyde Kluckhohn developed what he called an "obsessive fascination" with the Southwest. In the summer of 1923, Kluckhohn took a trip to the border region of southern Utah and northern Arizona, enticed by what he had read and seen in books, magazines, and movies, and through boyhood experiences. Kluckhohn's Holy Grail was Rainbow Bridge, then believed to be the world's longest natural stone arch spanning a waterway. The huge red sandstone arch stood in remote, rugged southern Utah, an area Kluckhohn characterized as "the last stronghold of Virgin Nature!"

After that trip and during the next three years at the University of Wisconsin, thoughts of that trip stayed with Kluckhohn—"a photograph in a magazine casually picked up would fan to flame the smoldering fires of memory, or a phrase in a book would catalyze the processes of the imagination, while I hardly dared go to a 'western' film lest I see too vividly those beckoning grey heights." Finally, a friend pointed out an article in *National Geographic* about thousands of unmapped square miles in southern Utah. The friend suggested they "pull a Grey" (after the author Zane Grey) and heed the "imperative call to adventure" beckoning from the Utah frontier. They embarked on their adventure with the same lust for discovery that had permeated their childhood. "We have heard of the grasshopper plague from grandfather," Kluckhohn wrote, "have played 'Cowboy and Indian,' have had Boy Scout epochs, have lived and dreamed *The Last of the Mohicans* as well as Bar X Bill's Revenge." Kluckhohn yearned for the outdoors and a physically demanding life, an antidote for his ailing middle-class body. All of that, Kluckhohn wrote, was "why the Utah Wilderness spoke to my partner and me."[1]

Now, skip ahead to 2005. A television commercial begins with a view of a mystical landscape in which tall spires and mesas of stone rise straight out of the ground bathed in bright sunlight through wisps of fog and rapidly moving clouds. A young Anglo man dressed in a white tank top and loose-fitting pants faces a soaring tower of stone on which is superimposed the image of a U.S. Marine in dress uniform. He begins to climb without equipment. About halfway up, the climber suddenly slips, loosened rocks tumble earthward, and he finds himself dangling by one hand hundreds of feet in the air. With an actor's resolve, he brings his free hand back to grab the rock, then swings his legs under him and continues to climb. The Iwo Jima scene of a U.S. flag being planted by a group of Marines during World War II is superimposed on the rock wall. The young man reaches the top. A deep-throated narrator intones: "The passage is intense. But if you complete the journey, you will find your destiny among the world's greatest warriors."

"The Climb," as the commercial was titled, was released to U.S. theaters on February 23, 2002, the anniversary of the famous Iwo Jima flag raising. Its target audience was young American males of the age for recruiting into the Marine Corps. The location where it was filmed was Monument Valley, which straddles the Utah-Arizona border on the Navajo Nation.

As the crow flies, Rainbow Bridge and Monument Valley are within forty-five miles or so of each other, part of the same area of the Colorado River Plateau, an eroded high-altitude desert of exposed rocks, deep canyons, mesas, and exotic stone formations. Though Kluckhohn's adventures and the Marines recruiting commercial are separated by some eighty years, the area they have in common has continually meant something in American culture. Most viewers of the Marines commercial likely didn't know its name, but they knew it. They had seen it in the vast array of images from television commercials for automobiles, sport utility vehicles, and other products. If they were older, they might remember it as the setting for Western movies. Monument Valley became the iconic image of the American West in popular culture during the twentieth century, and by the beginning of the twenty-first century it was, in the eyes of some, one of the great representative spaces of America itself.

This book is the story of how in the late nineteenth and through most of the twentieth century two cultures produced spaces and thus created meaning out of this area of the Colorado Plateau along the borders of Utah and Arizona, from Rainbow Bridge east to Monument valley, from the Glen Canyon of the Colorado River south to the north rim of the Grand Canyon. While most history seeks to describe changes over time, our lives and cultures also unfold in space, areas real or imagined that extend from our bodies. Spaces are the products of the societies in which those bodies are embedded. Social, economic, and cultural conditions produce space, give meaning to it, and determine not only how we use, see, and experience it, but also how we contest it. Thus, the rivers, canyons, deserts, mesas, and other landforms of the Utah-Arizona border country were not merely silent witnesses to human dramas unfolding within them. Rather, the perceptions and experiences and their use and reproduction through print or film were products of a particular society at a certain moment in time.[2]

The physical and imagined landscape of the Navajo grew out of that group's social organization, cultural imperatives, and local environmental and historical circumstances. Then, modern Anglo-Americans, with little or no regard for the area's natives, produced other spaces that owed their meanings to a different society and culture. There, Anglo-Americans went to experience and consume the space in accord with their own gnawing needs, the sense that their modern lives were somehow inauthentic and unmoored, awash in a constantly changing world as the United States went from a largely rural society to an urban, industrial one and then coped with the social, cultural, and historical phenomena of the twentieth century.

What is remarkable about Clyde Kluckhohn's two books of his adventures in the Utah-Arizona border country in the early twentieth century is how starkly they lay out the ways and means that modern America produced the space that is the subject of this story. It was boyhood experiences and what Kluckhohn read in books, magazines, and saw in movies that enticed him to visit. His middle-class background afforded him the leisure of travel, of putting his body in this area where he could use his received culture and senses to experience and then to narrate it.

So here is the formula of how modern America created new spaces and how it then experienced and reproduced them. Kluckhohn started with words and images from mass media and boyhood experiences that formed certain ideas about this space, its characteristics and meanings. Then, through the medium of money, he physically visited and experienced it through those words and images he packed with him from American culture, what are called "discourses." In turn, Kluckhohn, because of his education and social standing, had the power to circulate the ideas and images to a new audience in books, *To the Foot of the Rainbow* (1927) and *Beyond the Rainbow* (1933). Others followed his footsteps. Thus this space also became text and images that reproduced themselves in the minds and experiences of those who read, saw, and visited.

Kluckhohn evoked the discourses of the science of geology, the American Frontier (he capitalized it), the romanticism of the ruins of ancient Native civilizations, virgin nature, the popular culture frontier of James Fenimore Cooper, Zane Grey, and Western movies, as well as a modern fascination with the Native peoples who inhabited the region. Then, while he was actually there on horseback on remote trails, he encountered some of those who had created the words and images that attracted him in the first place. Along the trail to Rainbow Bridge, Kluckhohn met Zane Grey in a party with the movie producer Jesse Lasky and guide John Wetherill, who had packed in the 1909 party that "discovered" Rainbow Bridge. On his way to the Grand Canyon at the end of that first trip, Kluckhohn met tourists being shepherded about by the Fred Harvey Company, the leading commercial force in Southwest tourism, and a caravan hauling the cast and equipment of a movie company on its way to film Grey's *The Heritage of the Desert,* produced by Lasky. Thus, discourses, social circumstances, and people's physical presence interacted to produce this space.

These practices and discourses—the way we talk about and convey information that describes our world, narrates experiences, and regulates conduct, that tells us what is useful, relevant, or true at any given time—form an American Occidentalism.[3] The phrase is a play on the book *Orientalism* in which author Edward Said identified persistent themes in academia, government policies, and popular culture that guided European and American interactions with the Middle East and Far East. That book and a subsequent one detailed, in Said's words, "the invention and construction of a geographical space called the Orient."[4] Others have identified the Southwest as America's Orient and remarked upon a process similar to Said's Orientalism.[5] Using the term "American Occidentalism," however, permits the discourses and practices that produced the twentieth-century Southwest as an exotic space juxtaposed to modern urban life to be identified within their particular cultural context and historical moment. Like Said's Orientalists, American Occidentalists were, as they moved through Native spaces, engaged in a form of imperialism. Yet, the other aspect of this Occidentalism was that it exposed a hollow longing, an unremembered past, an emptiness at the heart of the very culture that modernization had helped to produce.

Behind the words and images of Anglo-Americans like Clyde Kluckhohn was the process of modernization. The appearance of tightly controlled corporate organizations as a new phase of industrialization toward the end of the nineteenth century, along with accelerated urbanization and the systematic organization of social life to serve capitalist production practices, unleashed deep changes in American culture that forged new ways of living in, looking at, depicting, and experiencing the world. The most salient feature of this modernization was its motor of "creative destruction," the environment of constant change in social and economic life that throws out the old and creates all anew—over and over again.[6]

Indeed, some historians describe modernization not in terms of development but rather, as one writes, "the social experience of a state of flux, a constant process of tearing down and building up that is rife with internal contradictions." Buildings were razed and replaced, whole companies dissolved in the onslaught of competition, urban areas expanded into what had been farms. Highways displaced neighborhoods. New products appeared as older ones disappeared. Technologies such as electricity or the internal combustion engine rapidly changed society. Historians looked to produce new explanations of historic events or eras. Human relationships dissolved, and others formed. Social movements rose and fell. Fashions were just that, fashionable yesterday but not today. This experience stresses the new, in which yesterday's modern is the past of today, and today must become the past to retain modernity as the "ever new." Modernity is "permanent transition." A definition of modernity is simply the constant production of the new.[7]

This dynamic process of the production of the new created great choices for those who were in a position to reap its harvests. In the United States, the market economy, the engine of modernization, over decades produced a growing middle class and offered it numerous options. "The market revolution," writes historian Daniel Walker Howe, "provided the opportunity for people to make choices on a scale previously unparalleled: choices of goods to consume, of occupations to follow, educational choices, choices of lifestyles and identities."[8] Modern people could be teachers, doctors, carpenters, archaeologists, and consumers of a whole variety of goods and experiences. Urbanization produced efficient systems of production and distribution, rising standards of comfort, and a rapid increase in the circulation of knowledge. Americans spoke of the grand story of modernization as "progress."[9]

Yet, while a great producer of wealth, tremendously dynamic, and culturally exciting, modernization led some caught in its grasp to feel that something hollow lay at its core. The scientific method provided the spark for industrialization, but science also secularized society. In the West, Darwin's evolution undermined the authority of the Bible to explain the world and its formation and left the modern American a spiritual life drained of religious mystery and wonder without the strict moral authority of an earlier Christianity.

"Lacking spiritual ballast," the historian T. J. Jackson Lears writes, "bourgeois culture entered what Nietzsche had called a 'weightless' period." American life, it seemed, had become overcivilized, weightless, and empty. "It appears," writes Marshall Berman in his description of modernity, "that the very process of development, even as it transformed the wasteland into a thriving physical and social space, recreates the wasteland inside of the developer himself."[10]

Modern life seemed inauthentic or artificial because of its inherent abstraction that has most people no longer participating in the production of their food, energy, clothing, shelter, and other necessities of human life. Clothing, food, shoes, knickknacks, and even art were mechanically reproduced and available on a massive scale, leaving the question of what was original, real, or authentic in an era of mass production.[11] For moderns, reality and authenticity were not found in their own urban worlds and time but in other spaces, historical periods, and cultures. Modern men and women sought out or, more accurately, created "primitive" peoples, experiences, landscapes, objects, and regions that fostered what supposedly were simpler, more primitive, and, therefore, authentic ways of life. In "primitive" peoples, landscapes, and objects, middle- and upper-class Americans created an authenticity they felt absent in their modern world. Indeed, one definition of modernism, the social and cultural forms of modernization, is the search for the authentic as something real, traditional, and organic as contrasted to the mass-produced, ever-changing world of contemporary life.[12]

By the turn of the twentieth century, much of the American West still was seen as open, natural space when contrasted to crowded Eastern cities. As such, the West became the museum of American primitivism, its lack of modern development an invitation to reimagine it as the site of an American past in which certain values might still hold sway beyond the reach of modernization and in which primitive landscapes and peoples could still be "discovered." With the closing of the frontier, modern American society made the West wild, a space of still-present wilderness and exotic places and peoples.[13]

The Southwest, with its hot deserts and difficult terrain, was not initially seen as part of the favored western landscape of mountains and seashores, like Europe's Alps and beaches. Even in the early 1880s, tourists disparaged its aesthetic qualities. By the end of the century, however, it was not so much Europe against which Americans measured themselves and their cultural landscape, but rather the modern world.[14] Anglo-Americans began to see the Southwest as a culturally valuable land. Key elements were the physical comforts of the new railroads and hotels and the sense that the region was ancient and still primitive.

The exposed land forms created over millennia, the presence of Indians still living in traditional ways, and the location of ruins of now-vanished ancient races contributed to this sense of the Southwest as a storehouse of the past and, therefore, primitive and authentic. Through the scientific discourses of archaeology and anthropology, Americans discovered in the region a history useful to their need of a national narrative and helped them chart progress from the past to the present. Geology enabled them to see the Southwest as an area of deep time and scientific interest, of history written in rocks.[15]

Like perhaps nowhere else in the United States, the geographical and social space of the Utah-Arizona border region particularly lent itself as a "blank" space on which these discourses could be animated. Its stark desert, deep canyons, spectacular land forms, and the Navajo occupation of much of it made this land remote, hard to reach, and particularly resistant to the encroachments of modern development. American Occidentalism found this space of Navajo culture and social power useful and willed a blankness on which to produce modern spaces.

In this process of creating and reproducing a landscape, certain meanings and images were adopted, and others were excluded. What Clyde Kluckhohn largely missed in his books about his 1920s visits to the Utah-Arizona border region was that the space he was evoking and experiencing through the texts of modern America also was Navajo. Kluckhohn later went on to become a noted anthropologist whose work focused mostly on the Navajo. But the notion that the celebration of an Anglo-American landscape was of an imperial nature did not influence the direction of the young Kluckhohn's books.

The Navajo landscape has a story of its own. In some respects, the process through which that space was created was the same as that of modern America. Stories intersected with environment, bodies, and social organization to make a space. Through time, Navajos developed a mythology whose main narrative is a story of emergence from other worlds into the present one. That story, in effect, mapped Navajo geography and linked the culture to the land that the Navajo physically occupied and used to sustain themselves and their society. Navajos traditionally read and experienced the landscape through tribal mythology and clan and family stories. The Navajo landscape made them Navajos. By the first half of the nineteenth century, Navajos had arrived in the Utah-Arizona border region. Chapter 1 discusses how, toward the end of the century, historical circumstances helped forge a new Navajo place at Rainbow Bridge.

In 1909, University of Utah archaeologist Byron Cummings and U.S. government surveyor William Boone Douglass led an expedition to Rainbow Bridge. They and their party were guided by trader John Wetherill of Oljato, Utah, and natives of the area. Soon, Cummings and Douglass began a long dispute over which of them was the actual discoverer of Rainbow Bridge. In doing so, they ignored the arch as a cultural space of the Navajos and also the evidence that they weren't even the first Anglo-Americans to see it. However, through newspaper accounts and magazine articles they were the first to publicize the find to a wide audience. In claiming the mantle of discoverers, Cummings and Douglass followed the template of European explorers, scientists, and adventurers who roamed the earth and claimed discoveries in the name of Western knowledge. Yet, the pair also acted within early-twentieth-century American culture. They followed the popular culture footsteps of historical figures such as Daniel Boone and other explorers and pioneers who battled harsh conditions and Indians to bring the American West into Anglo-American space. Chapter 2 looks at the social and cultural aspects at play in the "discovery" of Rainbow Bridge.

A former dentist struggling to make a living as a writer, Zane Grey arrived in the Utah-Arizona border country in 1907 to write about and photograph the capture of mountain lions. He returned the next year and from his experiences wrote *Heritage of the Desert,* the book that launched his career as a writer of Western novels. Grey was back in 1911 and rode horseback to Monument Valley and the ruins of Navajo National Monument. After that trip he wrote *Riders of the Purple Sage,* his most famous novel. In 1913, John Wetherill guided Grey to Rainbow Bridge, out of which came *The Rainbow Trail.* Later, Grey wrote *The Vanishing American* and other novels set in the area. Grey's stories fashioned Rainbow Bridge as a place to hold off the aspects of modernity that challenged his masculinity. Grey's settings provided a haven from modernity's challenges to gender roles and a site where the masculine imperative to adventure and control of female sexuality

Zane Grey in Monument Valley. Grey used Monument Valley as the setting for at least three of his influential Western novels, including *The Vanishing American* (1925), which also was made into a movie of the same name. (Reproduced with permission of the Ohio Historical Society.)

could be enacted. Chapter 3 shows how Grey helped create the modern space of the popular culture Old West and placed its heart in the Utah-Arizona border country.

It was, however, film director John Ford who made the Monument Valley an iconic site of a mythical America and a modern destination for American and European tourists. Ford arrived in 1938 to film *Stagecoach,* the movie that made John Wayne a star. After World War II, Ford returned six more times to make Westerns, among them *The Searchers,* perhaps his greatest work. Ford used Monument Valley as a mythical setting of a nationalist story of the European encounter with the American wilderness to resolve contemporary questions of race, sexuality, ethnicity, and class. Chapter 4 shows how Ford produced Monument Valley as the primitive space of a mythical American past in which he sought to meet the challenges of the Depression, World War II, the Cold War, and the racism inherent in American history.

In the 1950s, David Brower, the new executive director of the Sierra Club, was alarmed by a proposal to build a dam along a tributary of the Colorado River in Dinosaur National Monument in Colorado.

Brower and others who sought to preserve some of the remaining American wild lands negotiated an agreement that scuttled the Dinosaur dam but allowed the Bureau of Reclamation to build the Glen Canyon Dam downstream on the Colorado River as long as its waters did not intrude upon Rainbow Bridge National Monument. However, when Brower and other members of the Sierra Club rafted down Glen Canyon, they discovered a natural wonderland. The deal that the club and others negotiated that allowed Glen Canyon to disappear under the dam's waters became a lasting lament of the wilderness movement. When Congress failed to appropriate funds to protect Rainbow Bridge, wilderness groups filed a federal lawsuit.

Chapter 5 argues that the "nature" that wilderness advocates sought to protect at Rainbow Bridge was a notion that arose from the industrialization and urbanization that created modern America. In the eyes of Brower and like-minded wilderness advocates, Glen Canyon became the lost Cathedral of American Nature, and Rainbow Bridge its remnant representative space.

This American Occidentalism—the discourses of a wild nature being drowned by modernization, the Wild West, the nationalist mythology of the encounter with the wilderness, the Old West of popular culture, the sciences of archaeology and geology, and "primitive" Natives—also helped to produce the Utah-Arizona borderland as a space for consumption. T. J. Jackson Lears asserts that antimodernism represented a longing for psychic harmony that engendered a desire for self-fulfillment. So instead of a lasting and effective critique or alternative to industrialization and urbanization, antimodernism helped to ease Americans into an emerging economy of consumption that fed their desire for self-fulfillment.[16]

John and Louisa Wetherill proved to be remarkable brokers for the discourses that enticed Americans to visit the remote area of the Utah-Arizona border country in the first decades of the twentieth century. Louisa Wetherill's command of the Navajo language and her anthropological interest in Navajo culture were key to their success in playing host to Americans who wished to experience the landscape through the discourses of archaeology or anthropology or as they had seen and read of it in books, magazines, photographs, and movies. Chapter 6 also shows how Monument Valley gradually replaced Rainbow Bridge as the iconic scenic space of the region. Harry and Leona ("Mike") Goulding, a ranch couple from southwestern Colorado, arrived to start a trading post in Monument Valley in 1925 in a car and a truck, then symbolic of the changes occurring in America. Automobiles altered the nature of tourism in the area. With improved roads after World War II, the Gouldings were ready to receive modern tourists. Harry Goulding's success depended upon his ability to entice local Navajos to pose for photographs in ways that Anglo-Americans had come to expect, as "primitive" people still untainted by the modern world.

For many Navajos, the modern came in the form of wage labor and the trading post, which provided access to foods and goods not available previously but at the cost of altering traditional economic practices. Navajos themselves spoke in terms of modern and traditional. Navajos blended the modern and its new economic practices and access to goods in ways that made sense to them.[17] At Rainbow Bridge and at Monument Valley, tourism brought modern practices but also was a source of conflict over control, opportunity, and tradition. With a tribal park at Monument Valley, Navajos too helped to modernize their landscape.

By the last half of the twentieth century, the Utah-Arizona border region was a distinctive space in American culture. It has remained so to some extent up to today. This space was, in Zane Grey's phrase, the storehouse of unlived years. It held the unremembered past of modern Anglo-Americans, that vague feeling that there once had existed a place where men, women, and objects were authentic and close to the earth and where nature was sublime—at once alive, magnificent, and threatening. This storehouse was the repository of discourses and practices that spoke of the comforts and the displacements of modern American life. Yet the land remained Navajo even as the residents themselves negotiated with the modern.

CHAPTER ONE

Send Out a Rainbow

Making Rainbow Bridge a Navajo Place

Sometime in the mid- to late nineteenth century, a Navajo named Jayi
Begay was looking for stray horses along the slopes of Navajo Mountain just north of the present-day Utah-Arizona border when he came
across a huge natural stone arch. Navajos credit Begay, later known as
One Eyed Man of the Salt Clan and Blind Salt Clansman, as the first
among them to come upon the arch. The Navajos called the formation Tse Naniáhi ("Rock Spans"). In English, it became known as
Rainbow Bridge in the early twentieth century for its shape.[1] Decades
earlier, Begay would not have known that what he had found would
in the next century be known (inaccurately) as the world's longest
natural stone arch spanning a waterway. That it would be compared in
size to other such geological features worldwide likely would not have
been his concern. Instead, he led others to the rock formation or told
them about it. Tse Naniáhi then became a local Navajo place, associated with the grand myths that produced Navajo culture and their
tribal space. If "space" is the larger, dynamic area, both physical and
representative, produced by a society, "place" is a fixed entity created
within that space. So a specific Navajo place is produced within the
context of the Navajo world that includes their means of livelihood
and their social and cultural practices, including the central emergence
mythology.[2]

As part of this place making, local Navajos created a prayer or song that helped give meaning to Tse Naniáhi and made it Navajo. The first stanza of the prayer, probably recorded and translated in the 1920s, is:

Mountain where the head of the War-God rests.
Dark wind, beautiful chief, from the tips of your fingers a rain-
    bow send out,
By which let me walk and have life.
Black clouds, black clouds, make for me shoes,
With which to walk and have life.
Black clouds are my leggings;
A black cloud is my robe:
A black cloud is my headband.
Black clouds, go before me; make it dark; let it rain peacefully
    before me.
Before me come much rain to make the white corn grow and
    ripen,
That it may be peaceful before me, that it may be peaceful
    before me.
All is peace, all is peace.[3]

The prayer permitted Navajos to walk beneath the arch without violating the harmony of the special place. It was also used by sing-ers who made pilgrimages to it and performed ceremonies seeking to harmonize their world. The mountain of which the prayer speaks is Navajo Mountain, associated by locals with the tribe's emergence myth, which narrates Navajos' appearance from other worlds into this one. The black clouds evoke rain, which is the giver of life when it makes the white corn grow. So the prayer connected Rainbow Bridge to larger Navajo culture and specifically to Navajos' physical needs; the tribe was sustained by scarce rains in the high desert of the Colorado Plateau. Thus their own material needs intermingled with stories that narrated tribal identity to produce Rainbow Bridge as a marker of local Navajo space and culture. Historical events and cultural impera-tives and practices led to the creation of a Navajo place.[4]

Two general stories have been told of the Navajos' arrival in the Southwest and of how Navajos created social and cultural space there.

One story was told by archaeologists and historians, the other found in traditional Navajo mythology. In the first telling, ancestors of the Navajo—Athapaskan peoples, who shared a common language—occupied a region from the Arctic to central Canada from about 3000 B.C. to A.D. 200. Between A.D. 200 and 1100, a group of Athapaskans migrated south, reaching what is now the Four Corners area. At some time, they separated into Navajo and Apache communities, the only Athapaskan speakers in the Southwest.

The time of the Athapaskan arrival has been vigorously debated. One group of researchers suggests that Athapaskans came into the Southwest only a few years prior to Spanish explorer Francisco Vásquez de Coronado's 1541 arrival in present-day New Mexico. Others put the Athapaskan arrival before 1500. The Athapaskans gathered first in an area of the upper San Juan River in northwestern New Mexico, maybe around 1500. They were hunters, gatherers, and farmers.

When Coronado arrived at the Rio Grande in eastern New Mexico, his party met semi-nomadic bison hunters, one group of which were Athapaskan speakers called "Querechos." In 1583, Antonio de Espejo met a group of Querechos near Mount Taylor in present-day New Mexico. When Juan de Oñate colonized New Mexico in 1598, he assigned a priest to the Jemez and all the nearby "Apaches and Cocoyes." The first historical reference to the Navajo people was in 1626 by Father Zárate Salmerón, the Roman Catholic priest at Jemez, who indicated the "Apaches del Nabaxu" lived up the Rio Chama east of the San Juan River. The term may have been the name for an area of cornfields but later came to designate a large region from the Piedra Lumbre Valley on the east to the upper tributaries of the San Juan on the west and also was applied to the people who occupied that area.[5]

Dinétah is the Navajo name for their ancestral homeland, roughly bordered by the Continental Divide on the east, Chaco Canyon to the south, the Animas River to the west, and the present Colorado–New Mexico border to the north. It was here, according to some interpretations of archaeological evidence, that the culture of The Diné ("the people"), first became recognizable around 1500 A.D., with sites showing Navajos subsisting on an economy of hunting, gathering, and agriculture. "If anything," writes the archaeologist Gary M. Brown, "the distinctive constellation of traits that defines the Dinétah phase is interpreted here as the emergence of a local adaptation to the South-western environment by Athapaskan groups."[6]

In Dinétah, some studies have said the Athapaskans probably began the formation of clans and started the process of becoming The Diné, a group recognizable by its production of distinctive material and cultural forms. The earliest Navajo ceremonies, based on stories that narrate The Diné mythical arrival in this world, their description of it, and their place within it, were geographically based in Dinétah. Studies say that the emergence of the Navajo as a distinct ethnic group was forged in the crucible of Spanish rule from many disparate communities but mainly Athapaskan and Puebloan. However, Ronald Towner's more recent book asserts that the Navajos already had formed much of the tribe's distinctive culture before arriving in Dinétah.

The Dinétah phase was followed by what archaeologists label the Gobernador phase, roughly 1700–1775, when Pueblo Indians, fleeing the Spanish reconquest that followed the Pueblo revolt of 1680, lived among the Athapaskans. The Athapaskans adopted some Puebloan ceremonies, created rock art, and acquired European goods. During Dinétah and Gobernador phases Athapaskan peoples acculturated to the Southwest, with their culture grounded in that landscape.[7]

The creation of a culture and production of a Navajo space in the Southwest depended on words, images, and stories of what it means to be Navajo, which also set social norms and placed the culture in a landscape and then narrated it. The Diné emergence story oriented them to the world as it helped produce their space and as it reproduced Navajo culture. Navajo was and remains an oral culture, with myths passed from one generation to another through stories sung or told aloud. The emergence myth itself does not come in a single form and changes over time. Its telling depends on the singer or medicine man and on their geographic location and the time period in which the myth was told. Following is a broad outline of the story, condensed from one told by a Navajo singer named Sandoval in 1928.[8]

It is said that First Man and First Woman, supernatural mist beings who had definite form and would change into the humans and animals we know today, were in the first world, a dark place. Yellow corn was formed in this world along with First Woman. Others present included the Great-Coyote-Who-Was-Formed-in-the-Water along with Coyote, insects, and bats. Because of strife, the beings climbed into the second world and found others living there, including birds. But there was fighting and killing, and so they climbed into the third world.

In this world were various beings and the six mountains. In the east was the Standing Black Sash, known ceremonially as Dawn or White Shell Mountain and later named Blanca Peak, in present-day south-central Colorado. To the south was the Great Mountain or Mountain Tongue, its ceremonial name Bead or Turquoise Mountain, and called today Mount Taylor, in northwest New Mexico. In the west was Abalone Shell Mountain, later called San Francisco Peaks, near Flagstaff, Arizona. In the north was Many Sheep Mountain, its ceremonial name Obsidian Mountain and also known as Hesperus Peak, in the San Juan Mountains of southeastern Colorado. There also was Upper Mountain, also known as Center Place and later as El Huerfano Peak, in northeast New Mexico. The last of the six was Giant Spruce Mountain, also known as Gobernador Knob, in northwest New Mexico.[9] There was, however, no sun in this world, and the mountains and two rivers were not in material form.

The people planted and harvested crops. After harvest, Turquoise Boy went to visit First Woman and First Man and found the two together. Great-Coyote-Who-Was-Formed-in-the-Water told First Man to cross the Male River where it flowed through the Female River, so all the males were on one side and the females on the other side. This continued for four years, with the females satisfying their passions by various means. These sexual aberrations produced giants, monsters, and other creatures. The men killed the females among the mountain sheep, lions, and antelope and were warned they also would be killed. Because of these conditions, the women were finally brought over to the men's side of the river. First Woman became bored, however, and asked Coyote to bring her the two children of the Water Buffalo. After Coyote took the children a flood came, and the various peoples used the big Male Reed to climb into the fourth world with the rising waters behind them. There, the Water Buffalo recovered her children.

However, the fourth world was small, and there was too much water, so the beings emerged into the fifth world, the Earth. Here, First Man and First Woman found a cradle on one of the sacred mountains that contained Changing Woman. She mated with the Sun and gave birth to twins, Monster Slayer and Born for Water. After a trip to their father's house, where they received weapons, the twins slew the monsters that had come to plague the beings of the fifth world. The Navajos were then created, and Changing Woman, the Sun, and the Holy People took other forms.

This emergence story and related tales are told through Navajo ceremonials whose names almost invariably reflect some event, time, and place or beings mentioned in the origin myth. The stories of the emergence myth are associated with different holy people and reinforce and reproduce Diné identity, creating a nationalism and a culture of shared identity, beliefs, and practices. Ceremonies include praying, singing, making sandpaintings, and taking part in rituals. They are mostly performed to bring harmony back into the world for a sick patient or one exposed to bad events or places, or in the case of the Blessingway as a blessing for future life, health, prosperity, or to give thanks for recovering from an illness or for enjoying good fortune. Curing ceremonies are narrated through the emergence myth and are geographically bound, linked physically to specific places through the gathering of ceremonial materials. They bring people back into harmony with the Navajo world. The Enemy Way counteracts foreign influences.[10] Ceremonies bind bodies to space through the materials used. Every aspect of Navajo culture was linked to ceremonials. Navajo scholar Harry Walters asserts that ceremonies, when studied in the chronological order of their historical appearance, tell of the development of Navajo culture from a simple hunter-gatherer, patriarchal society to a complex, agricultural-pastoral, and matriarchal society. "Navajo ceremonies are Navajo history," he writes.[11]

Yet they also are history because they produce the landscape of Navajo life. It was in Dinétah where Changing Woman's birth and the twins' battles with the monsters primarily took place. In one version of the emergence myth, for example, the Sun, as a test of the twins' claim to be his offspring, asked them to point out their home. Monster Slayer looked down at the earth and became the four sacred mountains. The Pueblo War, described in the ceremonies known as the Enemy Way, Mountain Way, and Beauty Way, occurs later in areas

This Charles Kelly photo shows Navajos butchering a cow for a Squaw Dance celebration in Monument Valley. (Used by permission, Utah State Historical Society, all rights reserved.)

as far west as the Bears Ears, Ute Mountain, and the Abajo Mountains in Utah, and Canyon de Chelly and Round Rock in Arizona. Leland Wyman writes: "The geographical details of the long journeys of the protagonists of the myths almost literally bound the Navaho country; at least they state its landmarks."[12]

The stories and the landmarks they name also served as a kind of local knowledge, a form of mapping. Navajo stories, Wyman says, are full of detailed geographic information. "To a people who did not write, they served as an equivalent of our map, and they guide the Navajo to sites for hunting and for gathering foods, ceremonial plants, minerals, and other objects used in ritual."[13]

The mountains kept Navajo travelers and hunters oriented. Stories of places and events allowed them to avoid dangerous locations. In one version of the Deer Hunting Way the hero completes two journeys circling the Navajo world, naming many of the same places each time, with this oral tradition perhaps serving to claim the land.[14] The stories and ceremonies locate Navajos in a specific geography and make the geography the collective nation itself. A landmark can locate the territory of a clan or group of families, or The Diné as a nation.

To map the land base of the Navajo Nation as a whole, Navajos commonly mentioned the four sacred mountains associated with the cardinal directions and the outer limits of tribal territory, often together with the two other mountains in their midst, the birthplace and home of Changing Woman. These mountains also symbolize the largest social unit in preconquest times, the tribe. The sacred mountains define the national homeland and the social unit of The Diné.[15] Naol Nishi, a Winslow, Arizona, Navajo born about 1870, gave an interview in 1961 in which he explained how these mountains border Navajo country. He told of being asked at a tribal meeting about a plan to divide the reservation into eighteen administrative districts:

> I then stated that the country bounded by these mountains was where I live. Navajos were raised and created there and whatever placed them there told them they were to live within there and these mountains are sacred. Now the Navajos feel and say that these mountains are sacred and offer prayers to these mountains. Even though the reservation is divided into 18 districts, it won't change the traditions wherein they were named.[16]

The mountains house supernatural beings of the emergence stories and are pillars holding up the sky. For example, Sisnaajiní (Dawn or White Shell Mountain) in south-central Colorado was the first sacred mountain created by First Man and First Woman in the upper world. It is the property of the Talking God, and it is he who placed animals, plants, and other things upon it.[17] The name Sisnaajiní fixes the mountain within the Navajo world, associating it with stories, history, and a particular culture. Being known as Blanca Peak connects it to a different set of associations and another space.

These mountains and other Navajo places are often referred to as "sacred" in English. Anthropologist Keith Basso, however, cautions against applying the English concept of sacredness to American Indian lands. He points out that the Western Apache language does not have words that correspond precisely to the English words "sacred" and "holy."[18] And though Klara Bonsack Kelley and Harris Francis use the word "sacred" in the title of their book, *Navajo Sacred Places,* they too caution against the suggestion that some places are more significant than others. Rather, they write, "A place is usually important because it is part of a larger landscape constituted by a story, customary activities, or both."

Therefore, the use of the word "sacred" to describe a Navajo site says more about the modern division of some social and cultural discourses as "religion" and others as "science" than it does about the Navajo view of a world, in which religion and other forms of knowledge were within an organic whole.

Louise Lamphere also has cautioned against applying modern divisions to traditional Navajo worldviews. While Western society has divided nature and culture as separate concepts, Lamphere sees no such distinction among traditional Navajos. Instead, the Navajo world is a fusion of natural, supernatural, and human or social elements. Editha L. Watson defines Navajo sacred places as those "where Divinity is closest" and as any "legendary site."[19]

Navajo myths and ceremonies also produce a space of gender relations. Though scholars debate the time of its appearance, a matrilineal culture emerged among the Navajos either before or after their arrival in the Southwest, likely coinciding with the introduction of agriculture by 1600. Women owned a couple's land and property, and both they and kinship descent were passed down through the mother's biological offspring. Men became more powerful after 1770, when drought and intensified warfare, as well as the availability of sheep from the Spanish, pushed Navajos into an economy based largely on pastoralism. The society remained matrilineal, but its mythological practices still gave males important duties and positions.[20]

Even the traditional Navajo dwelling was constructed and used in accord with beliefs expressed through the tribal mythology, including that of gender roles. The hogan, a family residence traditionally made of wood and mud, was constructed in accordance with dictates from the Blessingway, the central emergence tale. Hogans are linked spatially to the sacred mountains.[21] They are to face east, and one is to walk around inside the hogan to the left when entering because that is the direction of the sun through the sky. During ceremonies that take place in hogans, men are seated to the left (when entering from the east), or the south side, with the singer seated on the west end of the men's side. Women are seated to the right, or north, with the person who is the object of the ceremony to the west of the women's side.

"Thus," wrote Edith S. Harrison in her dissertation on Navajo gender roles, "spatial orientation of women . . . conforms with dictates organizing the modality of proper cosmic order." The north is associated with danger, the south with safety and comfort. Males sit in safety but face danger, whereas females are amid danger but face the safety of the south, perhaps reflecting the ambivalence of a pastoral economy within a matrilineal society. Through the hogan ceremonials, Navajo space, in accord with mythology, also narrates aspects of gender relations.[22]

So it was that the Athapaskans created a new space for themselves and in the process became The Diné. Out of the arid lands with its mountains, red rocks, mesas, and desert, The Diné produced a space for the construction and reproduction of Navajo culture. The space was made from historical and material circumstances and was narrated as the time of the past found in the present. Emergence stories bind Navajos to the land and the land to the Navajos. Names of geographical features and their stories merge the Navajo past to the present. Through ceremonies that evoke time and space, the emergence story links Navajos in a physical and metaphysical geography. It obeys and enforces cultural norms and social relations. In the process, a Diné space is produced.

Beginning about 1716, Ute and Comanche raids likely forced a change in Navajo architectural, settlement, and subsistence patterns, eventually leading to abandonment of Dinétah by the 1750s and Navajo expansion beyond the original homeland.[23] Some scholars argue for occupation by Navajos in the Black Mesa area south of the present Arizona border with Utah by the early 1700s and in the Grand Canyon region sometime during the eighteenth century. A Mexican expedition was chasing Navajos north of Black Mesa in 1823. Navajos were herding in the Navajo Mountain area and associating with the San Juan Band of the Paiutes by the early nineteenth century. Most interpretations of historical and archaeological evidence have the Navajos migrating into the Grand Canyon area by mid-nineteenth century. Navajos, Paiutes, and Utes traded and had various conflicts in the area of southern Utah and northern Arizona during the late nineteenth century, a period of intense cultural interactions, dislocations, and conflict.[24]

Intersocietal conflict was the historical context for local Navajos who found and made Rainbow Bridge a Navajo place. Clashes with Anglo-Americans culminated in 1863 when Colonel Kit Carson led U.S. soldiers in a campaign against the Navajos. The objective was to force their surrender by depriving them of economic resources by destroying crops and livestock. The campaign culminated with the Long Walk, in which thousands of Navajos were forced to march to Bosque Redondo at Fort Sumner, 180 miles southeast of Santa Fe. Eventually, some eight thousand were held captive there. Many others starved to death or died of disease on their way to the fort.[25]

Some bands of Navajos avoided the march, however, particularly those from the more remote parts of their homeland near the Grand Canyon, at Black Mesa, north of the San Juan River, and in the Navajo Mountain area. One Navajo who would successfully evade the Army, Hoskaninni, was born in the 1820s in the Kayenta area south of Monument Valley. He was in his thirties at the time of the Carson campaign. When troops approached, he fled to the Navajo Mountain region with a group of seventeen people, including his wife and her two sisters (who also became his wives); twenty sheep; at least one horse; and an old rifle. Hoskaninni's son, Hoskaninni Begay, who was five years old at the time of the Carson campaign, remembered that the group had little warning that soldiers were coming. With their sheep and horses, they set out at night, sleeping during the day to avoid detection. They went north, then turned west toward Navajo Mountain. At the south end of the mountain was a stream with grass for the livestock. "Mother sat on the ground and said she would go no further. Father tried to make her go on but she would not, so we made camp there, and lived in that place for six years." Safe from soldiers and Utes, the group prospered, thanks to Hoskaninni's severe discipline, which earned him his name, which can be translated as "The Angry One." Hoskaninni Begay later told an interviewer, "In that time our sheep herds and horse herds had increased so that we had plenty of meat and many blankets. We also had lots of silver."[26]

Hoskaninni and his family were among various Navajos who used the Navajo Mountain area as a refuge from Carson's soldiers, as some families in the area trace lineages as far back as the 1820s. It became a soothing retreat in troubled times for the locals, just as Rainbow

Bridge, beneath Navajo Mountain's slopes, became a special place through Jayi Begay's stories and ceremonies. Navajo discourses integrated both sites into tribal mythology. Interviews in the twentieth century with Navajo medicine men or singers, those who through long study learned to perform Navajo ceremonies, demonstrated how Navajo discourse was used to produce such a place. One singer, Paul Goodman, related the local Navajo story of Rainbow Bridge. In it, Navajos made a home on Navajo Mountain for a supernatural being named Lageinayai, who was given lightning to create rain. In gratitude, Lageinayai promised to protect The Diné.

Later, a group of Navajos left home with a god named Danaiize, who had the power to create and to travel on rainbows. When the travelers reached a canyon they could not cross, Danaiize created a rock rainbow to serve as a bridge for The Diné. "Since that time," Goodman told an interviewer, "the bridge has been a protective shield for Navajo Mountain and The Diné. Prayers are offered which call on Tse Naniáhi to continue the beautiful way and provide rain for The Diné. In this way evil is kept away from The Diné and their livestock."[27]

Navajo Mountain residents told an interviewer a story in which holy men within a group of characters from the Navajo emergence story placed the rainbow in Bridge Canyon after having used it to find the twins and bring them back to the area hoping they would grow to battle monsters and evil spirits.[28] In 1950, medicine man Frank Goldtooth of Tuba City, Arizona, who was fifty to sixty years old at the time, related a slightly different version of the story that linked Navajo Mountain and Rainbow Bridge to the tribal story of the twins.

One day the twins were playing and they came to a canyon facing the north which is now Paiute Canyon. They could not get across when a worm came along and stretched his body across the canyon. It was a shooting worm . . . and it later became Rainbow Bridge. According to this bridge, all bridges have been made in the same way. The worm did this himself for he had power. After they were almost grown, both twins lived at Navaho Mountain. They ran around Navaho Mountain four times from the east to the west and from the south to the north. When they had finished, they were full grown.[29]

So through association with the tribal mythology and with ceremonies that took place there, Rainbow Bridge became a Navajo place. It would have been reproduced as such over successive generations when those medicine men or singers who knew the ceremonies passed them to understudies. Rainbow Bridge, however, was never known by the entire tribe, which stretched over a vast territory.

For Navajos who made their homes in the area, however, it was indeed a Navajo place, connected to physical well-being through spiritual practices. Goodman and others spoke about Rainbow Bridge, along with the prayer associated with it, as evoking rain. Goodman specifically mentions livestock that, since the introduction of sheep by the Spanish, had been a main source of Navajo sustenance. By performing Navajo ceremonies at the stone arch, Navajos sought rain to grow their corn and grass to feed their livestock. Rainbow Bridge is, therefore, not an abstract religious symbol but is tied directly to Navajos' health and harmony in their society.

When, after long efforts, trader Louisa Wetherill finally persuaded a Navajo to tell her the prayer for Rainbow Bridge, she also recorded another version of the story of how it came to have special significance in local Navajo culture. The bridge had been a path for mountain sheep but a man from the Red House clan of Navajo Mountain killed sheep there. Wind and lightning became angered and would not let it rain, and the clan had to move. After it moved, the rains returned. The prayer, which represents the colors of a rainbow, seeks to maintain harmony and continuance of the rains. The prayer to Rainbow Bridge ends:

Iridescent Wind, beautiful chieftainess, from the palm of your
    hand a rainbow send out,
By which let me walk and have life.
Iridescent clouds, iridescent clouds, make for me shoes,
With which to walk and have life.
Iridescent clouds are my leggings;
An iridescent cloud is my robe;
An iridescent cloud is my headband.
Iridescent clouds, come behind me; make it dark; Earth Mother,
    give me much rain,
To make the iridescent corn grow and ripen,

That it may be peaceful behind me, that it may be peaceful
behind me.
All is peace, all is peace, all is peace, all is peace.[30]

In the Navajo world were the ruins of other peoples who had made
the area theirs before The Diné. One was the Anasazi, the word from
Navajo meaning "ancestral aliens or enemies."[31] As The Diné spread
throughout the area, the abandoned dwelling places and the objects
found there were brought within the space of The Diné world. Many
of the sites were identified as homes of the gods and woven into stories, songs, prayers, and ceremonial practices. As in most of the traditional Navajo world, the ruins were ascribed with certain powers. The
traditional Navajo worldview revolves around harmonies present at
the beginning but now lost. In the present world, the Navajos were
traditionally concerned with maintaining harmonious relationships
between the gods and the earth-surface beings. Within this view, the
Anasazi ruins served as parables illustrating the rise and decline of
the older civilization because its inhabitants did certain things to anger
the gods, just as the Navajos could do if they failed to follow the proper
social and cultural practices. The Anasazi ruins became places evoking
and enforcing Navajo social relations through their narration as places
where people once lived but who had fallen into bad behavior.

For the most part, traditional Navajos avoided Anasazi ruins because
the dead, both Anasazi and Navajo, were buried there. Navajos feared
entering a hogan where a person had died, believing the living would
be made sick,[32] and this fear extended to ruins where the spirits of the
dead were thought to dwell. Navajos who knew the proper ceremonies
and cleansing practices, however, could enter ruins and gather objects
for use in their own ceremonies. And some Navajos simply didn't sub-
scribe to the taboo; they would enter and gather objects for their own
use, for research, or for sale.[33] At the end of the nineteenth century and
into the twentieth, these ruins and their artifacts would attract another
culture into the area, one that would overlay a new space on that of the
Navajo. And its agents would discover Rainbow Bridge.

CHAPTER TWO

"Discovering" Rainbow Bridge for Modern America

On August 14, 1909, a party of Anglo-Americans on horseback guided by two natives of the area rounded a bend in a deep, narrow red rock canyon of southeastern Utah and beheld Rainbow Bridge. The group was led by two men whose professional and rival personal agendas prompted their participation. One was Byron Cummings, a University of Utah dean and professor of Greek and Latin who three years earlier had embarked on a new academic career as an archaeologist. Cummings dispassionately wrote in his field notes that day that the party "finally dropped into Nonnezoshieboko [Canyon] and followed it down until we came to the bridge which is a graceful arch across the wash which has been cut through the sandstone." As Cummings searched the area for archaeological objects, noting an altar and a human skull,[1] the other leader of the party, government surveyor William Boone Douglass, set to work measuring the arch. Douglass, who would claim to be the first white man to reach the bridge, wrote: "A graceful, rainbow-like arch of buff sandstone, with a span of 278 feet, towers 309 feet above the bed of the small stream that winds its way through the rugged gorge below. The width is but 33 feet and the thickness of the arch only 42 feet."[2]

Cummings's dry notes were in keeping with his role as an archaeologist performing as an objective scientist; Douglass's were in accordance with his mission of describing in numerical terms the arch and
how the area connected with the grid system of land division laid out
over the United States by government surveyors. The use of professional discourses masked, however, personal antagonisms and fierce
rivalry that erupted in public only a few weeks later. On September 3,
1909, the *Deseret Evening News* of Salt Lake City told of the expedition under the headline: "Discover Bridge of Great Height, Utah
Archaeological Expedition Reports Valuable Find in San Juan County.
Is Bigger Than All Others."[3] On September 23, the *Cortez Herald* in
Colorado reported, "The Greatest Natural Bridge in the world has
been discovered in southern Utah by William B. Douglas [*sic*] examiner of surveys of the General Land Office."[4] So began a lively, vitriolic,
decades-long dispute between members of the Cummings party and
Douglass over who should be credited with the discovery of what they
believed to be the world's longest natural bridge, which the president
would soon declare a national monument.

Of course, years before the Cummings–Douglass expedition, Rainbow Bridge had been known to local Navajos. And according to
archaeological evidence, humans had been nearby a thousand years
before. Even Anglo-Americans, miners and traders, claimed to know
of the bridge's existence prior to 1909. Cummings and Douglass
later acknowledged that natives of the area knew of the bridge. Still,
they claimed to be "discoverers." A few months after the expedition,
Cummings wrote in *National Geographic* that he and the rest of the
party were "evidently the first white men to have seen this greatest of
nature's stone bridges." Douglass admitted his Paiute guide had known
of the bridge, but still, to the General Land Office (and, by extension,
to him) "belongs the credit for the discovery to civilization, and for its
preservation as a National Monument."[5]

So there's the rub. Though Cummings, Douglass, and their parties
did not discover the bridge, they certainly were the first to publicize its
existence to a wide audience in modern America. And in the modern
world, to be able to circulate knowledge through words and images
about a place was to shape it into the forms by which it would be
known, talked about, and pictured. Through discourses from their own

This is the first known photo of Rainbow Bridge, taken in 1909 by Stuart Young, a member of the Byron Cummings party that "discovered" Rainbow Bridge that year. (Reproduced with permission of Northern Arizona University, Cline Library, Stuart M. Young Collection.)

Anglo-American society, Cummings and Douglass were the first to give Rainbow Bridge meanings that fit the imperatives of their own culture. It then became a place in modern America, overlaid on top of the Navajo place. Yes, Rainbow Bridge had been discovered (again).

The discourses that emanated from and shaped America in the twentieth century animated Cummings and Douglass, even propelled them to the discovery, and gave meaning to the place they produced. Cummings, and to a lesser extent Douglass, was motivated by science. By the nineteenth century, science had become a dominant way of knowing the world. Its methodology motivated adherents, mostly European men, to wander the globe "discovering" peoples, plants, animals, ancient artifacts, and geographic features.

On September 2, 1909, the same day the *Montezuma Journal* of Cortez, Colorado, published the first account of the Rainbow Bridge expedition, the *Salt Lake Tribune* carried these headlines: "Cook, American Explorer, Reaches the North Pole, Century-Old Dream of Scientists and Daring Navigators Finally Becomes Reality, According to

Well-Authenticated Reports." On September 7, the newspaper reported "America Once More Is Victor in Quest of Pole, Commander Peary . . . Reached 'Top of the Earth' Nearly Year after Dr. Cook Did." On September 9, "Peary Tries to Discredit Cook" and "Frederick A. Cook Stands By Guns."[6] The dispute between Peary and Cook demonstrates the cultural assumptions and imperatives under which Cummings and Douglass operated, and the rewards that might be expected for the discoverer of Rainbow Bridge.

The North Pole conquest brought to a close what historian William Goetzmann labeled the "Second Great Age of Discovery." That age began in the eighteenth century with the emerging practice of science as an exclusionary emphasis on empirical observation. It was characterized by discovery as a pretext for adventure and imperial conquest. The explorers and scientists carried not just food and gear, but the discourses of their culture. The knowledge they sought created blank spots on the earth in which local ways of seeing, talking about, and experiencing the world were ignored or wiped away, leaving a void that could be filled with "discoveries." The division of nature by Western science into parts that could be easily cataloged allowed for the mostly educated, male, European, urban explorers to "naturalize" new sites immediately upon contact, to fit them into the language of their system and thereby bring them into the European world. Writes Goetzmann: "Once the powerful scientific method was devised, gentle bespectacled men like Charles Darwin or towering figures of erudition like Alexander von Humboldt could roam the earth, establishing this scientific method—the western mind-set—as the only way of comprehending the realities of Nature and Nature's Earth."[7]

The scientists and explorers brought these discoveries into the knowledge and, therefore, the space of European civilization through texts; their exploits made popular reading, and they became cultural heroes. Yet Cummings and Douglass also were performing within an American space, guided by a mythology of national origin. Their text was an emergence myth that had Europeans interacting with the wilderness and becoming Americans in the process. That tale also made heroic the white men who pushed into "unknown" territory and brought it into the national knowledge. By the beginning of the twentieth century, the American West was the representative space of this emergence tale, both in academic accounts and the popular culture of pulp novels and magazines that glorified the exploits of white frontiersmen who blazed new trails, fought Indians, and brought civilization to the frontier. Science, nationalism, and the West of popular culture guided Cummings and Douglass on the trail to Rainbow Bridge, gave the stone arch meaning, and created a new place in modern America.[8]

Byron Cummings was born September 20, 1860, in Westville, New York, the youngest of seven children whose father died of typhus in 1864 while serving during the Civil War. Cummings lived with his mother and stepfather until age fourteen, when he left after a dispute. Following that hard-knocks beginning, he joined the rising middle class when, around age 16, he attended the Potsdam Normal Teacher Training School and became a teacher. Then in 1885, he began a course in the classics at Rutgers College in New Brunswick, New Jersey, working in the library to pay his way through school. Upon graduation, he taught at the Rutgers preparatory school until, as he later wrote in an unfinished autobiography, "I thought I would like to get a position somewhere in the West." Cummings wrote to the National Teachers Association seeking a teaching position. The chance came when the president of the University of Utah in Salt Lake City offered him a job teaching Greek and Latin.[9]

In 1893, Cummings headed west by train to take up his new post. On the way, he stopped in Chicago to see the World's Fair, held to celebrate the four hundredth anniversary of Columbus's "discovery" of the Americas.[10] Apart from welcoming the World's Fair, Chicago played host to two other summer events that were engaged in a conversation about American culture as the nineteenth century drew to a close. The historian Frederick Jackson Turner presented a scholarly address that summed up in poetic language a national tale of the emergence of American democratic institutions and character. Also on hand was Buffalo Bill's Wild West show and its performance of a popular culture version of American frontier history. These three events, with their dialogue about science, nationalism, and the West of popular culture, shed light on the nature of the civilization that claimed the discovery of Rainbow Bridge.

Cummings did not record what he saw at the World's Columbian Exposition. His presence, however, provides a moment in which to explore the ideas, words, and images of modern America that he carried on his journey. If Cummings went by rail to the World's Columbian Exposition seven miles south of downtown, he would have gotten off at the station on what had been the empty shore of Lake Michigan before the fair was built. From the railroad station, he would have walked through the Midway Plaisance section, with its carnival atmosphere and re-created native homes for American Indians, Africans, Egyptians, and other "exotic" peoples, to arrive at the White City, a gleaming construction of classical architecture and ersatz marble. That stroll from the Midway to the White City was a text that could be read as a journey from the primitive to the civilized, from the inferior to the superior—distinctions that exist at the heart of modernity. Of course, the two are intimately connected. The idea of progress that helped to narrate industrialization contains the notion that America moved from the primitive state of the frontier to become modern.[11] So the walk through the peoples on exhibit in the Midway to the modern White City told the story of the rise of the modern, making the "primitives" quaint and their worldviews antiquated.

The Midway was under the direction of the fair's Department of Ethnology, which was presided over by Frederic Ward Putnam of Harvard's Peabody Museum of American Archaeology and Ethnology. His imprimatur and the participation of anthropologists Franz Boaz and John Wesley Powell in creating exhibits gave, in historian Robert Rydell's words, "ethnological, scientific sanction" to the primitive/modern, inferior races/white race juxtaposition of the Midway and the White City.[12] The science of anthropology, of which archaeology is considered a branch, had its American origins in the mid-nineteenth century in encounters between educated whites and Indians. Its mission was to save from the contamination of modernization and its artificiality the authenticity supposedly found in "primitive" peoples. In studying these Others, scientists implicitly contrasted their own civilization—particularly the modern city—with primitive spaces: the jungles of Africa, the deserts of the Middle East, or the wilds of the American West. Ostensibly, researchers sought out primitive peoples and their objects in hopes of salvaging "authentic" cultures. Such authenticity was, however, a willful invention of the modern, and it became a tool for bringing peoples and cultures into the knowledge of and under the power of Western civilization as primitives.[13]

At Chicago, it is likely that Cummings visited the exhibit mounted by the Utah Territorial World's Fair Commission (Utah did not become a state until 1896). If so, he doubtless saw the fruits of archaeological fieldwork, the artifacts of ancient Indian cultures excavated from various sites for the fair, including Nine Mile Canyon and San Juan County, places Cummings would later work as an archaeologist. In addition, Cummings may have seen two of Richard Wetherill's collections, including artifacts taken from Grand Gulch in San Juan County that were displayed at the Chicago Art Institute. One of the collections featured a sixty-five-foot artificial cliff, with a reproduction of a cliff dwelling ruin. The fair served as a catalyst for archaeology of the Southwest and perhaps too for Byron Cummings. When Cummings returned to Chicago in 1896 and enrolled at the University of Chicago to begin a Ph.D. program, one of his classes was in archaeology.[14]

Archaeology was particularly suited as a tool of a nationalist mythology of progress that helped to animate the late-nineteenth-century United States as represented at the Chicago fair. As a scientific discipline, it was intimately linked to nationalism from its beginnings, when nation states emerged and the industrial revolution created antagonisms that seemed to threaten social order. Western European intellectuals and other elites wanted to regard the historical, cultural, and biological heritage of a nation as a unifying force in the face of this social fragmentation. Archaeologists in this era interpreted the record of the past as the history of their nations instead of that of humankind. Curtis Hinsley, Jr., has written that archaeology is, as a form of storytelling, "a particular and powerful form of origin myth." In the 1840s, as industrial capitalism and the political philosophy of liberal democracy came to dominate Europe and the United States, archaeology became a "legitimatizing mythology" in which progress was illustrated by its distance in linear time from its predecessor, the primitive past.[15]

In the United States, interest in indigenous cultures was piqued in the nineteenth century as Americans searched for a cultural basis for a national identity, particularly in comparison with Europe. Not blessed with strong literary, artistic, architectural, or other cultural traditions,

Americans turned to their landscape and to ruins of the indigenous past as a source of pride and identity. Accounts of government surveys, paintings, and photographs brought attention to ruins of the Southwest beginning in the 1870s. Americans began to include the ruins and the region's inhabitants into a story of progress. The re-creation of cliff houses and the exhibition of artifacts at the World's Columbian Exposition helped bring ancient cultures and their artifacts into this national space, to domesticate them as the American past. Then, at the turn of century, instead of comparing their cultural heritage with Europe's, Anglo-Americans began contrasting it with the modern world that had arisen around them. As they sought out the authentic in primitive cultures and spaces, the discovery and interpretations of ruins in the Southwest provided Anglo-Americans with material to construct a past and a cultural identity. Archaeology was at a peak in American consciousness, able to explain the relationship of the past to the present and make the chaotic world of American society seem orderly.[16]

On July 12, as the World's Fair drew huge crowds to Chicago, University of Wisconsin historian Frederick Jackson Turner presented an essay at a meeting of the American Historical Association held at the Art Institute of Chicago. The essay, "The Significance of the Frontier in American History," quickly became famous and has influenced generations of historians by sanctioning a history centered on this continent rather than one emanating from Europe. It validated regional histories, particularly of the frontier West, with its often-quoted core argument: "The existence of an area of free land, its continuous recession, and the advancement of American settlement westward explain American development."[17] In Turner's construction, the advancement of the frontier into the open space of the wilderness was the experience that accounted for the development of American character and institutions. Turnerian frontier history was a space-time configuration in which linear time, in the form of progress, was directional, east to west, from civilization to the primitive land, from Europe to the New World. Turner mentions Indians only as savages. In Turner's story, Indian lands were thinly occupied spaces inviting the Anglo-Americans' physical presence and imaginations.[18]

Turner's essay also was an American emergence tale, a national-ist mythology of heroic white pioneer men and women conquering wilderness and being reborn in the process. The essay amounted to a national mythology, which Richard Slotkin has defined as "a complex of narratives that dramatizes the working vision and historical sense of a people or culture, reducing centuries of experience into a constel-lation of compelling metaphors."[19] Turner's narrative was, in effect, an emergence tale in the same sense that the Navajos had an emergence tale: both were stories of how people came to create a particular space and to occupy it. But Turner's essay would not have been so dramatic and influential had the mythic tale not already been known to Ameri-cans. Turner set down an already formed collective memory in poetic prose. His thesis was meant for a scholarly audience but relied on metaphor and myth from American popular culture and political dis-course reaching back to the colonial era.[20]

While Turner was presenting his essay, William F. Cody ("Buffalo Bill") was offering an equally powerful—and in some ways similar—discourse on the American frontier through his Wild West show right outside the gates of the World's Fair. Like Turner, Buffalo Bill glorified a past that saw the history of the American West as that of heroic con-quest of dangerous wilderness within the march of civilization. Buf-falo Bill, Daniel Boone, Kit Carson, John Fremont, and Davy Crockett were compared in the Wild West program to Columbus as "guides to the New World of the mighty West." They were strong white male characters who brought wilderness into American civilization. They differed from Turner's characters, however, in one major respect: Buf-falo Bill's Wild West was populated with Indians. His white men were the targets of aggressive savages, and they became heroic conquerors when they prevailed. Cody's Wild West show thus put race war at the heart of the American emergence story. The presence of his show in Chicago in 1893 complemented Turner's presentation, adding the ele-ment of justified racial conquest of primitive peoples by heroic white men to Turner's national emergence myth.[21]

Turner had opened a new space of intellectual inquiry, and Buffalo Bill had shown that the entrepreneur could make the frontier past into a cultural commodity. Both Turner and Buffalo Bill produced cultural products out of the national past[22] but ended their tales on a note of decline. Both declared that the frontier phase of U.S. history was in the past. Turner cited the 1890 census as showing the end of the frontier. And Cody's Wild West program described the frontiersman as "a class that is rapidly disappearing from our country." Both the essay and the show evoked a history experienced as nostalgia, as something fast fading as the modern world spread and developed. Turner and Buffalo Bill's Wild West show can be seen, then, as modernist. They were nostalgic re-creations of the past in the face of a rapidly modernizing world.

We can think of the stories, sights, smells, textures, and sounds of the Chicago fair—its discourses—as showing aspects of what animated the larger space of American society of the late nineteenth century. That was the space in which Byron Cummings operated when he went West, and again sixteen years later when he and William B. Douglass fixed Rainbow Bridge as a small place within that larger space. When Cummings and Douglass embarked on the expedition to Rainbow Bridge, they were performing these discourses on display in Chicago. They were animated by science and its heroic discoverers, by the nationalist story of Americans conquering the frontier, and by the popular-culture version of the West in which savage Indians were overcome by white men to make way for modern civilization. In the West, where some Indians still inhabited traditional spaces, Cummings and Douglass performed as mythic American and scientific adventurers seeking discoveries. Out of these discourses, they extended the space of modern America and created a particular place at Rainbow Bridge.

At the University of Utah, Cummings rose rapidly to become chairman of the ancient languages department, dean of men, and dean of the School of Arts and Sciences. But his interest in American archaeology had been aroused. Cummings helped found the Utah branch of the Archaeological Institute of America, working with Edgar L. Hewett of the institute, himself a budding archaeologist. Hewett would be instrumental in Cummings's expeditions and an important figure in making the Southwest into a modern space of primitive peoples and ancient artifacts. In 1906, Cummings taught his first class in archaeology. Cummings also sought to build popular interest in archaeology through lectures around the state, during which residents may have shown him local ruins. Those ruins, Cummings declared, were a hidden part of American history that should be told.[23]

In the summer of 1906, Cummings undertook his first archaeological field trip, alone and on horseback, to Nine Mile Canyon in central Utah, where artifacts had been gathered for the World's Columbian Exposition. He acted on behalf of the Archaeological Institute. His mission was to determine how far north the Pueblo culture had reached in Utah. He apparently did no digging.[24] Beginning that year, Cummings spent nearly every summer of his professional life in the field.

In the summer of 1907, Cummings set out on his second season of archaeological exploration. He and a group of University of Utah students visited ruins in Montezuma Creek Canyon in San Juan County in remote southeastern Utah, then went on to White Canyon, where there were three natural stone bridges. Cass Hite, a prospector and explorer of the Colorado River system, claimed to have been the first to see the bridges in 1883. In 1903, local cattleman Jim Jones Scorup took an engineer, Horace J. Long, to see the bridges, a trip that became the basis of a 1904 article in *Century* magazine. Its title, "The Colossal Bridges of Utah: A Recent Discovery of Natural Wonders," immediately framed the bridges as a "discovery." It was probable, the author wrote, "that they had never been seen by any of the white race, save perhaps a half-dozen cattlemen and cow-boys." The size of the formations was emphasized. A drawing compared the height of the largest bridge to that of the U.S. Capitol and the Great Pyramid of Egypt, demonstrating that America's nature was as great as its institutions and held works comparable to the ancient wonders of the world. In 1905, the Commercial Club of Salt Lake City sponsored an expedition to the bridges because "these were too important as scenic attractions to be overlooked by the citizens of this state."

A *Deseret Evening News* headline above a section of a story on the 1905 trip, "Beginning of Knowledge," recognized, even if inadvertently, that one had to circulate a discovery to a larger audience for it to become a place in the modern world. A member of that expedition, Edwin F. Holmes, wrote of the bridges in *National Geographic* in 1907, his account seeking to undermine the earlier expedition as a "hurried view of the bridges." Having wiped the slate clean, Holmes placed himself at the center of a narrative of discovery that re-created pioneer treks by describing the hardships faced in riding to the bridges on horseback. The article also said one of the bridges, then named Caroline, is "the longest span in the world."[25]

So by the time Cummings arrived at White Canyon in 1907, he had before him a cultural model of the Euro-American explorer-scientist and a specific case of huge natural stone bridges found, studied, and publicized in southeastern Utah. They were a model of discovery based on the first to see a geological wonder, the first to publicize such a find, or the first to scientifically analyze a site. Press accounts of bridges having the "longest span" or being among "nature's greatest" provided cultural and social incentive to someone who might discover a stone arch even longer or greater.

Cummings and other Americans also had been conditioned to perceive the bridges as not just interesting or aesthetically pleasing, but also representative of the forces of nature in accord with the American nation. Features of the landscape had long held fascination for Americans flooding across the country. Weary travelers on the Oregon Trail in the mid-nineteenth century went out of their way to visit areas where a river had cut through a ridge so that they could climb, sketch, explore, and describe it.[26] The science of geology was at least partially the basis for this fascination with unusual landscape. It brought to the modern condition the concept of "deep time," of a geological history that extended backward for millions of years.[27]

In 1907, Cummings went to Washington, D.C., to lobby for protection of ruins and the White Canyon bridges. Later in the year, he and a party of recruits, including nephew Neil Judd, traveled on horseback to White Canyon. Two of the students he had recruited surveyed the bridges and created a topographical map while Judd and another surveyed archaeological ruins in the canyon and drew another map. These maps and a report were sent to Edgar Hewett in Washington, D.C., and were forwarded by him to U.S. Senator Reed Smoot of Utah. The senator in turn sent them to the General Land Office, and they were the basis on which President Theodore Roosevelt issued a proclamation on April 16, 1908, creating the Natural Bridges National Monument.[28]

Natural Bridges was the first of three national monuments that Cummings had a hand in creating through the Antiquities Act, an instrument for the production of modern places (through protection and limitations on access) that emerged from the historical milieu of the Progressive era of American history at a particular moment in the professionalization and institutionalization of archaeology. As modernization displaced the old rural power structure, it created a new urban middle class of professionals and specialists. Among the new pursuits in this era was that of the professional archaeologist. By the turn of the century, archaeology was evolving into a profession with its own institutions, vocabulary, and books and articles. Practitioners of archaeology increasingly had to have graduated from a university program, a requirement that excluded the poor, the working class, African Americans, American Indians, Jews, and most women. These largely middle-class white male archaeologists began to look for places where they could perform field work.

To enable the practice of archaeology, universities, museums, and professional organizations sought to protect artifacts from commercial exploitation. Richard Wetherill, who had gathered artifacts for the Chicago fair, was now labeled a "pothunter" who stripped ruins of their scientific value for crass commercial gain. A bill proposed in Congress in 1904 to protect archaeological sites had the backing of university presidents and heads of other institutions. "Every person interested in scientific research, sociology and race development will no doubt heartily approve a measure such as contemplated in this bill," wrote J. T. Kingsbury, the president of the University of Utah. "My colleagues, mostly interested in archaeological studies, and myself heartily recommend that the bill be passed without delay and that the law then be strictly enforced."[29]

After the failure of antiquities protection legislation in 1904, General Land Office Commissioner W. A. Richards asked a young archaeologist from the West, Edgar L. Hewett, for a new study of American ruins. His report attached the ruins to the discourse of progress through science: "Every cliff dwelling, every prehistoric tower, communal house, shrine and burial mound is an object which can contribute something to the advancement of knowledge, and hence is worthy of preservation." Hewett proved to be a unifying force for the passage of the

Antiquities Act in 1906. The bill for the first time introduced the concept of the national monument. It allowed the president to protect
areas of historic or scientific interest along with those of spectacular natural beauty. Congress passed the bill, and President Theodore
Roosevelt signed it into law on June 8, 1906.

Archaeologist David Hurst Thomas writes: "With the Antiquities
Act, Congress had legally defined the American Indian past as part
of the larger public trust, like Yellowstone and the American bison."[30]
The places created by the act, the national monuments, also were thoroughly modern. They were places abstracted from ordinary life and
set aside for aesthetic purposes or for scientific study. They were conceived of through modern discourses of a freakish nature, of ruins of
ancient civilization that helped tell a story of a faded past, as a way to
salvage them and save them from the onslaught of modernization.

In the summer of 1908, after having provided the means by which
Roosevelt had proclaimed the Natural Bridges National Monument,
Cummings was again in the field in southeastern Utah. Judd also
returned. Hewett had authority over the expedition and had appointed
a recent Harvard graduate, Alfred V. Kidder, to lead it. The fledgling
archaeologists spent two weeks exploring and mapping ruins in San
Juan County before deciding to excavate a ruin on Alkali Ridge. Two
of Kidder's friends from Harvard joined them, and after hiring some
local help, they set to work. Altogether, the group gathered 350 artifacts and enough skeletons to fill a box. They sent everything to the
Smithsonian Institution in Washington, D.C.[31]

Judd later admitted that the crews digging in those early years
would not be considered archaeologists as the profession came to
be practiced. Still, they were conquering new territories where later
archaeologists could follow. Using the language of the frontier, Judd
connected archaeological field work to the American emergence
myth. "The country was wild and untamed; the trails traveled were
mostly Indian trails. There were no maps. . . . During those three sum-
mers Doctor Cummings blazed a trail for others to follow. Indeed, his
first half dozen expeditions were all pioneer undertakings."[32]

For men like Cummings, the exploration of geological features or
ruins of ancient civilization not yet known within general American society offered the twentieth-century white middle-class male the

opportunity to engage in the rituals of the national myth as Turner and Buffalo Bill had presented it. American frontier mythology was an instrument for the physical intrusion into Indian territories in the name of science and its production of knowledge. The budding profession of archaeology also allowed the members of Cummings's summer expeditions to engage the vigorous outdoor life promoted by Theodore Roosevelt. In lectures, magazine articles, and books about his hunting, military conquest, and travel, the West for Roosevelt was a place of regeneration of manhood and the nation. Roosevelt urged others to take up the vigorous life. Cummings once confessed to a student that he was "a worshiper at the shrine of Theodore Roosevelt."[33]

The emphasis on a vigorous outdoor life lived by men among men led to some physical transformations that had nothing to do with building muscles. A photographer sent along on the 1908 expedition by Hewett, Jesse L. Nusbaum, grew a beard. "At home in the city he shaved three times a day," Judd wrote, "but out there among the cedars and pinon he could be himself." Kidder, the Harvard man, "began cultivation of a facial covering that soon equaled, or surpassed, every other of its kind known west of the Pecos River . . . like the mane of a bull bison."[34]

As pioneers in the West as understood though popular culture, the Cummings men enjoyed hazing the Easterner "tenderfoots" who accompanied them, including Kidder's friends from Harvard. The Easterners first had to ride horseback thirty-five miles to the archaeologists' camp, a feat that, Judd suggested, served as the beginning of their transformation: "Both were still alive when they dismounted and, to the surprise of all, were ready for work in a day or two." While in camp, a hired man, a drifter named Nick, "took it upon himself to educate Kidder's friends in the ways of the West." He pointed out "Indian" moccasin tracks that one of the party had made by wearing slippers backward on the trail to the ruins. The hoots of owls were Indians signaling each other. Tall tales were told around the campfire, and tricks played. "Our Harvard friends were neither used to the wild country nor to the Indians and so the tall tales sank in rather deep. So much so that in a short time they were not able to sleep at night or endure anything by day." Cummings finally had to put a stop to the fun. "Our chief victim had lain awake night after night in the snoring camp, fully dressed and with both a Boy Scout hand ax and a Spanish War trenching blade unsheathed beside him." The soft Eastern men were remade as classic males of the frontier myth. "Not long after," Judd wrote, "it was learned that, in consequence of their Alkali Ridge schooling, the Harvard visitors never batted an eye when two of our workmen were indicted for murder shortly after leaving camp or, in an Espanola tavern a fortnight later, when a Mexican at the next table was killed during an argument."[35]

In performing the American male frontier myth and enforcing its codes, these early archaeological expeditions intruded upon spaces of the natives of the area. This act first required seeing the spaces as absent of modern ways of seeing the world, which allowed the intruders to bring modern, scientific knowledge to them. Frederick Jackson Turner had imagined the frontier as "free land." Geologists, archaeologists, and other scientists and explorers also wiped Native knowledge and practices from the space as they intruded.

The Cummings party set out to produce spaces in the name of science, and in so doing provoked repeated resistance from Utes, Paiutes, and Navajos. Those conflicts were absent in their later scientific texts because they violated the veil of dispassionate, objective, and apolitical discourse. In the nonscientific writings of Cummings and Judd, however, these conflicts, recast within the myth of the American frontier, play a prominent role. "At that time white men were not wanted in the Navajo country, where memories of Bosque Redondo were still fresh," Judd wrote. Bosque Redondo was a reservation in which Indians of various tribes were interned, and there was a forced march of Navajos to Bosque Redondo in 1864 (which Navajos refer to as the "Long Walk"). "But the Dean [Cummings] was on the trail of ancient history and he had no fear. Repeatedly challenged and threatened, he called more than one Indian's bluff." Thus Judd cast Cummings as an Anglo-American cultural hero in the vein of Buffalo Bill to legitimize intrusion into Indian lands. To Judd, the Indians were exotics, backward in time and outside of the American nation. "Local Indians were troublesome and antagonistic. Men wore their hair long and clung to the old ways." Cummings took a paternal attitude in his book on his encounters with Natives, *Indians I Have Known:* "I have found them to be not only human beings, but also men who measured up well in intelligence, industry and justice with other races in the world, even with Europeans and Americans."[36] Of course, that was not true of all of the American Indians Cummings encountered.

The conflicts with Natives began with Cummings's 1906 exploration in Nine Mile Canyon during which he apparently had some sort of confrontation with Utes. In 1908, while excavating in San Juan County near the town of Bluff, Johnny Benow, a "renegade" and "troublemaker," confronted the party over its presence in Ute territory. Cummings used the gathering of artifacts under the authority of archaeology to justify the intrusion: "You had better be careful and not make any more trouble for any of us who have a right to be in this country." Judd also remembered another incident during that summer. A Ute rode into camp and asked the party what they were doing. The archaeologists told him they were looking for "ancient ones," or dead people. For a dollar, the man offered to show Judd where he could find other places to dig. Judd followed him with a shovel for quite a distance. "Finally, when I was becoming a bit weary with this endless pursuit, he stopped outside a wire fence, grinned, and pointed to the Bluff City cemetery. I never trusted another Ute."[37]

Though comic, the story from the perspective of the Ute may also have posed a question to the Cummings party had its members been more reflective: Why concentrate your efforts on ancient Indian dead instead of the corpses in the white cemetery? Why not dig up your own? The joke points to the cultural assumptions and power relations that animated the Cummings archaeological expeditions.

In August 1908, after finishing the excavations at Alkali Ridge, Cummings and some members of the party rode their horses across the San Juan River to Oljato and the trading post where John and Louisa Wetherill and partner Clyde Colville carried out business with Paiutes and Navajos. The University of Utah group wanted Wetherill to point them to "archaeological possibilities" in northeastern Arizona for the next season's work. During one conversation, Louisa Wetherill told Cummings of a discussion she had with Blind Salt Clansman (Jayi Begay), who had wanted to know why white men had been in the country visiting White Canyon. "Why do they want to ride all the way over the clay hills to see—just rocks?" he asked. Told of the interest in stone bridges, Begay said to Wetherill, as she later remembered, "They aren't the only bridges in the world. . . . We have a better one in this country."

Blind Salt Clansman informed her of the Rock Rainbow that spans the canyon near Navajo Mountain.[38] Louisa Wetherill in turn told Cummings of the arch, and he made arrangements to return the following summer to mount an expedition to "discover" the natural bridge, which he thought might be even larger than those he had helped make a national monument just months before in White Canyon.

That same summer of 1908, William Boone Douglass was in Cortez, Colorado, making a survey for a reservoir and studying the feasibility of a road to Mesa Verde National Park, the extensive ruins of Anasazi villages in southwestern Colorado where Richard Wetherill and his brothers, including John, had first dug. On July 3, officials assigned Douglass to do a formal survey of the Natural Bridges National Monument to supplant the informal one made by the Cummings party.

While surveying the White Canyon bridges, Douglass employed a Paiute or Ute named Mike's Boy, later called Jim Mike, who told Douglass of a bridge even bigger than those they were surveying. He bent a twig and stuck both ends in the ground to convey the shape of the bridge. Douglass then wrote to the commissioner of the General Land Office reporting a bridge "larger and prettier" than those at White Canyon, a "white sandstone arch 'like a rainbow.'" Douglass went on, "If this bridge exists, and I believe it does, it should beyond doubt be preserved. . . . Mike's Boy says no white man has ever seen this bridge and only he and [unreadable] Indians knows its whereabouts." Douglass recommended that he be assigned to investigate it and ruins in the area that he had heard about from John Wetherill. That same month, he was assigned that task.[39] So within a few weeks of each other, both Cummings and Douglass became aware of a stone arch said to be even larger than the ones of Natural Bridges National Monument.

In December 1908, after finishing his survey of Natural Bridges National Monument, Douglass went to Oljato with the intention of finding the stone arch described by Jim Mike. Jim Mike, however, failed to appear at Oljato as planned, and Wetherill begged off making the trip with Douglass. "Frankly," Douglass later wrote, "Mr. Weatherill [*sic*] said Jim was lying, and that we would find nothing." Wetherill instead employed a Navajo named Sam Chief to guide Douglass to an arch that the trader vaguely suggested might be the one Jim Mike had mentioned. Sam Chief, according to Douglass, "discovered nothing of greater interest than Sam's own former corn-patch, to which he led the party." They returned to Oljato with the intention of trying again, but snow blocked the trails.[40]

Wetherill had just months before learned of Rainbow Bridge through his wife. His statement that Jim Mike was wrong shows that Wetherill wanted to divert Douglass away from the bridge and preserve its discovery for himself or for his client, Byron Cummings. Indeed, Wetherill and his business partner, Clyde Colville, each made attempts that autumn to reach the bridge. Wetherill may have been successful but never publicly claimed he was the first, perhaps because Cummings already had hired him for the next season to look for the arch. (Wetherill's son, Ben, later claimed his father had reached the bridge that year.)[41] Wetherill and Colville did, however, provide Douglass with a description of the extensive ruins in nearby Tsegi Canyon. Douglass wrote to the General Land Office and requested that the ruins be withdrawn from possible private claim. They should be preserved, he argued, along with "every article that comes from them, with accurate data as to its exact location in the building and the condition under which it was found." Douglass, however, also had another motive for writing. He knew that Cummings had seen the ruins and planned to return the following summer to excavate. "I have reliable information of a pseudo-scientific expedition planning to excavate here in the summer, which is principally concerned in accuring [*sic*] a price-less archaeological collection." Washington officials ordered Douglass to survey the ruins the next summer. They were declared a national monument even before the survey.[42]

Douglass was back the following summer. On August 9, 1909, he and a crew that included Jim Mike started for Oljato with the intention of finding a trail to the big rainbow-shaped arch. First, however, Douglass had learned that Cummings and a crew of summer recruits from the University of Utah, along with Edgar Hewett, had indeed returned and were digging in Tsegi Canyon. He wrote to Washington, D.C.,

Stuart Young, a member of the 1909 expedition to Rainbow Bridge, took this photograph of the party. Pictured in the back row, left to right, are Ned English, Dan Perkins, Jack Keenan, Vern Rogerson, Neil Judd, and Don Beauregard. In the front row are Jim Mike (aka Mike's Boy), John Wetherill, Byron Cummings, W. B. Douglass, and Malcolm Cummings. Not pictured is Nasja Begay, a Paiute who helped guide the expedition to the bridge. (Reproduced with permission of Northern Arizona University, Cline Library, Stuart M. Young Collection.)

seeking to have Cummings's permits revoked and his party forced out of the ruins, which he touted as "the most remarkable ever located in the United States." "The expected has happened," Douglass wrote Walter Hough of the U.S. National Museum in an August 4 letter. "I learned here that Prof. Hewett and Prof. Byron Cummings went into the reserve ruins about six weeks ago, and as they have not come out I fear they are excavating." He warned that Cummings "has obtained a very remarkable collection and unless stopped will land it in the museum of the University of Utah. I have written a long letter to the G.L.O. [Government Land Office] protesting this." Douglass would not receive replies for a while, and so it was with high expectations for himself that he set out on August 9 with guide Jim Mike and other crew members to discover Rainbow Bridge.[43]

Cummings's party had left Salt Lake City on June 7 with the intent of working ruins they had seen the year before and making the pack trip to Rainbow Bridge. The group, which included Cummings's son, Malcolm, and university students Neil Judd, Donald Beauregard, and Stuart M. Young, first went to Tsegi Canyon (also called Tsagie ot Sosie) to excavate while waiting for Wetherill to take them to the new bridge. Hewett joined them but departed the region before the group started for the bridge. Through June and July, Cummings and the party explored and mapped ruins and gathered artifacts.

At some point before they started for Rainbow Bridge, members of the Cummings party set up camp near some ruins and used wood taken from the structures for campfires. A Navajo who lived in the same area, Hosteen Jones, was "horrified and assured us we would be sick and 'maybe all the Indians get sick.'" Jones brought the group other firewood so they would not use timber from the ruins. As Cummings noted, Jones was attempting to "protect us from our ignorance and to save his family from possible suffering or death. In those days a Navajo would not use anything from prehistoric ruins." But Cummings's diary also indicated that a confrontation had taken place of such import that he made a note to himself to write the Tuba City Indian agent to complain about Jones. Trying to take advantage of the Navajo taboo against contact with the dead, the party also placed a skull conspicuously in camp to prevent the theft of their equipment.[44]

The incident and the use of the skull underscores the contrasting cultural spaces within which Navajos and archaeologists regarded and used the ruins. By custom, Navajos were admonished to avoid ruins because of their association with death. It was taboo for Navajos to enter places where people had died or were buried. Archaeologists' pursuit, excavation, and use of objects also are bound to beliefs of their own culture. Fieldwork achieved "the rank of the sacred archaeological ritual" in the twentieth century. For archaeologists, an object is discovered, marked, and brought into a lab for cleaning, study, and cataloging. It then becomes an artifact and is "buried" in a museum or other storage, thus making it a sacred object in the name of science. That science, with its truths and facts, is thus a conditioned or situated form of knowledge, dependent upon the historical and cultural moment. But the conflicts between area Natives and the Cummings's parties seem to indicate that archaeology was not just a science but also a form of political discourse.[45]

On August 8, Wetherill arrived back in camp from a trip to Bluff. He brought a letter from a Bluff resident informing Cummings that Douglass had written and telegraphed Washington in an attempt to get the Utah group's archaeological permits canceled. Wetherill also informed Cummings that Douglass was on his way to Oljato to find the big rock bridge. The camp packed up and headed to meet Douglass, either at Cummings's insistence because he wanted to resolve their conflicts, or because Wetherill had already made arrangements with Douglass to include him in the Rainbow Bridge party. First, however, there was a "discovery" to be made.

Earlier in the season, Louisa Wetherill had asked a Navajo family whether there were any more ruins in the area and had been told of some nearby. But the Cummings party was unable to go at that time. On August 9, however, as Cummings and the university students were returning to Oljato to start to Rainbow Bridge, they paid $5 to a Navajo who showed them the ruin. They claimed the discovery of Betatakin, a big picturesque cliff dwelling that was part of Navajo National Monument. The party spent less than an hour there, then hurried on to Oljato.[46]

The Cummings party paused at Oljato for a few days, during which expedition member Donald Beauregard had time to write an article and send photographs to the *Deseret Evening News* in Salt Lake City. He wrote of the group's discovery of the Keet Seel ruins, not in terms of being the first to find them (Richard Wetherill is credited), but rather as scientists bringing modern knowledge to public notice. "The most important cliff ruin brought to the notice of the world since the discovery of the Cliff Palace in the Mesa Verde, Colo., has for the first time been thoroughly examined, and photographed by our archaeological expedition."[47]

On August 10, Douglass having failed to appear, the Cummings party set out for Rainbow Bridge. A Navajo sent from Oljato soon caught up and informed them that Douglass had finally arrived, and they paused to wait until he joined them with, in Cummings's words, "four men and an Indian." For Douglass, it was Cummings who joined his party: "He was preparing to start in search of the bridge, having learned of my proposed trip from Mr. Wetherell [sic]." In any event, the two groups resumed the quest together. The terrain was extremely difficult. Judd later complained that Douglass's farm-raised pack animals were too big for the narrow trails carved in the rock for smaller Navajo horses, so the party had to remove the packs on Douglass's animals to squeeze through narrow points. "Douglas's [sic] party was pretty slow and we were held back all the time by them," Stuart Young wrote in his diary. The going was tough for all as they traveled through sand under a scorching sun. Moving at times over bare rock, Douglass was forced to cache some of his equipment when it proved too heavy and slowed the party. Wetherill sniped at Douglass that Jim Mike, who was supposed to be the guide, obviously did not know the way. The party became discouraged. However, at the end of the third day, August 13, Nasja Begay, a Paiute who lived nearby and had earlier been contracted to guide the party to the arch, joined the group. Once in camp, Nasja Begay assured the party they could reach the bridge the next day, and the mood brightened.[48]

The following day, the group entered the canyon where the arch was located. Douglass, according to Judd, constantly tried to keep out ahead in a "wild race" and "exhibited the uncontrolled enthusiasm of the amateur explorer and he was so utterly disregardful of the possible danger to other members of the party as to arouse the disgust of all." Douglass, for his part, saw Cummings as an eager participant in the race: "A spirit of rivalry developed between Professor Cummings and myself as to who should first reach the bridge." Douglass at one point suggested that Cummings fall back and take care of his son, Malcolm, who was riding with others in the rear. Cummings declined. It is unclear from the various accounts what order members of the party were in when they neared their goal.

In Cummings's telling, Nasja Begay suggested Cummings ride ahead with him. "As we reached the point and I saw the object to our long trek just a little way ahead, I turned and shouted, 'Eureka, here she is!'" Douglass spurred his horse to try to reach the bridge first. Wetherill, seeing what Douglass was up to, sped ahead on his horse to be the first to the massive stone arch. "Thus," Cummings later wrote, "I was the first white man to see Rainbow Bridge and John Wetherill was the first white man to pass under this great arch." Douglass, however, erased Wetherill from his account, giving Cummings and himself, as the two leaders of the expedition, the right to claim any discovery. He ignored Cummings's first sighting, making the criterion for discoverer the first of them to physically arrive at the arch. "Fortune favored me at the close, the Professor being some hundred feet in the rear when I reached the bridge."[49]

On August 14, 1909, only that small party of white men knew the arch had been "discovered." Douglass, with Judd to help guide him, stayed to survey, then went on to survey the Keet Seel, Inscription House, and Betatakin ruins. His work was the basis for President Taft's declaration of the Rainbow Bridge National Monument. Cummings and Wetherill and the rest of their party returned to Oljato. From there, after Judd rejoined them, the students made their way back to Bluff en route to Salt Lake City and fall classes. While in Bluff, they spoke with the *Montezuma Journal* of Cortez, Colorado, which publicized the first account of the discovery. The *Journal* wrote that students led by Cummings had spent the summer in the vicinity of Navajo Mountain. "They also brought back photographs of another natural bridge which spans a deep canyon running out of Navajo Mountain towards the south and from their measures it is bigger than the Great Augusta natural bridge of White Canyon northwest of Bluff."

The next day, on September 3, the *Deseret Evening News* of Salt Lake City also told of the find, crediting Cummings and company. However, on September 23, the *Cortez Herald* shot back, "An early report . . . from Salt Lake City credited the representatives of the Utah Archaeological Society with the discovery of this bridge. This report is entirely erroneous. The honor belongs to Mr. Douglas [*sic*]." That prompted Cummings to write the Wetherills asking if they had seen Douglass's statements in the paper: "Douglass has an article in it claiming all the credit and slurring us. Of what . . . material some men are made!" The *Grand Valley Times* weighed in with the headline "Jealousy Besets Gov't Official," and quoted Cummings as saying, "I am disgusted with the petty little spirit shown by Mr. William B. Douglas [*sic*], examiner of surveys of the general land office, in the interviews given out by him on the discovery of the new natural bridge in San Juan County."[50]

On October 2, Neil Judd wrote Douglass to explain why he was refusing to supply promised photographs of ruins they had visited after the discovery of the bridge. "Despite the fact that the Utah party was very much responsible for the success of your summer's work you very ungratefully refuse to mention it in your report. The 'oversight' is obvious. The pettiness of your claims is laughable; their smallness beyond belief." On the same date of his letter to Douglass, the *Deseret Evening News* also published an article by Judd complaining Douglass was trying to take credit for the discovery of Rainbow Bridge when the honor was due Cummings. Even the newspaper's headline heaped sarcasm on Douglass: "How W. B. Douglass, U.S. Examiner of Surveys, 'Discovered' the Big Bridge."

For his part, Douglass continued to try to stop Cummings from digging in the ruins. He wrote John Wetherill on September 19 after he returned to Cortez, "I believe it would be very unwise of him to remove anything found in the area withdrawn in the Presidential proclamation until he gets express permission from the Secretary of the Interior. I had a telegram about that which I intended showing him but forgot it in my hasty departure." In fact, the chief of the Bureau of American Ethnology of the Smithsonian had replied the previous month that Cummings was apparently legally working under the authority of Hewett. Another official in Washington asked Douglass for more information. Still Douglass persisted. In November he wrote Hough, "I am doing all in my power to stop him [Cummings]. That he, with all the fruits of the Garden of Eden before him, in the matter of excavations, must eat of the forbidden tree, is disappointing indeed."[51]

That the Cummings party and Douglass argued for years over who had discovered Rainbow Bridge pointed to their desire to mimic the scientific and cultural figures of the Second Great Age of Discovery, to which the Rainbow Bridge expedition was but a postscript. Discovery allowed the pair to perform the American emergence mythology as told in some intellectual circles and in popular culture. Discovery created Rainbow Bridge as a modern place and required that meanings be attached to it. As Blind Salt Clansman reportedly asked Louisa Wetherill, "Why do they want to ride all the way over the clay hills to see—just rocks?" Rocks, after all, have no intrinsic meaning. Rock arches only are given meaning, are produced as places, by a particular culture at a moment in time. In producing a place through "discovery," the Cummings/Douglass expedition gave it meaning. They wanted to be inscribed within the pantheon of mostly male heroes who brought the world into Euro-American space. They also wanted to place themselves at Rainbow Bridge as the equals of the white American males enshrined in popular culture as conquering adventurers within the national emergence mythology.

In bringing Rainbow Bridge into the knowledge of their civilization, they hoped to circulate it as a place to observe how ancient forces, defined by the science of geology, created a natural wonder. By casting it as a place for practicing archaeology, they in effect set Indians who had lived in the area in sharp contrast to the modern world. In assisting in the creation of a new national monument, they made it a place where American nationalism could dwell, with its story of progress from the primitive to civilization, where America's nature was in harmony with its institutions and people. In trying to inscribe these meanings there, however, Cummings and Douglass inevitably produced Rainbow Bridge as a place of modernity. It contained not ancient forces but modern sensibilities.

Discovery depended upon the reproduction of words and images by mechanical means to a wide audience, one whose daily lives were far removed from the place thus created. Navajos had circulated knowledge locally and used tribal mythology to make Rainbow Bridge a place in their culture and connected it to the vital rains that sustained their bodies. The Anglo-American discoverers used their own culture to create a different place, and they circulated it to people whose bodies would never depend on the rains of the area and whose interest was decidedly abstracted from their daily lives.

In 1914, Cummings once again was back working out of John Wetherill's trading post, now moved to Kayenta, Arizona, some twenty miles south of the Utah state line. There, Cummings and his crew, dirty and disheveled from digging in ruins, met another Wetherill client in the company of six young women. The man, Cummings wrote later, "instructed his 'cousins,' as he called them, not to have anything to do with our crowd. . . . For some reason he seemed to be somewhat afraid of us." On the way back from attending a Navajo ceremony, one of the young women lost control of her horse. A member of Cummings's party charged out and slowed it. "Mr. Grey, it seems, was very indignant, and said that the young lady in question was in control of her horse, that she could have managed it, and the man from the 'greasy sack outfit from Utah' should have minded his own business."[52] The Mr. Grey the Cummings's party encountered was Zane Grey, by then the famous author of the 1912 novel *Riders of the Purple Sage*. The year after the encounter, Grey would publish a sequel, *The Rainbow Trail,* a story of cowboys and their women that culminated at Rainbow Bridge.

CHAPTER THREE

The Storehouse
of Unlived Years

Zane Grey and the Modern Old West

In 1910, a *New York Times* review of Zane Grey's new novel, *Heritage of the Desert,* said the book had earned the author the right to be classed among the best of American novelists who took the frontier as their focus of exploration. The review drew a map of sorts of the United States: "From the Aroostook to San Diego and Snohomish to the Florida Keys, the story tellers have ranged this country until one would have thought there was not left in it one corner anywhere that had not been used as the background of a novel." *Heritage of the Desert,* however, had "staked out a region hitherto unknown in American fiction . . . that almost inaccessible country of Southern Utah and Northern Arizona bordering on the rim of the upper reaches of the Grand Canyon of the Colorado." On top of the Navajo place and over Cummings's and Douglass's site of science and Anglo-American discovery, Zane Grey overlaid a very different kind of narrative, and by inscribing it with new meanings he remade Rainbow Bridge as a place in modern America.[1]

Heritage of the Desert marked Grey's emergence as a popular writer and put him firmly on the path to establishing his formulaic Western as a dominant literary form in twentieth-century American popular culture. In several trips to the Utah-Arizona desert, he had found a recipe for producing novels that worked: a ride into wild areas, notebooks full of descriptions of the landscape, and local characters and stories that could be translated into an adventure/romance novel that a New York publisher would buy. Personal and cultural conditions became a story, which, through mechanical reproduction and wide distribution of books, produced a new place. It was not the frontier of old, but a new, modern place, reflecting and reproducing its age.

Although Owen Wister's *The Virginian* of 1902 invented the modern Western, it was Grey who brought the Western fully into the twentieth century and made it widely popular. Grey's novels, according to one cultural historian, were "instrumental in actually defining the Western as a genre. . . . He all but single-handedly confirmed the shape of a powerful new narrative form." Grey's books appeared regularly on bestseller lists from 1917 to 1925, accumulating sales during that period of more than 40 million copies, and his popularity continued well into the 1930s. He wrote more than sixty novels and more than 250 short stories and outdoors articles. At least 116 movies have been made from his stories, and there were 129 episodes of a TV series, "Zane Grey Theater," from 1956 to 1961, as well as a magazine and newspaper comic strips based on his work. In 1925, *Publishers Weekly* placed Grey sixth out of one hundred best-selling authors from 1900 to 1924; a 1927 article ranked Grey first from 1919 to 1926. Zane Grey established formulas and plots followed for decades by pulp fiction and screenwriters when the Western was at its height of popularity as an American genre.[2]

The heart of Zane Grey's West was the remote border area of southern Utah and northern Arizona from Kanab, Utah, in the west to Monument Valley in the east, from Rainbow Bridge in Utah to the north rim of the Grand Canyon in Arizona. During his many trips there, starting in 1907, Grey kept journals in which he described landscapes and people, and used these in his fiction. The modernization of economic and social life in the second industrial revolution of the late nineteenth century, with its ideas about the roles of men and women, disputed Grey's vision of the world in his fiction. In his stories, the Utah-Arizona borderlands became the stage on which these conflicts were performed. He fashioned Rainbow Bridge and other areas into sites for an authentic masculinity in a primitive past of the American West of popular culture.

Pearl Zane Gray (spelled with an "a") was born in 1872 in Zanes-ville, Ohio, a town named for one of his ancestors. His father, Lewis M. Gray, was a traveling preacher who became a dentist. Lewis Gray's office-bound profession was of little interest to a son who spent his days outdoors playing and fishing with friends. Zane lived among boys who flourished away from mothers at home and fathers at work, in the forests and fields and orchards of small towns. As a boy, he read *Robinson Crusoe* and *The Last of the Mohicans.* The latter, he later said, exerted tremendous influence on his storytelling.

When the elder Gray went broke from bad investments in 1890, the family moved to Columbus, Ohio. It was there that Lewis Gray apparently changed the spelling of his last name to Grey, likely to put the stigma of bankruptcy behind him. The experience deeply affected the young Zane. In a diary entry, Grey described himself at that time as "disgraced and ostracized . . . receiving a bitter education never to be overcome."[3] Zane played baseball and went to work in his father's office. He then attended the University of Pennsylvania and played baseball on the college team while he studied dentistry. He had dis-liked his father's business, but the university gave him an escape from home. Dentistry offered him a profession with which he already was familiar and required only three years of study.[4]

In 1896, Zane opened a dental office in a poor, immigrant neigh-borhood in New York, a location that brought him little money and helped enforce a sense of isolation. To alleviate his loneliness, he turned to books and became an avid reader. He also joined the Campfire Club, an elite group of outdoors enthusiasts. Among its members were Ernest Thompson Seton, a founder of the Boy Scouts of America; Dan Beard, founder of the Sons of Daniel Boone and later an organizer of the Boy Scouts; Gifford Pinchot, the first director of the U.S. Forest Service; and various editors of outdoors-theme publications.

Grey also began to take vacations away from the city. A conversation with his mother about his ancestors, the Zanes of the Ohio frontier, brought back memories of stories from his youth and of his interest in the frontier tales of James Fenimore Cooper and the pulp fiction of Harry Castleman. Writes biographer Thomas Pauly, "If there was any single epiphany that transformed the has-been baseball player and unhappy dentist into a writer, this was it." Grey contrasted his unhappiness with his dental practice and his life in the city to the seeming freedom of the frontier of American fiction and his own ancestors. He began to write at night and to long to be able to do so without the interruptions of a dental practice.[5]

If, as Pauly asserts, this was the moment that Grey's desire to become a writer was born, then such a calling sprang too from his personal frustrations with modernization and with his urban experience. Modernization is narrated by twin discourses of progress and nostalgia. "Progress," writes historian Christopher Lasch, "implied nostalgia as its mirror image."[6] Nostalgia yearned for a past that was romanticized as purer, simpler, and authentic in contrast to a modernization in which the old is tossed out and everything is made anew over and over again.

Particularly at the end of the nineteenth century, nostalgia manifested itself in "antimodernism," the term used by historian T. J. Jackson Lears for the discourses, styles, and practices that arose in reaction to the tremendous changes brought on by modernization. Some—such as writers James Fenimore Cooper and Henry David Thoreau, historian Francis Parkman, and painters Thomas Cole and Albert Bierstadt—attempted to "fix" the changing landscape in a moment of preindustrial time, to preserve the primitive before it disappeared.[7] At the turn of the century, middle-class men joined fraternal organizations such as the Improved Order of Red Men to engage in faux primitive rituals. Theodore Roosevelt extolled vigorous physical activities of hunting and the outdoor life to regenerate Anglo-American manhood, which was seen as endangered by the ease of modern life. Other forms of antimodernism were sports, a tonic of fresh air, a rediscovery of nature, a worship of wilderness, an emphasis on camping, creation of the Boy Scouts, an admiration of romanticized Indian cultures, hunting by middle- and upper-class men, romantic literature, the simple life, arts and crafts movements, an admiration and emulation of certain aspects of medieval and Middle Eastern culture, and a search for authentic experience and "real life."

Antimodernism was not, however, a force counter to prevailing values. Rather, it was fully in accord with its contemporary world. Antimodernism was a modern pursuit, moving the nation into the new economy and new social roles. Because it provided progress with a visual and narrative timeline, the discourses and practices arising from antimodernism's various forms were not only fully compatible with the modern world but were at its very core.[8]

By about the mid-nineteenth century, acquisition of new territories in the West coincided with modernization, including an increase in the mechanical production of books, magazines, and images. The intersection of the westward national expansion and the means to reproduce images and words about that process set the stage, according to historian Alfred Runte, for the East to narrate western expansion as a nationalist adventure, with stories, travel accounts, and dramatic paintings placed within a wild and spectacular nature. "Indeed, Americans conquered the region precisely as popular literature, art, and professional journalism came of age. While the frontier passed into history, the nation watched intently, if not in the field then through its dime novels, its newspaper correspondents, engravers, artists, and explorers."[9]

In this modern moment, Zane Grey contrasted the lives of the frontiersmen of fiction and family memory to his own life as a struggling dentist. Whatever influence he had on formation of the twentieth-century Western came in this intersection of the city and frontier nostalgia. But this was, of course, a modern nostalgia: a vague, nagging memory of a life at some time in the past that had been authentic. In the Old West, at the moment of industrialization and its changing of the physical landscape and economic and social roles, Anglo-Americans found a past in which human beings were close to nature, to their economy, and to their social roles. Wrote Grey, in his 1952 novel *Captives of the Desert,* "This desert solitude was the storehouse of unlived years, the hush of the world at the hour of its creation."[10]

In 1902, Grey published his first magazine story and in 1903 completed his first novel, *Betty Zane,* about the adventures of his ancestors on the early American frontier. Unable to get the book published, he borrowed money from Reba Smith, his brother's girlfriend, to pay for the printing. In September 1904, Grey purchased a house in Lackawaxen, Pennsylvania, at the confluence of the Lackawaxen and Delaware rivers. Along with other family members, Grey moved to the new house, which he viewed as refuge from the city and modern life, a return to the "simple life" of premodern times.[11]

Grey likely borrowed the money for the house from Reba Smith and a patient, Lina Elise ("Dolly") Roth, whom Grey had been courting since 1900, when she was 17 and he 28. Even while courting Dolly, Grey continued to see and have sexual relations with other women.[12] Nonetheless, Dolly and Grey were married on November 21, 1905. Dolly's inheritance of some $10,000 would support them for several years as Grey struggled to make a living as a writer. The couple went West on their honeymoon in early 1906 and stopped off at the Grand Canyon on their way to California. It was Dolly, however, and not Grey who wanted to travel to the West. "I really don't want to go," Grey wrote in a journal.[13]

In letters before and after marriage, Grey attempted to set the terms of his masculinity. Despite vows of monogamy, he wanted to leave open the possibilities his attraction to other women might bring. Grey amassed a collection of nude photographs of nearly all the women with whom he had sexual relations, some of which also showed Grey during intercourse. In addition, Grey kept journals in code that contained explicit descriptions of his sexual acts.[14]

Grey's other journals and his letters reveal grave insecurities and fears fed by periodic, crippling bouts of depression. He describes a long history of dark periods that led to intense self-loathing. His diary from 1917 provides the best description of these depressions. "For many years I have had these. All my notebooks are full of them. . . . The tendency to morbid brooding is an insidious terrible disease." The next day he wrote, "A hyena in ambush, that is my black spell! I conquered one mood only to fall prey to the next. And there have been days of hell. Hopeless, black, morbid, sickening, exaggerated mental disorder."[15] The disorder caused him to question his sanity and masculinity time and again. These periodic outbreaks shaped Grey's writing. His principal male characters often suffered some illness or problem that only the West could cure. They entered the West, struggled, and became men by throwing off sickness and weakness.

Grey's mental illness also found explanation in the modern world in which men were confined for long periods in offices and spaces of commerce, where it was difficult for the Victorian ideal of the independent man to perform. Doctors of that period diagnosed a condition called "neurasthenia," a nervous disorder attributed to excessive brain work and the strain on professionals and businessmen from a challenging bureaucratic economy in which work was done mostly inside and without physical labor. Some contemporary commentators concluded that middle-class men had grown decadent in contrast to working-class and immigrant males, who still exercised "primitive" customs that maintained their virility. Even the shape of the male body was a concern. Zane Grey once explained his attraction to hunting and fishing in terms of the effects of modern life on the male body: "Not to practice strife, not to use violence, not to fish or hunt, that is to say, not to fight is to retrograde a natural man. Spiritual and intellectual growth are attained at the expense of the physical."[16]

Grey's prospects as a writer and provider for his family were at their lowest ebb in 1907. His fledgling writing career brought in little money, and he and his wife, now with a son, were still living on her inheritance. Grey's depression seemed particularly acute early that year. He later wrote, "At the end of five years I appeared to be as far away as ever from finding acceptance of my work. Disappointments had multiplied until their combined weight was crushing." That year Grey attended a lecture at the Explorers Club in New York by one Charles Jesse Jones. "Buffalo Jones" spoke of his work along the Arizona Strip on the north side of the Grand Canyon to preserve wildlife he once had hunted. Jones was in New York to raise money for his efforts but had been ridiculed for his claim of having captured wild animals by roping them like a cowboy would a steer. Afterward, Grey offered to write a book of Jones's exploits to prove their veracity. Jones agreed that Grey could join him in the West, in part because Grey could help defray his expenses. Grey later wrote that he hesitated to use more of Dolly's money, but she insisted, and Zane Grey went west to try to revive his dwindling prospects, as some of the characters of his novels would.[17]

Passing through Salt Lake City in March 1907 on his way to meet Jones, Grey wrote Dolly a letter that captured his mind-set as he went about what would become, after two trips to the Utah-Arizona border country, a cathartic experience that would launch his career as a writer. In the missive, Grey pined after a masculinity stuck in modern

boyhood dreams that embraced classic tales of the chivalrous, romantic heroism of Western civilization. Upon awakening to a snowy day,
he wrote Dolly that he had "dreamed many dreams, and wrote many
books, and fought many battles, and loved many women, and was a
hero—for I went in search of and found the Golden Fleece. To overcome fierce beasts and kill evil men; to expand the hearts of men, and
subdue those of women; to overthrow greed and poverty and prostitu-
tion; in a word, to be heroic, that is in my blood. That, perhaps, is the
great secret of my discontent."

For all of that bravado, however, there was a troubling disquiet. Grey
feared mental illness; he feared that his opportunities for making a
living as a writer were slipping away, if not gone. Grey wrote of his
unwillingness to be faithful in his marriage, not a year and a half old.
He doubted his capacity to love:

> Under proper guidance in my youth I should have lived to be
> a great poet. I knew it. But, now, with bitter past, hemmed in
> by narrow confines, limited by poisoned habits, bound by all
> the stone-set laws of slow developing years, what can I do? I
> actually sicken for knowledge.
>
> . . . I have tried to kill the deadly sweetness of conscious
> power over women. A pair of dark blue eyes makes me a tiger.
> I loved my sweetheart in honest ways more than any other; I
> love, I love my wife, yet such iron I am that there is not change.
> I do not melt.
>
> . . . All is quiet. I feel lonely and sad without you, yet were
> you here quite likely I would be cold. I cannot help it.
>
> . . . I shall go down, because man is not immortal, but it will
> be in the last ditch, spent, bloody, unyielding.[18]

In that mess of contradictions—boyhood fantasies and masculine
bravado as well as modern self-doubt, sexual aggression, and emotional
indifference—Grey arrived about a week later in Flagstaff, Arizona.
Buffalo Jones was there to meet him. Before they departed, Jones took
Grey to observe the trial of Jim Emmett, who owned a ranch at Lee's
Ferry, a Mormon-founded crossing of the Colorado River just south

of the Utah state line. Emmett was acquitted of charges of rustling from the Bar Z, a rival cattle company. Grey was introduced, and he hired Emmett to bring the party through the desert.[19]

Grey, Jones, and their party accompanied Emmett back to Lee's Ferry on the Colorado River, upstream from the Grand Canyon. The prospect of the trip had him, as Grey wrote Dolly, "quivering with joy. . . . I have lost all my blues and am actually happy." Grey wanted to study the Mormons with whom he was riding and the Indian villages he would visit, but writing a novel was not on his mind. "This ought to make great material for the occasional short story I want to write." While Grey joked with Dolly about a polygamous Mormon with the group (Emmett had several wives, as did another member of the party) who wanted the fledgling writer to meet his two families and fifteen unmarried daughters, Grey assured his wife he could be faithful. "I thank the Lord I'm so much of a man."[20]

Grey and the group of men and horses set out on April 12, 1907, for the trip to Lee's Ferry. Grey's diary of the trip shows a modern man inventing a journey back in time to a premodern landscape. Such a landscape was "reminiscent of something not remembered," which by the early twentieth century was a desire to see the world as it once was at its most powerful and primitive before modernization glossed it over. Here was "the hush of the world at the hour of its creation." The horseback ride was for Grey the physical acting out of words and images of American culture that told how to see and to give meaning to the experience. Grey saw the area not as a home, as natives would, but as a space of primitive places, peoples, sights, smells, and food. Thus on April 19, Grey noted, "We are twenty miles farther on into the desert and the ghastly skeleton of the earth is becoming visible." After the first day's ride, "Jones cooked me a steak in the old buffalo style, and I never tasted anything so good."[21]

Grey's diary showed him physically and emotionally tested by the conditions. "I am a sight to behold," he wrote at noon on April 15. "Never thought I could get so dirty, or hungry, or thirsty." The other men in the group initiated Grey into the West by playing tricks on him. Emmett, Grey later related, sent him to inspect ruins "only a few miles" from camp that turned out to require hours of walking to reach.[22] There also were numerous other experiences, including a buffalo that threatened to charge Grey's horse and a sandstorm "so bad that it was impossible to see a road ahead. I had to cover my face and let the horse find his way home." Grey wrote one night after a hard day of riding, "I am very tired. My legs are so sore from sitting on a horse that I can hardly sit down."

The party reached the north rim of the Grand Canyon and tried to capture the cougars that Jones was trying to preserve. Grey spent his time pursuing cougars chased by dogs, photographing Jones and the others, and taking notes. During one still night the cry of a cougar left Grey terrified. One of the cowboys on the trip later remembered that Grey's inexperience meant the hired hands had to watch and guide him. Grey also appeared sickly to the others. Former cowhand Rowland Rider remembered: "When I first met him I realized that he hadn't been in too good health."[23]

Grey, with his inexperience and weakness, was a sharp contrast with the men with whom he rode. Grey ignored some of Jones's obvious flaws as a leader, his unfamiliarity with the northern Arizona land-scape, and his aging body to describe him as "erect, rugged, brawny." Grey wrote, "He had a dark, bronzed, inscrutable face; a stern mouth and square jaw, keen eyes, half-closed from years of searching the wide plains, and deep furrows wrinkling his cheeks."[24] Grey later lionized Emmett, a huge, bearded man, in a piece titled "The Man Who Influenced Me Most." Emmett "stood well over six feet, and his leonine build, ponderous shoulders, and great shaggy head and white beard gave an impression of tremendous virility and dignity." By ignoring certain characteristics or behaviors, Grey made these men into the heroes of his boyhood reading, sharply contrasted with his father and the confining profession of dentistry. In the meanings he projected upon them, Grey found models for later fictional characters.[25]

Grey also experienced a Wild West moment. The Bar Z fore-man, known as Dimmick, had testified against Emmett at the trial in Flagstaff. By Grey's account, he and Emmett had ridden to a place where they planned to spend the night when they were confronted by Dimmick, who was already there. Dimmick brandished a rifle, and Emmett pulled out a pistol. Grey recounted that he stepped between the two and, with his face "white as a sheet," yelled, "Don't kill each other! It'll spoil my trip." Emmett then put away his gun and turned.

Dimmick greeted him with, "Howdy young feller! You shore took chances heah!" But Rowland Rider, the cowboy who was with Dimmick, remembered the situation differently: "When he [Dimmick] saw who it was, of course, he drew his six-shooter and he would have shot Jim Emett [*sic*] had I not kicked the gun out of his hand." Grey then begged Emmett not to shoot Dimmick, and Rider told the pair to "move on because I can't hold this man forever."[26]

By May 9, it was time for Grey to go home, beginning with a return to Flagstaff. The thought of "going back across these terrible canyons, and that terrible desert makes me sick," Grey wrote as the group was about to embark. "It could take ten or twelve days to get home, and that is enough to lay me out." There was beauty to write about along the way, but by the next day, Grey was remarking of the hardships: "My God! What I have been through since 5 o'clock this morning." The group crossed the Colorado River and began the journey up the other side on a difficult trail until they halted for the night. The day's journey left him exhausted and thinking of Dolly. "I am writing this in a little box canyon some distant from the river, and I am barely able to write."

In a letter a few months later, Grey summarized the experience, which had left him physically spent but with an interesting cast of characters in mind: "I starved on the desert, was lost on the desert, buried in sand on the desert and I lived on the desert. I met some real men, men who lived lonely terrible lives, who are silent, who perform heroic deeds as a matter of course, and men who have hearts, who have loved and lost. I met Mormons and I hate them. I learned something of their women and I pity them. I met the strange nomadic Navajos;— and as an anti-climax, I had some associations with big mountain-lions."[27]

By Christmas 1907, Grey had written seven chapters of *Last of the Plainsmen,* his account of the trip with Buffalo Jones. Another bout of depression, however, left him in a dark state.[28] In April 1908, he returned to northern Arizona and southern Utah to take more photographs for the book. The trip was the same mixture of physical challenges, sensual observations, and encounters with stark, strange land forms and exotic people. This time, however, with one such trip already behind him, Grey was ready for the challenges. He visited Kanab, Utah—"beautiful little village. Mormons interesting"—and Fredonia, Arizona, across the state line. Both towns were Mormon enclaves where polygamy was practiced in defiance of the church's 1890 ban. He described roping mountain lions with Jones ("Great Day! Hard work!"). He went down the trail into the Thunder River area north of the Grand Canyon. He bought blankets from Navajos, visited with Paiutes, and assisted in the capture of wild horses.[29]

The two trips made Grey an experienced traveler on horseback into some of the wildest country left in the continental United States. The first left Grey exhausted, and he also had felt himself a boy among "real men," whom he fit into his image of American masculinity gained from frontier fiction. But the second made him, in his own description, "thin, black, wiry, and hard as iron." Grey wrote a friend that he also had discovered a personality within himself that was "wild, savage, fiery, and strong."[30] The transformation of Grey's body to tanned and hard made him "Native," in contrast to the softness of the modern American middle-class male. His discovery of a "fiery" personality was a counter to the bouts of depression that left him brooding and self-pitying. Grey felt his body and emotions regenerated in the desert of the Utah-Arizona border country.

In 1908, Grey and Jones took the manuscript of *The Last of the Plainsmen* to the New York offices of the book publisher Harper & Brothers and editor Ripley Hitchcock. Several days later, Grey was summoned, and Hitchcock told him, "I don't see anything in this to convince me you can write either narrative or fiction." Grey left the office stunned; according to his later description, his sight failed, and his body went cold. He reached the street and clung to a steel post—"the most exceedingly bitter moment of my life." Grey quickly recovered, however, and he narrated the experience as a transformational moment. Of the publisher, Grey cried, "He does not know! They are all wrong!"[31] After *The Last of the Plainsmen,* which later would be published, Grey wrote a friend that he had no desire to write another "lion story." "I'd much rather write a big novel, and fill it with the desert, the Mormons, and their relations." Grey said his disappointment at Hitchcock's response prompted him to sit down and write through the winter his breakthrough Western novel, *Heritage of the Desert.* In reality, Grey went into a prolonged depression and took two more trips, including the return to northern Arizona for more photographs, before he started writing in mid-November 1909. Grey worked feverishly, sometimes past midnight, on the book, and he completed it on January 23, 1910. This time, Harper gave Grey a contract.[32]

Heritage of the Desert opens with a man discovered prone on the ground in southern Utah, almost dead. "My name is Hare," the character tells would-be rescuers. "I am twenty-four. My parents are dead. I came West because doctors said I couldn't live in the East." Like Grey, Hare is given to depression, and he suffers "blind, sickening headaches." Hare had passed through Salt Lake City, secured a job with a cattle outfit, and ended up sick and near death in southern Utah. Luckily, he is found by August Naab, a tough but kind and fair Mormon who owns a ranch along a river. Naab is a man who had conquered the desert: "His chest was wide as a door, his arms like the branch of an oak," a description matching that of Emmett, the owner of the ranch at Lee's Ferry. Dene, the fictional cattle thief, and Holderess, a non-Mormon rancher and Dene's partner, create the tension of the novel as they try to take Naab's land and animals from him. The characters could be based on Emmett's enemies, owners of the cattle company that accused him of rustling, or even on Emmett, who was being tried on rustling charges when Grey first encountered him.

In the novel, Naab helps heal Hare and restore his masculinity. Naab provides Hare with a gun to protect against outlaws, thereby "giving him a man's part to play. The full meaning lifted Hare out of his self-abasement; once more he felt himself a man."[33] Hare's health begins to return: "The wilderness of this desert cañon country, and the spirit it sought to instill in him, had wakened a desire to live." Like the hardening of Grey's body, the desert and the work at the Naab ranch transforms Hare. "The leanness of arms, the flat chest, the hollows were gone," Grey writes. "He did not recognize his own body." In scenes like those described by Grey during the 1907 trip, Naab also teaches Hare about the desert and how to see; "his eyes had adjusted themselves to distance and dimensions."[34]

Hare is attracted to Mescal, the exotic half-Navajo, half-Spanish girl living with Naab. Her touch "rioted in his blood," Grey writes. "His heart swelled in exquisite agony." Mescal, however, had already been promised to one of Naab's sons. Hare rescues her and then undergoes the last part of his rebirth when "he too had been overcome by the desert's call for blood." The tensions culminate in a quick-draw shootout—perhaps inspired by the confrontation of Emmett and Dimmick during Grey's actual visit to the area: "Gleam of blue—spurt of red—crash!"

In the final chapter, Hare marries Mescal in an Eden-like scene at the Naab ranch. They camp on their wedding night on a plateau above the ranch like one Grey described in his 1907 diary. With the campfire burning and their horses nearby, they prepare for bed, and "a lonesome coyote barked. The white stars blinked out of the blue and the night breeze whispered softly among the cedars."[35] A regenerated man and the object of his desire could reproduce in blessed matrimony along the Colorado River in the Utah-Arizona border country. Their progeny would be the true sign that Hare was now a complete man, reborn in the primitiveness of that Western space, his masculinity restored, his desires fulfilled.

In 1910, Grey wanted to return to the canyon country. He wrote soliciting the services of David Dexter Rust, a tourist guide from Kanab, Utah. "My purpose in going to Utah is to have a fine exciting interesting trip, and incidentally get some material for another book." Grey wanted to tell of the "wonder and beauty" of the Mormon struggles in the desert. "I will have to 'go some' to beat 'The Heritage of the Desert', and you are going to help me do it." Along with the guide, Grey wanted "a boy or an Indian to help." Grey offered to pay a boy $1 a day or a man $2 plus expenses. "An Indian or someone who knows Indians a little would be just what I want." Grey also urged Rust to make sure he had a horse to ride but added, "Don't get me a bucking bronco, for Lord's sake."[36]

The letters reveal another specific ingredient of the 1911 trip crucial for Grey: money. Money enabled Grey to travel to the desert. The novels he produced would not have existed had he not been able to pay Emmett, Rust, or other guides, and the income he received from Harper & Brothers or magazines for the stories he wrote was a key component of the formula that opened the trail from New York to one of the remotest parts of the forty-eight states. The money trail helped to make the places that Grey produced with his novels extensions of the city and of publishing houses and their ability to connect presses, writers, and consumers. And because the books were meant to sell, the writing had to accord with stories and images that, in various ways, already were familiar to readers.[37]

Rust, for whatever reason, did not make the trip; when Grey returned to Flagstaff, he hired another guide, Al Doyle, to get him to southern Utah. They planned to see Rainbow Bridge and the ruins of Tsegi Canyon, by this time the Rainbow Bridge and Navajo national monuments. Grey rode to Kayenta, Arizona, just south of the Utah state line, where in 1910 John Wetherill had moved his trading post from Oljato, Utah. Grey wanted to visit Rainbow Bridge in 1911, but Wetherill, the packer for the 1909 expedition that discovered the modern wonder, could not or would not take Grey that year. Shown a photograph of the bridge, Grey concluded he had "missed the grandest sight in the world." Grey did, however, ride from Kayenta along Marsh Pass and into Tsegi Canyon. He viewed the Anasazi ruins of Keet Seel and Betatakin, which Byron Cummings's archaeological party had explored in 1909. After completing this trip, Grey returned to Lackawaxen in May, and by August he had finished writing *Riders of the Purple Sage,* the book that became perhaps the single most important source of modern Westerns.[38]

As the novel opens, Venters, a cowboy working for Jane Withersteen, an unmarried Mormon woman trying to operate her late father's ranch, is about to be whipped by the evil, polygamous Mormon leader Tull, who wants to marry Jane. Just when Venters is about to feel the lash, Withersteen sees a "horseman, silhouetted against the western sky, coming riding out of the sage." The scene became a classic Western motif, the rider against the western sky, a vertical play between ground, man and horse, and the heavens that depicts a heroic and masculine landscape. The lone man is Lassiter. Unlike the easterner Hare in *Heritage of the Desert,* Lassiter emerges upright from the land. Lassiter is a mythical western man who rides a blind horse, never sleeps indoors, and never errs. He also knows when to shoot.

The plot of *Riders of the Purple Sage* revolves around two sets of would-be mates. Jane and Lassiter try to save the ranch from Tull, while Jane cares for a little orphaned girl named Fay, who turns out to be Lassiter's kidnapped niece. Venters is attracted to Bess, the daughter of the outlaw Oldring. The purple sage marks the openness of the desert of southern Utah, which holds opportunities for some, but also dangers, particularly for women. They are threatened with kidnapping, even rape, by evil Mormons.[39] Jane risks becoming Tull's polygamous wife in the closed, corporate Mormon society of Cottonwood— "Your body's to be held, given to some man, made, if possible to bring children into the world."[40] Jane is a modern woman who in the end must accept Lassiter and his guns to protect herself from Tull and his sexual designs and greed.

The open desert also holds the possibilities of romantic sexual union, however, which often in Grey's works are intermingled with images of nature. Yet these opportunities presented a challenge to societal norms of sexual contact sanctioned only within marriage. To protect his characters from modern dangers, Grey produced a new place. From Deception Pass, Grey's name for Tsegi Canyon, Venters finds and names Surprise Valley, an Edenic retreat reached through a hidden canyon passage up stairs carved in stone by ancient Indians. It is a valley guarded by a huge rock set so it can be toppled to shut off the outside world. In creating Surprise Valley, Grey appears to have combined descriptions of the canyon where the Betatakin ruins of Navajo National Monument are located off Tsegi Canyon that he had visited in 1911 and the ruins he encountered in Snake Gulch on the north side of the Grand Canyon in 1908.[41]

Venters takes Bess to Surprise Valley, where she heals from a gunshot wound and has wild animals for pets. Here too, Grey blends the ancient cliff dwellings, the objects of archaeologists, into a Utopian modern present. But that present depends on finding gold in the valley of ancient history. In contrast to the lessening of individual opportunity in corporate capitalism, Venters declares, "I'm free! I'm a man—a man you've made—no more a beggar!"[42] Hearkening back to Grey's shame over his father's bankruptcy and his own struggle to make a living away from his dental office, Venters finds independence from modern capitalism.

"Meantime, at the ranch," Tull and his Mormons prove to be too much of a force, so Jane and Lassiter, with little Fay in tow, retreat into Surprise Valley, while Venters and Bess leave across the purple sage to return to the Midwest with their gold and plans for marriage. Pursued by the evil Mormons up the stone stairs to Surprise Valley, Lassiter hesitates in dislodging the rock that would seal them inside. Jane cries, "Roll the stone! . . . Lassiter, I love you!" The stone tumbles, and the three are forever safe in Surprise Valley.[43]

If we think of the open space of the purple sage as the challenges of modernizing America, Surprise Valley is a place carved out of, but also isolated from, this America. When Lassiter rolled the stone, Surprise Valley was sealed, and in it a kind of primitive masculinity was protected from those social challenges. Grey made Surprise Valley a place of male dominance in which man, woman, and child could live harmoniously in primitive nature—the natural way, as Grey saw it.

Grey had a difficult time convincing Harper & Brothers to publish *Riders of the Purple Sage,* apparently because of its brutal depiction of Mormons. But the publisher agreed to a deal after Grey appealed to a senior officer. The book became a best-seller and brought Grey fame and money. The novel was most popular in urban centers but did not make the best-seller lists of any city west of Ohio.[44]

In the spring of 1913, Zane Grey was back in northern Arizona at John Wetherill's trading post in Kayenta. This time, Wetherill agreed to take Grey to Rainbow Bridge. For this trip, money was not in short supply, and Grey took along guests and extra help. Besides a cook, two young women also were present, identified in the Flagstaff newspaper as two of Grey's cousins, Misses Wilhelm and Swartz. Lillian Wilhelm, a thirty-year-old painter who was invited on the trip to illustrate Grey's next book, was a cousin of Dolly's. She had first met Grey in New York while he was dating Dolly. Her traveling companion was Elma Schwarz, a cousin eight years younger than she. The two women's participation was the culmination, it seems, of two years of Grey's daydreaming about beautiful women. His 1913 trip and subsequent ones with them and other women were an escape from what he obviously saw as the constraints on his masculinity imposed by a family that now included two children. Wilhelm and Schwarz both had long affairs with Grey.[45]

Grey and his entourage traveled to Kayenta and from there to Monument Valley and then on again to the ruins of Navajo National Monument in Tsegi Canyon. After a visit to the Keet Seel ruin, Grey found the trail to the canyon holding the Betatakin ruins where he had left

Zane Grey and a companion are shown in the foreground at Rainbow Bridge during one of Grey's several expeditions to the National Monument in the early decades of the twentieth century. Grey called Rainbow Bridge the "one great natural phenomenon, the one grand spectacle which I had ever seen that did not at first give vague disappointment." (Photograph in author's possession.)

Lassiter, Jane, and little Fay in their Surprise Valley. "With the sight of those lofty walls and the scent of the dry sweet sage there rushed over me a strange feeling that 'Riders of the Purple Sage' was true," Grey wrote of his return to Betatakin. He climbed about the canyon where, perhaps helped by the presence of two young women, his imagination found "Fay Larkin once had glided with swift sure steps." He left the area, "haunted by its loneliness and silence and beauty, by the story it had given me."[46] After the visit to the ruin, the party, which included Nasja Begay, the Paiute who had guided the Cummings-Douglass party to Rainbow Bridge in 1909, started for the huge stone arch. Also along was a big Mormon cowboy named Joe Lee.

Just as Grey ignored the noise of his companions at Betatakin to describe it as silent and the trail as lonely, Wilhelm and Schwarz were dropped from his nonfictional account of the trip. Instead, there were dangerous trails and descriptions of Joe Lee and Nasja Begay. Grey put himself in the role of the white explorer. "My party was the second one, not scientific, to make the trip," he claimed in one account. Later, he wrote: "And I was the first fortunate man, not scientific or

archaeological, to accompany Wetherill to see this magnificent phenomenon of nature." In fact, quite a few other parties preceded his
after the 1909 Cummings-Douglass discovery of Rainbow Bridge.[47]

The experience at the stone arch proved exhilarating and cathartic
for Grey, "the one great natural phenomenon, the one grand spectacle
which I had ever seen that did not at first give vague disappointment, a
disenchantment of contrast with what the mind had conceived." Rainbow Bridge, Grey wrote shortly after the visit, "silenced me. My body
and brain, dull from the toil of travel, received a singular and revivify-
ing freshness."[48] For Grey, Rainbow Bridge was his special place, one
where he took special friends.[49]

Out of this trip, and another in 1914, came a new novel published
in 1915, *The Rainbow Trail,* a sequel to *Riders of the Purple Sage.* Grey's
experience at Betatakin, in which he reimagined the little girl Fay as
a real person in his fictional Surprise Valley, became the basis for the
new book. The protagonist, John Shefford, like Hare of *Heritage of the
Desert,* is a man from the East in need of regeneration. Like Grey, who
wanted to be a writer and outdoorsman but first was stuck in a dental
practice, the fictional Shefford was forced to become a preacher by
his family. Shefford failed miserably and lost both his profession and
his faith. He is clearly a man struggling with modernity, in which for
many geology had supplanted Genesis and Darwin had called into
question literal readings of the Bible. Modernization and its seculariza-
tion of society led some to search for an alternate, authentic spirituality among primitive peoples and in nature.[50] So Shefford goes to the
desert to reconstruct his primitive male self and his spirituality, chasing
a story he heard in Illinois about Lassiter, Jane, and Fay sealed off in
Surprise Valley.

Shefford wants to find Surprise Valley and the three, particularly Fay,
who has grown into a young woman in the intervening years. Other
characters include Nas Ta Bega, an educated Indian who has returned
to his traditional home, and the Mormon cowboy Joe Lake. They teach
Shefford about the nature religion of the Indians and regenerate him
as a man. After a convoluted story in which Shefford finds Fay, who
had found a way out of Surprise Valley, about to be forced to submit to
a polygamous Mormon, Shefford and Fay flee to Surprise Valley. There
they free Lassiter and Jane, who take with them sacks of gold from the

place where they had been trapped for years. The entire group then heads toward Rainbow Bridge to escape pursuing Mormons via the Colorado River. Grey makes the fictional party the first to "discover" the bridge.[51]

At the stone arch, Fay remarks on how Shefford has been transformed by the challenges. He asks Fay to marry him, and she agrees. Shefford finds, along with love, a renewed religious faith, a combination of the primitive land and worldview of the Navajo. There was a spirit in the cañon and "the truth for Shefford was that this spirit was God. Life was eternal. Man's immortality lay in himself. Love of a woman was hope—happiness. Brotherhood—that mystic and grand 'Bi Nai!' of the Navajo—that was religion."[52]

Like Surprise Valley in *Riders of the Purple Sage*, with Grey's new novel Rainbow Bridge became a new modern place.[53] There, a masculinity displaced by a changing world could once again encounter a primitivism in which male values and social prerogatives were dominant. One could reconnect to nature through primitive Indians and reconstruct a religion of God *and* nature. One could join in traditional marriage and find true romantic love and happiness.

In 1925, after three more trips to Rainbow Bridge, Grey published another novel, *The Vanishing American*. In the years between the books, World War I and changes in American society left Grey disillusioned. "This approach of war is horrible to me, in its distressing necessity, in its threat of blood, hate, agony, in its destruction of ideals, hopes, in its awful forcing of doubt in self," he wrote in his diary as the United States prepared to enter the conflict. "I know that I am no coward, but I am sickened at the thought of war." Grey was deep in depression when the United States declared war on Germany in April 1917. "I feel like an atom whirling in a universe of winds." In October his mother died, and he was deeply affected. Grey felt modern society was moving beyond him and his values. His publicly displayed attitude of women as objects of a romantic idealism was offended by the more uninhibited behavior of women in the 1910s and 1920s, the flappers' shorter dresses and manners and cigarettes. Women also formally entered the political arena, claiming the right to vote in 1920. In 1917, the 45-year-old Grey declared, "I am at war with the times, with the ways of people, with the customs of life, with the ideals of men. I believe in the innate goodness and nobility of women, and I see salvation for the world only though them. Yet women today are wild, drifting, on the wrong track."[54]

That Grey should complain about a more open female sexuality seems to contradict his years of sexual involvements with numerous women, including teenagers, outside his marriage. Plus, the women with whom he had affairs were modern in the sense they were open to new adventures and to sex. Grey romanticized his affairs as just rewards for his successes, and, according to Pauly's biography, they helped relieve his recurrent depression.[55]

In a February 1923 diary entry, Grey wrote that his attraction to young women had been the basis of his work. "From every angle in which I view the matter I come back to the fact that therein lay my source of inspiration. I always knew it. But life has changed, and therein lies the staggering truth." At age 51, Grey lamented that modern America had passed him by, that he could no longer write books for "a legion of eager romance-loving dreaming girls. The movie, the motor, the jazz and dance, the suggestive magazine and novel, have done away with that type. I am a faint little voice in the cataclysmic roar of the age!"[56]

By June 1922, Grey had finished *The Vanishing American*. The main character is the Indian Nophaie, who grew out of Grey's experiences on the Navajo reservation, particularly with his first guide to Rainbow Bridge, Nasja Begay, and from the flu epidemic that swept much of the world killing millions of people, including the guide. Grey fictionalizes Nophaie as kidnapped by whites as a child while herding sheep in Monument Valley. His education culminated at an eastern university. Nophaie returned to his Monument Valley home to rediscover his Indian soul, which had been shrouded by the white man's education. For Grey, however, it is not the Indian who was vanishing but modern middle-class Anglo men's masculine self in the tempestuous waters of modernity. Nophaie represents the modern Anglo man's desire to reconnect to his primitive self in the authentic landscape of the American West. Through Nophaie, Grey sought to reconcile nostalgia for the American manhood of the past with the pursuits of modernity.[57]

Nophaie's love interest is Marian Warner, a white woman he met at the university who has come West to try to marry him and to get away from fallen modern women in the East: "The laxity of Marian's social set in no wise gave her excuse for wildness and daring. She hated the drinking and smoking of women, the unrestrained dances, the lack of courtesy, the undeniable let-down of morals."[58] The story involves Nophaie's struggles to bridge his education and his Indian primitive worship of nature. Science and progress had robbed modern Americans of a spiritual connection to nature. "Scientists would not grant nature a soul." Nophaie declares, "I am an American" and enters the service during World War I. But just as he returns a hero, influenza devastates the tribe. Nophaie too contracts influenza and is dying. But the trader Withers says, "I must tell you the strangest thing. Many of these Nopahs who died of this plague turned black. . . . Nophaie talked of turning *white*." Becoming white "must mean he is true at last—to the mind—the soul developed in him." Nophaie has begun to reconcile his Indian soul and his Anglo education, the prescription for the American middle-class man adrift in the modern world.

Nophaie takes a mystical journey to Monument Valley, yet still finds he has "no home, no kin." He then sets out on the trail to Rainbow Bridge, and the final transformation begins. Nophaie spends the night awake under the arch he calls Naza and experiences "the last dying flash of Indian mysticism and superstition." Geology has told him that, like the Vanishing American, the arch itself would not endure; it too "must in time pass away in tiny grains of sand, flowing down the murmuring stream." With that realization he understood the secret of the arch's great spell. As long as he could stay there, at Rainbow arch, he would be free and satisfied with his life. For Nophaie, and for Grey, the arch meant freedom because of its "isolation and loneliness and solitude." In the shadow of the devastating war and in the face of modernity's challenges to masculine privilege, Rainbow Bridge was produced as a place where American middle-class men could recover their primitive, privileged selves: "The world of man, race against race, the world of men and women, of strife and greed, of hate and lust, of injustice and sordidness, the materialism of the Great War and its horrible aftermath, the rush and fever and ferocity of the modern day with its jazz and license and drink and blindness—with its paganism—these were not here in the grand shadow of Naza."

At Rainbow Bridge, Nophaie becomes a modern Anglo man who embraces his education yet retains the primitive soul. If the arch was disappearing a grain of sand at a time on the water and the wind as understood by geology, there still was a universal God in which the primitive spirituality of nature was available for the educated white man. Nophaie succumbs to exhaustion and is dying. He tells Marian that at Rainbow Bridge, he found "your God and my God." And now, "All is well!"[59] Rainbow Bridge was Grey's ultimate storehouse of unlived years. Kept there, in that place, was the modern angst of an unremembered past. There dwelled the timelessness of the primitive, authentic Anglo middle-class masculinity of a mythical America, kept safe and fresh from the ravages of modern life.

If Zane Grey brought the Western to a fully formed but still evolving genre that would dominate much of American popular culture in the twentieth century, it should be remembered that although the Utah-Arizona border region's deserts, canyons, stone arches, and ruins became his mystical Old West, it was a thoroughly modern Old West. While Grey's stories used the outward forms of the nineteenth-century American West, they were thoroughly engaged, as was he, in the social and cultural questions of the early twentieth century. Later in the twentieth century, social issues increasingly became the subject of another medium, film, and they brought new meanings and concerns to the area that Grey had ridden through as he imagined his stories. The canyons, mesas, and stone spires would become still another place in modern America.

CHAPTER FOUR

John Ford and Monument Valley

The Production of a Mythical National Space

Approaching the soaring buttes and towering spires of Monument Valley from the south, a traveler first encounters a massive volcanic rock plug that rises dramatically from the desert sands. Its Navajo name, Agathla, can be translated as "Much Fur." In local Navajo culture, Agathla helps to hold up the sky. Agathla is one of the sites where early members of the Western Water Clan camped in their wanderings seeking their relatives, a story related in the Bead Chant. While the Western Water Clan camped at the rock, hunters disguised themselves with deer heads and hides and killed many deer. While the hides were being dressed, the fur blew against the rock, practically covering it. Hence its name. North of Agathla a short distance is Monument Valley, whose Navajo name has been translated several ways, as "Stretches of Treeless Areas," "Clearings among the Rocks," "Stretches of White Area (or Clearings) among the Rocks," and "Rough Rocks Standing Up." The mesas, buttes, and rock formations of the Navajo landscape came from the battle in the tribal emergence story in which the twins fought Yeitso, or Big God, one of the monsters whose vanquishing ushered the people into this world. Yeitso was sliced up during the battle, and parts of his body and blood became the rock formations. The large monuments also represent to the Navajos barrels or pots that store water that emerges as springs at their base.[1] These stories from the tribal emergence myth and collective memory imbue the landscape with meaning and create Monument Valley as a specifically Navajo place.

Past El Capitan, as Agathla became known to Anglo-Americans, Zane Grey rode on horseback in 1913. Inspired by the stone mesas and columns of Monument Valley, the author set several novels there. Over the next few decades, filmmakers, artists, writers, and tourists crisscrossed Monument Valley, helping to make it a place within the context of their own culture and time. However, not until film director John Ford arrived toward the last of the Great Depression did the area get "remade" as an iconic place in twentieth-century American culture. Ford used Monument Valley as a major location for seven of his Westerns, beginning with the 1939 release of *Stagecoach* and ending with *Cheyenne Autumn* in 1964. All brought into Monument Valley the contemporary social and cultural challenges of the United States, whether the Depression, World War II, the Cold War, or the Civil Rights Movement. At Monument Valley, the national emergence myth was modified to take on the challenge of contemporary problems as Ford used the setting to redefine what it meant to be an American. In each film, a successful resolution by male protagonists allowed the uniting of a young Anglo-American couple who then symbolically can reproduce the nation. Monument Valley became a place where many of the anxieties and challenges of the twentieth-century United States were played out, the nation was again sanctified, and the collective memory reconsecrated.[2]

The Western genre allowed for stories that symbolized the founding of the nation in the encounter of Europeans with the wilderness and its inhabitants. Western intellectuals, Krista Comer writes, "have long observed that the West operates in nationalist discourse as a symbol not only for region but also for nation. It is commonplace of both western history and literary studies to note that the story of western settlement serves as the nation's founding myth."[3] The Western was the Anglo-American emergence mythology acted out through the motifs that identify the genre: cowboys, horses, Indians, plots, specific clothing styles, and so on. And, of course, there was the landscape.

At the end of the nineteenth century, Americans began to picture the Southwest as a national space valued for its aesthetic and cultural resources. Its uniqueness fed a sense of exceptionalism. Indeed, the Southwest became a valuable cultural space for Anglo-Americans just as anxieties were rising over the closing of the frontier, the tale of which had sustained the American narrative for nearly a century.[4] The West in general, but particularly the Southwest, became the site of an "Old West" of authentic men and places, of the ritual reenactment of the American emergence mythology, of spectacular nature and untrammeled wilderness, and of still "primitive" Indians. The Southwest more than any other area lent itself to the Western film because of its bareness of flora, exposure of naked land, and lack of development. The resistance of the land to the development of cities left much of the Southwest, in the modern formulation, as a primitive and, therefore, authentic landscape seemingly untainted by the stains of modernization. This "blank slate" of the Southwest was not really blank, of course. It held numerous American Indian cultures and their spaces. But the emptiness many Americans saw there itself was a space produced by modern America, filled with sensibilities that defined the primitive and authentic against the modern urban world.[5] The primitiveness of the Southwest enabled moviemakers to claim their tales as authentically grounded in a time before modernization had altered the wilderness.

Monument Valley provided Ford a linear space along the desert floor with its sparse vegetation. Ford's stagecoaches, cavalry troops, ranchers, and gunfighters moved horizontally along the desert floor as stories developed chronologically through time. But the stories traveled among mesas and stone spires soaring toward the heavens, which bestowed on the narrative a mythological weight and epic proportion, as in a cathedral where songs and prayers rise to the great space above. By using the genre of the Western set among natural towers of stone, Ford's stories created a mythical nationalist space out of Monument Valley.[6]

Monument Valley and nearby areas had a history of filmmaking at least two decades before Ford arrived with his company to make *Stagecoach*. As early as 1916, Zane Grey encouraged movie producers to use the actual locations for the film versions of his Westerns, most of which at that time were set in the Utah-Arizona border region. Grey's novel *To The Last Man* was filmed in the area about 1922. *The Water Hole,* based on a magazine story later published as the book *The Lost*

Pueblo, was filmed in the area in 1928. The most noted movie filmed in Monument Valley before Ford was based on Grey's novel *The Vanishing American,* released to theaters in 1925. The film was produced by the Famous Players–Lasky company of Jesse Lasky, whom Grey had escorted to the area to scout for locations.[7]

The Vanishing American, a silent film with cards for narrative and dialogue, begins with a quotation from Herbert Spencer's *First Principles* espousing a Social Darwinist survival-of-the-fittest trope in which the natural order dictated that stronger races conquer weaker ones. The narration continues, "In a Western state far from the present haunts of men, lies a stately valley of great monuments of stone." Monument Valley is shown. "Gateway from North to South—since the dim dawn of human life it has been the mighty corridor through which race after race has trod its way from darkness into dark. . . . Through the ages since the Great Beginning of it All, how many races have crept within the shadow of the Monuments?"

Shaggy early-human figures ascend out of a womb of rock. The procession evolves into cliff dwellers who are eventually overwhelmed by a warrior tribe before the arrival of Spanish conquerors and then Kit Carson, who subdues the tribe. The story progresses as the Indian leader Nophaie falls in love with the white school teacher, goes off to World War I with members of his tribe, returns a true American, but dies in the end. The last card reads, "—for races of men come—and go. But the mighty stage remains." The movie closes with a shot of Monument Valley.[8] In *The Vanishing American,* the "mighty stage" is a site where Anglo-Americans come to dominate the land because they are stronger. The land they possess as a result of their superiority as a race is symbolized by Monument Valley.

"My favorite location is Monument Valley," Ford told an interviewer in 1964. "It has rivers, mountains, plains, desert, everything the land can offer."[9] John Ford already had a long history of directing Westerns and movies from other genres when he came to Monument Valley in late 1938. His attraction to the Western genre began in childhood.

Ford was born John Martin Fenney in 1894 to Irish Catholic immigrants near Portland, Maine. John Fenney was the youngest of the six of eleven children who survived beyond childhood. In sharp contrast to the dominant Protestant Anglo culture, the family's multiethnic

Manjoy Hill neighborhood blended Yankees, Irish, Jews, Scandina-
vians, Scots, Canadians, and blacks.

At age 12, Ford contracted diphtheria and was confined to bed for
months. During that time, his sister Maime read to him such books as
Treasure Island, Huckleberry Finn, and *Grimm's Fairy-Tales.* The books
helped to develop Ford's sense of narrative. In his teens, Ford ushered
at a movie theater showing silent films. "At that time the things I loved
most were Westerns," Ford told his grandson in an interview late in
his life.

The early Ford also was stage-struck, and he worked and occasion-
ally acted in local theaters. In elementary school, a favorite teacher
started his education in artistic composition. The subjects he most liked
to sketch were cowboys and Indians, and he tended toward heroic,
idealized figures. Also influential was the high school principal and
history teacher William Jack, whom Ford remembered as a wonderful
speaker.[10]

History helped Ford invent himself and his America. In Jack's
classes, Ford learned that Irish immigrants had fought in the American
Revolution, a fact he used to galvanize his own sense of being American in contrast to his identity as a son of Irish immigrants in Yankee-
dominated Portland. Over the years, Ford mythologized his family
history, declaring that his father had come to America to fight in the
Civil War when it actually ended before his father immigrated. Ford's
exaggeration revealed a desire to construct a past harmonious with his
emotional needs. Often, that need was to define who qualified as a
good American, to be part of the "We" of "We the people."[11]

After high school, Ford wanted to enter the Naval Academy but
failed the entrance exam. Ford also claimed to have had a short-lived
experience at the University of Maine. So with few prospects in Portland, Ford went west in 1914 to be with his older brother. Francis
Fenney had left home and made his way from New York theaters to
Hollywood, where he acted in and became a notable director of silent
films, including important early Westerns.[12] John went to work for his
brother, first doing manual labor, then taking on other production jobs
and acting in films. He also worked for other companies in a variety of
jobs. Francis Fenney had changed his last name to Ford sometime after
he left home. John soon also became a Ford.

John Ford was an actor or stuntman in at least sixteen silent movies. One of his roles of this period was as a member of the Ku Klux Klan in D. W. Griffith's *The Birth of a Nation;* he appeared in a scene in which he played a man trying to keep a hood from falling over his glasses while riding a horse. Ford directed his first movie, *The Tornado,* in 1917. When the United States entered World War I that same year, Ford signed up for the draft. He was rejected for service but later fabricated a war record. From 1917 until the release of *Stagecoach,* Ford was a cast or crew member, writer, or director in 116 films. He directed at least thirty-four Westerns leading up to *Stagecoach.* Ford won an Academy Award as best director for the 1935 film *The Informer.*[13]

In the years before *Stagecoach,* the production of quality Westerns hit a slump as the Great Depression deepened. From the heady days of the 1920s to the Depression years of the '30s, Americans experienced a loss of faith in institutions and in their history as a story of progress. Even historian Frederick Jackson Turner's national emergence myth of the frontier as the formative space of American development had fallen into disrepute. Historian Walter Prescott Webb labeled the Great Depression "the crisis of the frontierless democracy," and questioned the authority of Turner's 1893 thesis. Webb wrote, "Either historians have claimed too much for the frontier as a cause of what is considered American or they must now face the very difficult task of telling us how we can preserve the frontier virtues of individualism, self-reliance and other virtues."

Archibald MacLeish in the Depression era captured that feeling of the closing of the American frontier in his poem "The Land of the Free": "We looked west from a rise and saw forever./ . . . Now that the land's behind us we got wondering/We wonder if the liberty was land and the/Land's gone: The liberty's back of us." In a 1932 campaign address, Franklin Roosevelt also resorted to the closed frontier metaphor: "Our last frontier has long since been reached, and there is practically no more free land. . . . We are now providing a drab living for our own people." Roosevelt's New Deal policies were heavily influenced by the discourse of the closed frontier. For ordinary citizens, the Depression was more than a financial catastrophe. It also seemed an overwhelming natural disaster complete with floods, dust storms, and erosion. Even the land itself seemed to have turned on America.[14]

The Depression did not, however, prompt a revolutionary response to the obvious failures of American capitalism. Intellectuals were unable to articulate a popular agenda for radical change, and the working class clung to whatever it could. Instead, Americans found security in their institutions and myths and reinforced existing values through rediscovery of tradition, folklore, national identity, and the common man. Henry Wallace's 1934 book, *New Frontiers,* recycled the myth to suggest ways America could transform to fit new realities of a modernization that had failed: "The great difficulty in designing social machinery is that it must be so fashioned to operate in two worlds: it must utilize the habits and beliefs of our old individualistic pioneer world; simultaneously it must operate in a new world where powerful economic forces have made mincemeat of many established habits and beliefs." Historians have noted a trend toward historical dramas and biographies that coincided with the New Deal's support of regionalist painters, folklore studies, and state guidebooks. Writers also turned to the past for material, including frontier literature. At the same time, the rising threat of war with totalitarian and militaristic regimes in Germany and Japan brought new demands for a coherent national mythology to face the challenges.[15]

So it was under these historical and social circumstances that American culture turned to its modern emergence myth to fortify the nation in the face of the challenges of the twentieth century. Threatened from within during the Depression and from without during World War II and the Cold War, American culture turned again toward its primitive landscape, the West, where it located tales of mostly male heroes battling the land and savage Indians. In 1938 and '39, the major studios enlisted in the campaign by reviving the Western. Statistics show the percentage of such films rising, beginning a thirty-year period in which the Western was the preeminent American mass-culture genre.

In 1939, Ford released three films grounded in American frontier history: *Young Mr. Lincoln, Drums along the Mohawk,* and *Stagecoach.* Two years earlier, Ford bought the film rights to a short story in *Collier's* by Ernest Haycox titled "Stage to Lordsburg" and hired a writer to turn it into a movie script. Ford had not made a Western since 1926. As he prepared a script from the short story as a big-budget Technicolor project, however, Ford found it difficult to interest a studio in risking the capital. Finally, producer Walter Wanger agreed to make it as a modest, black-and-white movie.

The magazine story was set in the nineteenth-century West and concerned a perilous journey by a disparate group of passengers: a cattleman, a young woman on her way to marry an Army infantry-man, an Englishman, a young man named Malpais Bill, a gambler, a whiskey drummer, and a prostitute, plus the driver and a guard. The story is understated, with spare dialogue and little character develop-ment. The prostitute is ostracized by the rest but shows a humane side as Bill falls in love with her. Indians attack. Several characters die. At Lordsburg, Malpais Bill shoots an enemy for an unstated reason; then he and the prostitute unite and, we can assume, marry.[16]

Ford and screenwriter Dudley Nichols altered Haycox's rather sketchy story by changing characters and adding plot elements. The alterations created the tension of the movie by pushing questions of class, respect, and identity to the forefront and posing a central ques-tion: Who deserves to be considered a good American?

Though Ford proved to be a mess of political contradictions over the years, his sympathies during the Depression years were with Roosevelt. Ford was involved in Hollywood labor battles during the Depression, and he helped form the Screen Directors Guild. In a speech to the guild, Ford blamed the problems of Hollywood workers during the Depression on Wall Street bankers, whom he accused of using the situ-ation to make gains against labor. Ford also aligned with Irish rebels against the English, and with Spanish Loyalists over Franco's Fascists in the Spanish Civil War. His strongest emotional and political stance, however, was his sympathy for the underdog.[17]

In the movie script, the cattleman of the magazine story is absent, and those boarding the stage include a banker with a satchel holding $50,000 stolen from his bank. The audience knows Gatewood is a thief, yet the pompous banker spouts conservative platitudes ("And remember this: What's good for the bank is good for the country" and "America for Americans") as he calls for reduced taxes and complains about a proposal for implementing bank examiners. Haycox's girl on her way to marry a soldier is replaced with Mrs. Mallory, a pregnant woman traveling to meet her husband, who is an officer. Mrs. Mal-lory, a daughter of southern aristocrats, shuns the prostitute, Dallas,

John Ford and a camera crew get ready to film "Apache" Indians for a scene from his 1939 movie *Stagecoach*. The Apaches were actually local Navajos who were recruited by Ford through the years to play various tribes in his movies. (Reproduced with permission from the Wisconsin Center for Film and Theater Research, United Artists Corporation, series 5.6.)

even after Dallas helps with the delivery and care of Mrs. Mallory's baby. The gambler of the magazine story is in the movie as a southern card shark named Hatfield. He wears fine clothes and puts on aristocratic airs despite his disreputable profession. Hatfield accompanies Mrs. Mallory out of respect for her father and participates in the shunning of Dallas.

On the other side of the divide of class and identity among the passengers, Haycox's Malpais Bill is transformed into the Ringo Kid, who was wrongly imprisoned at age 17 after the Plummers killed his father and brother. Ford and Nichols softened Haycox's prostitute with a story of her parents massacred by Indians. "Well, you gotta live no matter what happens," Dallas says in explaining how a catastrophic event caused her to become a prostitute, her plight echoing the desperation of many Americans during the Depression. Dallas is forced to leave town on the stagecoach by the sheriff at the insistence of the upright women of the Law and Order League, one of whom is married to the corrupt banker. At the same time, the drunken Doc Boone is run out of town for not paying his bills. He tells Dallas, "We're the victim of a foul disease called social prejudice." The Ringo Kid and Dallas fall in love as the story progresses, but their coupling cannot take place until the central conflicts of the story are resolved.

Using these various characters and caricatures, the movie script commented on class conflict and mocked pretensions of social and moral superiority, making it a parable for the Depression. Yet the Ford and Nichols script was far from a radical response. As the movie begins, a bugle blows, and an American flag is raised over Monument Valley, signaling that this is a nationalist space. The narrative takes place within the parameters set by patriotism of a kind that questions its forms but never the existence of the nation or its capacity for ultimate good. The question then becomes who should be considered a good American and worthy of inclusion in the national mythology, not whether the general order should be overturned. The journey of the stagecoach became metaphorically that of the nation during the Depression and the questions posed were of the nature of class and identity, or who is a good American.

Wanger and Ford established a budget for the movie of nearly half a million dollars. Claire Trevor, who played Dallas, received $15,000, the highest salary among the actors, and John Wayne, still a mainstay of B-grade Westerns, was at $3,000 the lowest paid. The budget also reveals a surprising shooting schedule. Only six days of photography were allotted for the Monument Valley sequences, and no sound was recorded there. In contrast, fourteen days were scheduled for studio shooting, and ten days at locations in California. Of the thirty days of filming scheduled from October 31 to December 7, 1938, only one-fifth were in Monument Valley. None of the main actors appears in the actual Monument Valley footage.[18] Yet Monument Valley dominates the film.

As the movie begins, the conflicts of the story are established and questions posed in the town of Tonto. As the stage leaves town, it passes a fence marking the end of civilization and heads toward Agathla, the volcanic plug at the southern entrance to Monument Valley. Looking at the story in terms of the use of Monument Valley, the overall space of the journey of the stagecoach is that of the American nation during the Depression. The towns at either end of the journey, Tonto and Lordsburg, are where the social issues of the Depression and American identity are present. So the journey between the two is meant to comment on those issues.[19]

During the passage, Dallas becomes the character with the most warmth and charity as she shows she is worthy of the real love of a man and motherhood. The drunken doctor redeems himself by sobering up in time to deliver Mrs. Mallory's baby. Ringo demands respect for Dallas as a woman and heroically shares in the fight against the Apaches to save the coach. On the other hand, Mrs. Mallory never grows beyond her disgust with Dallas. The gambler is killed, and the banker is arrested when the stage reaches Lordsburg. After Ringo kills the Plummer brothers in a shootout, and the conflicts have been resolved, he and Dallas reunite. They ride off together out of Lordsburg and into Monument Valley, where they will reproduce the nation. With the revival of the "A" Western to meet the cultural demands of a twentieth-century America during the Depression, *Stagecoach* established Monument Valley as a mythical national space in which the challenges of the era could be located and played out within the Anglo-American encounter with the wilderness.

Ford did not make another Western until 1946. Between *Stagecoach* and *My Darling Clementine* was World War II. With U.S. entry into the war imminent, Ford entered active military duty. He was 47 years old, but the opportunity fed a lifelong fascination with the Navy. Ford was assigned to the Navy's Field Photographic Branch, from which he filmed battles, made training films, and helped with intelligence projects for the Office of the Coordinator of Information, which in 1942 became the Office of Strategic Services and was the predecessor of the Central Intelligence Agency. Ford was wounded by shrapnel while filming the Battle of Midway and received a Purple Heart. He also directed the filming of the D-Day invasion of Normandy.[20]

At the request of his superior, William J. Donovan, director of the Office of Strategic Services, Ford produced *December 7th* about the attack on Pearl Harbor. Donovan believed that the failure of the Army and Navy to keep him informed of intelligence they had gathered allowed the Japanese to surprise the U.S. base. The original version of the film argued that the military was unprepared and had been blind to spying by Japanese Americans in Hawaii. Admiral Harold R. Stark, who had been chief of naval operations when Pearl Harbor was attacked, complained about the film. President Roosevelt issued an order that all Field Photo material would be subject to censorship. Ford edited the picture to a shorter, less polemic version, negotiating between historical events and their representation on film.

One aspect of the film goes to the heart of the questions Ford asked in his postwar Monument Valley films. At the end of the battle sequences in *December 7th* the film arrives at the "hallowed graves" of those who died in battle. The narrator asks rhetorically the identity of these American dead. Then a roll call is performed that includes an ethnically, racially, and geographically diverse group of sailors, soldiers, and Marines who are Jewish, Irish American, black, and Hispanic. The narrator asks why their voices all sound the same. The reply: "We are all alike. We are all Americans."

Later in the war, Ford landed on the French coast shortly after D-Day, which his crews had filmed. Years after that, when asked why he had featured a black cavalryman in a Monument Valley film, Ford replied: "When I landed at Omaha Beach there were scores of black bodies lying in the sand. Then I realized that it was impossible not to consider them full-fledged American citizens." Ford's sensitivities to questions of belonging to the national mythology may well have stemmed from his own experiences growing up as the son of Irish immigrants in Maine. His participation in World War II seemed to have led him to greater exploration of those questions of American identity among the divisions of race, ethnicity, and class, though, significantly, not gender.[21]

For Ford, participating in military life, photographing battles, and witnessing death proved transforming yet enigmatic. The experience deepened Ford's sense of patriotism and his attraction to rituals that marked military life. Ford's association with the military and the Office of Strategic Services fed a growing political conservatism and anti-communism. He accepted the tremendous sacrifice of life for a greater good. Yet the strict military hierarchy and bureaucracy also strained his antiauthoritarian streak.

Ford left the service on September 29, 1945. In the immediate aftermath of the war, he returned to Monument Valley to make another Western, *My Darling Clementine*. For Ford, Monument Valley became a place to regenerate and to ponder the war in which he had just participated. Westerns, Ford once told an interviewer, "are a chance to get away from Hollywood and the smog. You live in the open, sleep under a tent, eat from a chuck wagon, barbecue your meat. It's great fun. At night, we get together and sing songs."

The script of *My Darling Clementine* took as its historical subject the rivalry of the Earps and Clantons that culminated in a gun battle at the O.K. Corral in Tombstone, Arizona, in 1881. Ford saw the photographic possibilities of a primitive frontier town set against the vertical rock mesas and spires of Monument Valley: "In the background there were the mountains and the buttes, and the street was very cheap to erect but it was very effective."[22]

In Ford's version, when the Earp brothers arrive, Tombstone is a rough frontier town, first seen in dark shadows that give it an air of evil. The music and wild sounds coming from the bars peg it as a rough and rowdy place, still wild and untamed, full of Mexicans, drunken Indians, and whores. The Clantons kill one of the Earp brothers and steal their cattle. They must be dealt with, and Wyatt Earp takes on the job of sheriff. As the United States took on the post–World War II role of superpower and opposition to totalitarian communism, so too, in the figure of Wyatt Earp, its cowboys come to the rescue of Tombstone. Clementine's arrival on the stage represents civilization. She is to become the town's schoolteacher. Clementine and Wyatt are attracted to each other, but before they can marry and have children, evil must be vanquished.[23]

There are three circular spaces to contend with in the film. The outside one that encloses the others is the space out of which emerge Wyatt and his brothers, the nation through which they are moving their cattle to California and, more appropriately, the American West. Inside that outer ring, there's Monument Valley. Finally, at the center, is the town of Tombstone, which consists mostly, it seems, of rowdy bars. So the question posed is who will control Tombstone at the heart of the space, within the mythical landscape of Monument Valley and in the context of the national project: the Earps, the righteous men of the West; or the Clantons, who are pure evil. If the Earps win, then Wyatt can marry Clementine and reproduce a nation of civilized people. If the Clantons kill the Earps, then evil reigns. Tombstone is thus poised between immorality and chaos and a civilization of laws and reproduction.

In the transformative moment of the movie, Wyatt agrees to take Clementine to a dance at the church, which is still under construction. As they walk, the soundtrack plays Ford's favorite hymn, "Shall We Gather at the River." As the pair, now obviously fated to be united in blessed union, turns a street corner, the church is a short distance away. The final script described the scene: "They come up to a skeleton of the church building. The only thing completed is the floor and some studding that supports the bell tower. There is considerable activity about the church as a cross-section of Tombstone's citizens gather for the first service." The script had an American and an Arizona flag flying over the building. Ford filmed it with two American flags.

Under Ford's direction, the unfinished church set against the sandstone mesas represented America in its infancy, balanced between civilization and the wilderness seen through the skeletal bell tower. The scene is a magic moment full of possibility; civilization had not yet fully arrived, and big American men still walked the land. Here, Ford again produced Monument Valley as a mythical nationalist space where America always is poised between civilization and the primitive space of its mythology, eternally there and always full of promise.

In *My Darling Clementine,* the violence at the O.K. Corral was necessary to conquer evil and sanctify the community. The American heroic male, the cowboy coming from the western landscape, brings civilization to town by applying violence when necessary to protect the community. In the end, though, Wyatt and his remaining brother leave town, with Wyatt telling Clementine he will be back, presumably to marry and reproduce the nation.

After the war, Ford and producer Merian Cooper formed their own production company, Argosy Pictures, to exercise independent control of their films. Ford and Cooper knew they needed a commercial success even before they released their first picture, *The Fugitive,* which left the company about $500,000 in debt. Cooper bought the movie rights to a *Saturday Evening Post* story titled "Massacre," by James Bellah, in February 1947. Ford hired a former *New York Times* movie critic, Frank Nugent, to help turn the story into a script that became *Fort Apache.* Research included gathering iconic stories and images of the West. Frederick Remington's "Navajo Raid" and "Caught in a Circle" were among the prints obtained as visual models, along with some by Western artist Charlie Russell. Books such as Elizabeth Custer's *Boots and Saddles* were consulted, as well as histories of the U.S. Cavalry and the American Southwest.[24]

According to production documents, the intent of *Fort Apache* was "to recreate a little-known phase of American history." Ford and those making the film saw Fort Bowie, as the frontier outpost was first called in production documents, as a framed picture along the time line of American development, "merely a point of rest in the march of history." If it was merely a point, the fort was, nevertheless, understood as a representative space of the American story and its encounter with open space, "a mere dot on the Arizona plains, all but swallowed up by the great stretches of desert. . . . But when studied closely, as we intend to study it, it will prove to be a dramatic stage no less impressive because it is in miniature."[25]

This movie is built around four concentric spaces, through which runs the linear time of the narrative. The film opens with a stagecoach traveling through Monument Valley. The dialogue of its occupants, Lieutenant Colonel Owen Thursday and his daughter, Philadelphia, shows they are traveling from their home in Washington, D.C., to Fort

Apache because the War Department has sent Thursday there. The East and Washington, D.C., therefore the nation, are established as the outer space that encloses the others. On the second day of the shooting schedule, July 28, 1947, Ford produced a second space: Monument Valley.

In *Fort Apache,* Monument Valley is the space within which the action and resolution of conflicts could take place. As Thursday and his daughter are taken to his new assignment in an Army ambulance, a third space is introduced, Fort Apache, which appeared in a scene scheduled to be shot September 18 at the Corrigan Movie Ranch in the Simi Valley of California. Fort Apache is masculine, martial space, where rituals are symbolic of the nation's military that had just participated in World War II. Within the fort is an interior space.

On August 21, on a studio stage, two married women help Philadelphia furnish her and her father's quarters, signaling this as domestic, feminine space at the heart of the concentric circles: the nation, Monument Valley, the fort, and, finally, the home, the site of reproduction. Women, therefore, are confined to the cyclical time of reproduction, outside the linear time of progress and excluded from politics played out in Monument Valley.[26] The storyline revolves around this domestic sphere, which is at the heart of the conflict of *Fort Apache.* That conflict is over whether two people, Philadelphia and Lieutenant Michael O'Rourke, the son of the Sergeant Major O'Rourke, will marry and have babies who carry the future of the nation.

The biographies that Ford ordered for each of the main characters showed Thursday as a graduate of West Point, a major general by the end of the Civil War sent to Europe to observe the Prussian-Austrian War. He is a "High Episcopalian . . . the son and grandson and great-grandson of Regular Army soldiers and in politics is a Republican." It was Ford himself who added the character of the elder O'Rourke, an Irish immigrant who joined the U.S. Army, an "Old Irish Sergeant . . . with a West Point Son."[27] The O'Rourkes timed their arrival in the United States to ensure that Michael was born an American.

The script as developed by Ford and Nugent set up a romance between two people whose families were divided by ethnicity, religion, and class. Thursday cannot believe that the son of an Irish American sergeant was admitted to West Point. Class differences are further exposed when, in the presence of Thursday, the younger O'Rourke asks Philadelphia to marry. She immediately agrees, but her father interjects, "I tell you this is not a proper or suitable marriage for you." Then Thursday addresses the elder O'Rourke, "As a non-commissioned officer, you are well aware of the barriers between your class and mine."[28]

The character of Captain Kirby York, played by John Wayne, is in sharp contrast to Thursday. York's biography has him as a Midwesterner educated at Ohio Wesleyan College, a veteran of the Civil War who has spent much of his time with the Army in the Southwest. "He knows the country," is "a great admirer of the plains Indian," and "unconsciously has taken on some of the fighting attributes and characteristics of the Indian Warrior."[29] York's style of leadership, gained from his time in the open space of the West, is a stark contrast to that of Thursday, whose education in warfare came from time in tradition- and class-bound Europe with the Prussians.

The two clash repeatedly over military tactics and diplomatic relations with the Indians, their rivalry posing the question of who will be the leader of the project at hand, that of the American nation. If it is Thursday, then the film validates the aristocratic claim to leadership of privilege and arrogance and sanctions class as a defining divide, with Philadelphia and Michael unable to marry. If it is York, then the marriage of Philadelphia and Michael takes place, and American nationalism is reborn, bringing into its fold the patriotic immigrant, erasing class distinctions, and validating a claim to leadership based on experience and merit that was naturalized in battles with the "savages" of the American West.

Monument Valley is the site of the resolution of the conflict. The troop (but not York or Lieutenant O'Rourke) is massacred by the Apaches as a result of Thursday's arrogance and ambition. York assumes command. The question of leadership resolved, Philadelphia and Michael O'Rourke marry and produce a son—Michael Thursday York O'Rourke.

In a final scene presided over by a huge portrait of Thursday, now lionized for his sacrifice for the nation, York answers the questions of reporters sent to cover the new campaign against the Apaches. Asked about the heroic Thursday, York hesitates, shifts his eyes back and forth, looks down, then in a lowered voice says, "No man died more gallantly nor won more honor for his regiment." Since the audience already knows that Thursday was an ambitious, egotistical fool who needlessly led his men to slaughter, York's reluctant affirmation of the heroic image serves as an ironic commentary on the ways that popular culture forms, such as movies and the news media, treat historical events.

Having debunked aristocratic claims to leadership with his portrayal of Thursday, Ford reserved the true mythology for the common soldier. When a reporter comments that the other soldiers who died will be forgotten, York replies: "They aren't forgotten because they haven't died. They're living, right out there." On the glass of the window out which York looks is reflected mounted soldiers, the ghosts who live eternally in the American mythological space of Monument Valley. Thus, in the end, Monument Valley serves to hold an America where differences of class, ethnicity, and religion can be resolved, where common soldiers are never forgotten, and where the nation lives on to regenerate and reproduce.

Ford's World War II experiences had influenced *My Darling Clementine* and *Fort Apache,* and in the postwar years he found himself immersed in another maelstrom: the domestic politics of the Cold War. In 1947, the House Committee on Un-American Activities launched hearings on communist influence in Hollywood. The committee issued subpoenas in September to forty-three people in the movie industry. Ford's own work was questioned. His 1940 adaptation of John Steinbeck's Depression-era critique of American society, *The Grapes of Wrath,* was mentioned by committee members as one of those movies that showed the "sordid side of American life." Ford even came to be considered a security risk by the Signal Corps, though he apparently later was cleared. As chair of a Screen Directors Guild committee formed to respond to the subpoenas, Ford helped steer a course that defended civil rights but also declared opposition to communism, acceding to the rhetoric of the committee.

Though Ford's sense of Americanism was offended by the committee's activities, he also became more politically conservative and, as a son of immigrants, the "Mick" from Portland may have felt he still needed to prove the depth of his patriotism. At a Screen Directors Guild meeting on October 21, 1947, the second day of the Hollywood hearings by the House Committee on Un-American Activities, Ford called himself a "state of Maine Republican," a significant shift for a man whose father had been a Democratic Party ward boss. Ford also had almost casually dropped the name of a writer with "communistic leanings" to the military's Personnel Security Board in an attempt to help fellow director Frank Capra gain a security clearance to work on a defense project.

With John Wayne at its helm, Ford became increasingly involved in the Motion Picture Alliance for the Preservation of American Ideals and its anticommunist crusade, which included blacklisting. Yet when actor Ward Bond, another member of Ford's stock company, asked Ford to attend a party in honor of Senator Joseph McCarthy, Ford replied, "Take your party and shove it. . . . He's a disgrace to and a danger to our country."

In 1950, the Screen Directors Guild held a meeting on whether to support Cecil B. DeMille's proposal for a loyalty oath for members and a blacklist of those who refused. At the tumultuous meeting on October 22, after much debate, Ford raised his hand to speak. He made clear that he opposed imposition of the oath, and he made a motion calling for the resignation of board members who had backed the oath. The vote carried, but the next day Ford sent a fawning letter to DeMille.[30]

In October 1948, a year after the House Committee on Un-American Activities hearings and some eight months after Argosy delivered the print of *Fort Apache,* Ford began shooting *She Wore a Yellow Ribbon.* The movie was the second of Ford's so-called Cavalry Trilogy and, like the first, was filmed in Monument Valley. Ford used most of the same research from *Fort Apache* to prepare for the sequel. Unlike the previous movie, *She Wore a Yellow Ribbon* was in color. Ford also filmed more of the scenes in Monument Valley than he had for *Fort Apache.* Filming began October 25, 1948, on the new movie, which was based on the James Bellah story "War Party," published in the *Saturday Evening Post.*[31]

In *She Wore a Yellow Ribbon,* Ford again introduced a conflict of class and identity and the question of the mantle of national leadership with the rivalry between two lieutenants, Cohill and Pennell, for Miss Dandridge's hand in marriage. Cohill is to take over the troop when Captain Nathan Brittles, a competent and lovable Cavalry officer played by John Wayne, retires. Pennell is an upper-class kid from the East who wants to leave the Army and marry Dandridge. That rivalry for her hand in marriage takes place within a larger conflict, of both external and internal enemies.

At the beginning of *She Wore a Yellow Ribbon,* the narrator reports that Custer has been massacred. The narrator intones: "From the Canadian Border to the Rio Bravo, ten thousand Indians, Kiowa, Comanches, Arapaho, Sioux, and Apache under Sitting Bull and Crazy Horse, Gall and Crow King, are uniting in a common war against the United States Cavalry." American civilization is threatened by huge, hostile, savage forces—concerns of Cold War Americans facing the Soviet Union after World War II. Echoing the hearings of the House Committee on Un-American Activities, there also are internal enemies. A character named Karl Rynders is supplying the Indians with guns and whiskey. These concerns are all transferred to the national mythic space for resolution: "By military telegraph, news of the Custer massacre is flashed across the long lonely miles to the Southwest." The narration arrives at Fort Starke, and the American flag is raised above Monument Valley. The representative space of American nationalism—produced in *Stagecoach, My Darling Clementine,* and *Fort Apache*—is threatened.

So the concentric spaces here are of external enemies threatening the nation, then the nation itself, then Monument Valley, and at the center Fort Starke. Within that context, the question posed is whether Miss Dandridge will choose Lieutenant Pennell, the rich officer from the East, or Lieutenant Cohill, the heir to a leadership based on merit. Ford again used the comedy of the stereotyped, whiskey-drinking, and fist-fighting Irishman—Victor McLaglen as Sergeant Quincannon—to comment on ethnicity as part of a truly American identity. The movie also argued for national reconciliation, with Brittles allowing a Southern flag to drape the coffin of a former Confederate soldier as the music of "Dixie" plays softly. To oppose the massed enemy, Ford called for unity despite regional, class, religious, and ethnic divisions.

In the end, in Monument Valley Brittles outfoxes the Indians by driving away their horses so they cannot fight. Cohill takes over the troop and marries Miss Dandridge, while Pennell stays in the Army to earn his position by merit. As *She Wore a Yellow Ribbon* ends, mounted soldiers ride through Monument Valley. The narrator has the last word:

"The dog-faced soldiers, the regulars, the fifty-cents-a-day professionals riding the outposts of the nation. From Fort Reno to Fort Apache,
from Sheridan to Starke they were all the same, and only a cold page in
the history books to mark their passing. But wherever they rode, and
whatever they fought for, that place became the United States."

In *Fort Apache* and *She Wore a Yellow Ribbon,* Ford wanted to negotiate the terms of patriotism while still anchoring it in tradition. The
rebel in Ford refused to bow to claims of a hereditary leadership. The
son of Irish immigrants wanted the contribution of ethnic Americans
to be recognized as part of national history. The conservative Ford
wanted to validate the American past and create a mythological space
that would serve to support the military role America had assumed in
the postwar world to confront communism. As Richard Slotkin has
noted, "By transferring the ideological concerns of the World War and
its aftermath from the terrain of the combat film to the mythic landscape of the Western, Ford proposed a mythic response to the crisis of
postwar ideology that is at once a moral critique of our victory and
an affirmation of the importance of patriotic solidarity that made victory possible."[32] That "mythic landscape" was most often Monument
Valley.

After *She Wore a Yellow Ribbon,* Ford would not return to Monument Valley until 1955. In the interim he completed two Westerns, *Rio
Grande,* the last of the Cavalry Trilogy, and *Wagon Master,* the tale of
heroic Mormon pioneers. Ford had conceived the idea for *Wagon Master* when he used Mormon residents of nearby towns as extras while
filming in Monument Valley. Most of the outdoor photography for
those films took place near Moab, Utah, a town along the Colorado
River to the north of Monument Valley. With some of the same type
of eroded sandstone formations, Moab was Ford's "miniature Monument Valley," and the presence of motels and other accommodations
nearby made the location easier and less expensive for filming.[33]

In 1952, Ford signed an agreement with C. V. Whitney Pictures to
direct a movie called *The Searchers,* based on an Alan LeMay novel.
Ford returned to Monument Valley to film what is perhaps his best
movie, and one of the greatest of American cinema. Working again
with Frank Nugent, Ford crafted the screenplay and planned the production. Unlike the more straightforward stories of American nation-

alism of the cavalry pictures or of American identity of *Stagecoach*, *The Searchers* is a dark tale of race and sexuality.

Ethan Edwards, played by John Wayne, has searched six years for his niece, who was kidnapped as a youngster by a Comanche chief named Scar. The movie begins with the credits and title rolling off against a wall of adobe brick. The lyrics then pose a question: "What makes a man to wander? What makes a man to roam? What makes a man to leave bed and board and turn his back on home?" The screen goes to black, a door opens, and there in the pure stark light of the high desert is Monument Valley. Martha Edwards, Ethan's sister-in-law, emerges onto the porch and sees Ethan (John Wayne) riding toward her. That opening sequence was not in the final script; Ford improvised it after he began filming in Monument Valley on June 16, 1955.[34]

The Edwards cabin, constructed of adobe and wood, is described in production documents as "almost a fortress. It sits alone in a vast expanse."[35] The images situate the house as a site of American primitivism, that space in the emergence myth where American civilization was born in the encounter of Europeans with the wilderness. As the movie ends, Ethan brings his niece back to another house, a painted, clapboard home of the immigrant Jorgensens. The journey from a primitive cabin to a painted clapboard house makes the story a tale of linear progress. A memo from the planning stages states the premise of the movie: "The characters are not romantic Western figures in the accepted sense of the word. But they are the only race capable of holding their fortress-like houses in the face of the Comanches, blizzards, droughts, and heat so oppressive that it sometimes strikes dead the long-horned cattle that represent their only wealth." The motivation for these Anglo-Americans is "the same intangible urging that sent their Viking ancestors across the sea to England and their more immediate predecessors to the Atlantic Coast. Orators of this period called it 'Manifest Destiny.'"[36]

If the movie begins in primitivism and ends in civilization, the narrative connects these points through the space of Monument Valley, where most of Ethan's search takes place and where he finally succeeds. By the time the movie was made, Monument Valley was known through Ford's movies as the space of mythic nationalism. Yet by 1955, when Ford began filming *The Searchers,* questions were being raised about inherent racism in American history and contemporary life.

The American myth was being contested because savage wars on Indians, years of brutal slavery, and contemporary racism and lynchings did not fit neatly into a tale of heroic Anglo-Americans building a new civilization in the wilderness. Frederick Jackson Turner and popular culture's tale of America sprung from the wilderness did not work well if slavery and the South were included. Nor did it if one raised questions about the dispossessed Indians. Once slavery, savage war on American Indians, and racism and its pervasive influence on American history are brought into play, the emergence myth is challenged as the tale of national development. Ford went back to Monument Valley to try to reconcile the national mythic narrative with the stark reality of the nation's racist past. Filming at that location lasted until July 10.[37]

Ethan is an unreconstructed Confederate soldier who never surrendered and engages in shady activities until he returns to his brother's ranch after the Civil War. What is apparent immediately upon his return is that he and his brother's wife are in love. After the couple are massacred by Comanches, and Martha raped before dying, that love is transferred to a search for the two daughters, one of whom is later also raped and killed. Ethan's hunt for the remaining girl, Debbie, begins as an act of love for Martha but evolves into a journey to kill Debbie because she has become the wife of Scar, the leader of the Indians who killed the family and kidnapped the girl.

An early synopsis put it this way: "Later in the story we will realize that he intends to kill the girl Debbie when he finds her because she has been sullied by the Indians he hates." So the answer to the question posed by the theme song—"What makes a man to wander?"—touches on race, sexuality, and power. Debbie's body is the contested terrain.[38]

The character of Martin Pawley, the adopted son of the Edwards family, serves as a moral counterpoint to Ethan's racism. Pawley, who is one-eighth Cherokee, steadily matures through the movie. He is pursued by a neighbor girl, Laurie Jorgensen, but Martin refuses to stay put long enough to court and marry her because he fears Ethan will find and kill Debbie if he is not there to prevent it. Thus, the couple cannot reproduce a nation of Indian-Anglo blood until the question of Ethan's power in relation to race and sexuality is resolved.

In the end, however, it is not Martin who saves Debbie from Ethan. Ethan rescues Debbie as "Martha's song" plays on the soundtrack. He kills and scalps Scar, and with no child to attest the illicit union, Ethan now has control of Debbie and apparently sees no need to kill her. In the final scene, Ethan carries Debbie in his arms and gives her to the Jorgensens on the porch of their house. The Jorgensens and Debbie turn inside, followed shortly by Martin and Laurie, who will soon marry. By the end of the story, Martin has, production documents say, "grown into a man of [Ethan's] stature without the bitter undercurrents."[39] Martin is, in other words, the new American man, who can now marry and reproduce in the mythic space of Monument Valley, though it is now sullied by the exposure of Ethan's racism.

The Searchers proves a dark and disturbing commentary on American history. While the movie challenges the construction of Monument Valley as national mythic space, in the end, Ford reaffirms it even while acknowledging that racism has scarred the American past and present. In addition, the use of John Wayne, by that time *the* ideal of American masculinity, also serves to confirm that mythology even as the film contested it. "A modern man would find much about him [Ethan] psychopathic," according to a memo written during the development of the film. "But there is greatness in him, too. His courage, relentlessness and frontier skills are magnificent. He achieves his goals where more stable men fail."[40] So the movie's creators wanted to say that Ethan Edwards was perhaps the only type of man who could have built the American nation out of such a savage wilderness, as the national emergence tale would have it.

Ford sought not to destroy the myth of a great people rising from the wilderness by exposing the racism at its heart but rather to acknowledge and comment on it and, at the same time, to preserve the myth. At the end of the film, Ethan pauses on the porch of the Jorgensens' house, then turns and walks back alone into Monument Valley. The door closes and all is black again. The movie ends with John Wayne still wandering out there, in Monument Valley. The mythical space is made true and reconstructed once again, even as we acknowledge the racial-sexual politics inherent in American history that was increasingly contested in mid-twentieth-century America.

As race relations in the United States came to occupy a larger part of domestic politics, Ford returned twice more to Monument Valley to make motion pictures. Ford began filming *Sergeant Rutledge* there on July 16, 1959, and finished on July 25. Of the forty-three days of photography, only ten were in Monument Valley. Twenty-nine days were used on stage sets, with four at locations in California.[41] The movie alternates between scenes from the courtroom where Sergeant Rutledge, a black cavalryman, is on trial for the rape and murder of a white girl, and Monument Valley, where the black man proves his patriotism with a series of heroic actions. Ford again explores the deep-seated racism of Anglo America, and once again its central conflict is sexual. The movie exposes a series of assumptions and fears about black men's sexual appetites for white girls.

In the movie, Rutledge arrives at his commanding officer's quarters to report on Apache raids. He finds, instead, the naked body of the commander's teenage daughter. The commander enters and upon seeing Rutledge over the body assumes the black man had raped and killed the girl. He shoots Rutledge, who then kills the commander in self-defense and flees. Asked why he ran, Rutledge replies, "Because I walked into something none of us can fight—white woman business." The contemporary state of race relations at the time of the filming is starkly stated by one of the black soldiers when he tells another, "Ya, it was all right for Mr. Lincoln to say we were free. But that ain't so. Not yet. Maybe some day but not yet."

In *Sergeant Rutledge,* the couple who cannot reproduce until a question is resolved is Rutledge's defense attorney, Lieutenant Tom Cantrell, and Constance Towers. In the end, after Rutledge has proved his bravery in Monument Valley, the real killer is unmasked and confesses in a melodramatic courtroom scene. Ford redeems Rutledge and brings black men into the national mythic space with the same type of images he uses to consecrate white cavalrymen in *Fort Apache* and *She Wore a Yellow Ribbon. Sergeant Rutledge* connects to that symbolism when the accused man tells the black cavalrymen, "I ain't going to let none of this trouble rub off on you. You're Ninth Cavalry men. And like I've said again and again, the Ninth Regiment is going to speak for us all some day. And it's going to speak clean."

The final shots have the troop led by Rutledge riding through Monument Valley, silhouetted against the sky. Ford again used the space of Monument Valley to preserve American nationalism, this time to bring black men into the story of nation building and to dispel stereotypical beliefs about sexual appetites.

Ford returned in 1963 to film another movie, *Cheyenne Autumn,* his final movie in Monument Valley and his last Western. Ford was sixty-nine, and his vision was, literally and symbolically, darkening. He again chose the theme of race and the American story. This time, however, the film displayed Ford's pessimism about the idea of progress, contesting a clean telling of Anglo-American conquest of a virgin continent.

Ford and writer James R. Webb took the novel *Cheyenne Autumn* by Mari Sandoz and turned it into a more epic story. *Cheyenne Autumn* followed by two years *The Man Who Shot Liberty Valance,* one of Ford's great Westerns in which Monument Valley is conspicuously absent. Ford's coproducer of *Cheyenne Autumn,* Bernard Smith, convinced Jack Warner of Warner Brothers that a John Ford Western could make money for the company at a time when it had committed a huge investment to *My Fair Lady.* Like *Fort Apache,* the picture debunked a hero of American history. Unlike that film, however, Ford at the end did not endorse the myth.[42]

In *Cheyenne Autumn,* Ford demystified the Western itself, portraying the Cheyennes as dignified, morally superior victims of a corrupt U.S. government and white civilization. The film, a precursor of the "counterculture Westerns," was released as scholars were reexamining American culture and history, particularly race relations, and as representations of Indians were being used to critique modern America. In one scene, Captain Wessels points to the books of James Fenimore Cooper, the earliest of frontier novelists: "You're right Captain Archer. Fenimore Cooper knew little about Indians but his books first made me interested in them." The movie also debunked Ford's earlier portrayal of Wyatt Earp as a hero in *My Darling Clementine.* In *Cheyenne Autumn,* Earp is a comical cardsharp. Ford mocks the Anglo-Americans of Dodge City and shows the military as bloodthirsty. Ford also sought to expose stereotypical racial fears, just as he did in *Sergeant Rutledge*.[43]

Like the young Anglo couples in Ford's previous Monument Valley Westerns, the coupling of Captain Thomas Archer and Deborah Wright cannot take place until a central problem is resolved, and that is the successful removal of the Cheyenne people from Anglo-American space—the mythical American nationalist cathedral of Monument Valley—to their own traditional territory. Ford removed himself too from Monument Valley, finishing the photography of *Cheyenne Autumn* at Moab, Utah, where filming wrapped up November 23, 1963, the day after the assassination of President John F. Kennedy. Ford told a friend that not until Kennedy, also of Irish descent and a Catholic, had been elected president did he feel a first-class American citizen. *Cheyenne Autumn* was the most expensive film Ford made, and it was also a critical and financial failure, a stark exposure of Ford's diminishing powers as a filmmaker, his old age, and his pessimism. It also may have signaled the exhaustion of the Western as a genre.[44]

Ford wanted to cast American Indian actors in the major parts of the film, but at the studio's insistence, the roles went to non-Indians, notably Sal Mineo, Dolores Del Rio, and Ricardo Montalban. The favorable resolution of the Cheyennes' dilemma in the movie also was very much in the hands of the Anglos. It is ultimately the secretary of the Interior who decides to grant the Cheyennes' wish to remove themselves to their own homeland. The conflict resolved, the Anglo couple is free to marry and reproduce. Yet now the Indians, the "savages" against which the Anglo-Americans tested themselves, were gone from Monument Valley, and so after 1964 was John Ford.

As *Cheyenne Autumn* marked the end of Ford's Westerns, it also signaled the decline of the genre. Only an occasional Western is now released. The explanations for the decline, if not the death, of Westerns may lie in Ford's movies. Beginning with *The Searchers,* then in *Sergeant Rutledge* and *Cheyenne Autumn,* Ford commented upon the racism and racial violence in American history that undermined the narrative of the national mythic of a good, honorable nation sprung from the European encounter with the primitive wilderness. It seems the linear narrative of national development couldn't sustain the mythic treatment demanded by the spires and mesas of Monument Valley.

Western literary scholar Krista Comer writes that dialogue of the Western landscape no longer fit the needs of the "U.S. hegemonic nationalism," courtesy of the antiwar, gay, feminist, and civil rights movements. Ford tried to comment upon the nation's racial past, but his Westerns never made women the protagonists who resolved some problem in the space of Monument Valley. Women were not part of Ford's national myth except as reproducers of the nation along with the male heroes who traveled through the towering stone to revive and restore the national myth. Others have suggested that the proliferation of photographs of Monument Valley in advertisements also profaned its mythic image.[45]

In his seven films made in Monument Valley, Ford never explored it as Navajo space. The Navajos constituted for him a source for the savage primitives against which he could cast a story of Turnerian progress or of the American heart of darkness. In a letter to James Bellah as Ford was preparing *She Wore a Yellow Ribbon,* the director wrote, "At Monument Valley I have my own personal tribe of Navajo Indians who are great riders, swell actors . . . have long hair and best of all they believe in me." The Navajos became in Ford's mind part of his stock company of actors. "We can braid their long hair in the Cheyenne, Kiowa, Comanche or whatever hairdress we desire . . . choose particularly good costumes . . . have elaborate war bonnets and make them look good."[46]

John Holiday, a medicine man who participated in Ford's films as an actor and crew member, had a similar comment: "We changed our tribe during the different movies. Sometimes we were Apaches and wore braids, loincloths, and painted faces. I became the enemy, along with other Navajos, and we did plenty of scalping."[47]

Ford transformed the Navajos into any tribe he desired, but in his movies they were never Navajo. In *Stagecoach,* Monument Valley Navajos played Apaches, as they did in *Fort Apache.* In *She Wore a Yellow Ribbon,* they were Kiowa, Comanche, Arapaho, Sioux, or Apache. The Navajos played Comanches in *The Searchers* and Apaches again in *Sergeant Rutledge.* In *Cheyenne Autumn,* they were, of course, Cheyennes. For Ford, working within the Western genre, American popular culture did not accord the Navajo the "savage" status of the Apaches or other tribes. Instead, Ford used the Navajos as generic Indians, able to stand in for any tribe deemed savage enough to present an obstacle to be overcome in order to reaffirm the Anglo-American nationalist mythology.

Navajos welcomed Ford for the most part. His moviemaking provided incomes for playing bit parts, renting horses, or providing auxiliary services. Ford claimed over the years he had rescued the Navajos of the Monument Valley area from the effects of the Depression by filming *Stagecoach* there. For that movie, Ford was in Monument Valley for less than a week of photography and paid $1,800 (about $28,000 today) for the Navajos' services.[48] In the earlier Monument Valley movies, Ford paid "Indians" far less than he did the "cavalry," many of whom were residents of nearby Mormon towns.

With *The Searchers,* however, the "Indians" received $15 a day (the equivalent of about $120 today), the same as the "Rangers" were paid. The movies, according to one Navajo, helped the people of the area understand money and the wage economy. By the time he made *The Searchers,* Ford had an established relationship with the Navajos. When he arrived for the filming, he was greeted by three brothers—John, Jack, and Johnny Stanley—who had worked with Ford in previous films, including *Stagecoach,* and by Lee Bradley, who acted as interpreter and yelled out Ford's instructions in Navajo.[49]

Though Ford and his movie crew were welcomed by the Navajos of Monument Valley, Ford's use of a "medicine man" was not without controversy among them. Ford budgeted a salary for a man he called "Old Fat," Hosteen Tso, who was employed as a weather-maker. Ford later told stories of the Navajo changing the weather to fit the needs of his aesthetic vision for a day's shooting. Tso's son, Tallas Holiday, said that one day Ford gave Hosteen Tso $100 to make clouds go away. "But I think he made a mistake," Holiday told an interviewer. "That kind of ceremony is dangerous, because you can't control nature. Year after year after that, when there was drought the people blamed him. 'You're the one!' I told him as soon as the movie was over he should have done another ceremony to bring the clouds back, but he didn't." Hosteen Tso died sometime after, and some Navajos blamed his death on his interference with the weather on behalf of Ford.[50]

The association with death in Ford's movies also went against the greatest Navajo taboo. Scenes of death in movies in which Navajos participated "invited death to stalk the people," according to tribal beliefs. The wages, of course, helped overcome doubts for some. But many years later, John Holiday, who related fond memories of his employment as an extra and a crew member for Ford, told an interviewer that those who had repeatedly participated in death scenes, such as the Stanleys and Bradleys, had died premature deaths as a result.[51]

Navajos of the area who later watched Ford's films found their own meanings. Dolly Stanley-Robertson, a niece of the Stanley brothers, watched *Stagecoach* forty years after it was made. "For me it was almost like watching a part of Navajo history," she told an interviewer. *The Searchers* was a tale of American racism, but for the Navajos, the context was not history, race, or politics. Seeing family members on the screen evoked another reaction when it was shown in the Monument Valley area—howls of laughter. "Everyone was quiet until the Indian parts began," Stanley-Robertson said. "Then it was like watching home movies. Everyone would laugh and called out the names of who they saw on the screen. The whole movie became more like the funniest comedy ever filmed."

On July 4, during a holiday from the filming of *The Searchers,* Ford organized games, including races. He participated in the "old man's race," and won, if only because he cheated. Navajos presented him with a deer hide inscribed to Nahani New, translated as Tall Soldier, and inscribed with words adapted from the Night Chant: "In your travels may there be beauty behind you, beauty on both sides of you, and beauty ahead of you."[52]

When Ford finished shooting in the area for the final time, he left Monument Valley to the Navajos (and the tourists). Ford's films, however, had produced Monument Valley as the quintessential space of the American West, and in the context of his work through four decades of the twentieth century, as America's mythic national space, yet also compromised and contested, even by John Ford himself.

CHAPTER FIVE

Last Notes of the Canyon Wren

Saving a Remnant of Nature at Rainbow Bridge

Zane Grey says he is opposed to the Colorado River power project as it
"will spoil the desert and take the reservation away from the Indians."

Coconino Sun, November 4, 1921

In the early 1950s, the Sierra Club became alarmed about a proposal
for a dam at an area known as Echo Park in Dinosaur National Monument at the confluence of the Green and Yampa rivers upstream from
Glen Canyon on the Colorado River. A second dam was planned at
Glen Canyon. The dams were to be part of the massive development of
the Colorado River system by the federal government. David Brower,
the newly appointed executive director of the club, commenced a
campaign against the Echo Park Dam that was joined by dozens of
other groups. In a major victory, the coalition forced Congress to
strike a deal that deleted the dam from Dinosaur. The dam at Glen
Canyon remained, however. The accord also was designed to protect
other units of the national park system, specifically Rainbow Bridge
National Monument, which was in a side canyon some six miles above
the river as it flowed through Glen Canyon.

Then in the late 1950s and early 1960s, as the dam was under construction, Brower and others rafted the Colorado through Glen Canyon and were dazzled by the wild nature found there. They produced
slide shows and books about the canyon soon to be under the waters

of the Colorado. So began the long lament of the American wilderness movement.

In 1970, Brower and others filed a lawsuit to enforce the congressional requirement to protect Rainbow Bridge National Monument. With the efforts to preserve Rainbow Bridge, the stone arch became symbolic of something disappearing—wild nature. Through the lawsuit, newspaper and magazine articles, and books, Rainbow Bridge became a place where a remnant of that nature still existed. However, rather than being largely untouched by human intervention, the nature discovered in Glen Canyon and Rainbow Bridge by Brower and others was itself thoroughly modern, constructed through words and images obedient to the social and cultural context of late-twentieth-century America—a nature of nostalgia and regret, an abstract space made so by a modern America in which wild nature is valued precisely because modernization makes it scarce. In the 1960s, Glen Canyon became this American cathedral of modern nature, and Rainbow Bridge the echo of its lost song.

In 1869, anthropologist and geologist John Wesley Powell launched an expedition down the Green and Colorado rivers to explore and gauge the potential of the waters to aid development of the arid West. On June 18, his party rested on a beach at the confluence of the Green and Yampa rivers under an eight-hundred-foot rock wall. Powell recorded in his journal the echo from the wall and named the area Echo Park. The site, 220 miles upstream from Glen Canyon, is in what is now northwestern Colorado, a few miles from the border with Utah. In the summer of 1909 a paleontologist funded by Andrew Carnegie, the steel magnate who wanted a dinosaur fossil skeleton for his Pittsburgh museum, found a deposit of some four hundred fossils in the remote northeastern corner of Utah near the border with Colorado. To protect the area, President Woodrow Wilson in 1915 used the Antiquities Act to proclaim eighty acres around the dinosaur quarry a national monument. Publicity over the beauties of the Yampa River later led the National Park Service to propose acquisition of the area and its protection as a national monument. With officials in Utah and Colorado attracted by its potential for tourism, President Franklin Roosevelt in 1938 signed a proclamation expanding Dinosaur National Monument across the border into Colorado, including

Echo Park. The expansion of Dinosaur came, however, with a caveat. Private companies and federal agencies had identified the potential of the upper Colorado River and its tributaries to produce hydro-electricity and provide water for irrigation. Roosevelt's proclamation allowed for construction of dams within the monument.[1]

Since Powell's expedition, federal officials and private companies had eyed the Colorado River for its potential to aid development of the American West. Southern California Edison in 1922 had a federal permit for a dam at Glen Canyon, a plan that it touted as an alternative to the Boulder Dam near Las Vegas, Nevada. For Utahns, thoughts of a dam at Glen Canyon provoked visions of a grand civilization rising from the dry dirt of the desert. "The Glen Canyon dam would impound one hundred times as much water as the great Ashokan Reservoir in the Castkills [*sic*], from which the city of New York draws its water supply," noted the *Times-Independent* of Moab. "It would control almost twelve times as much water as the great barrages [*sic*] of the Nile control."[2]

The 1922 Colorado River Compact, an accord between states with lands drained by the river basin, divided the waters between upper and lower basin states at Lee's Ferry, just downstream from Glen Canyon and a few miles south of the Utah border in Arizona. By the 1930s, upper basin states, looking for water and electricity for economic growth and fearful of California's thirst, lobbied for federal projects that would allow them to use their allocation. Then federal spending during World War II aided a development boom in the West and greatly increased demands for electricity and water. Political leaders and opinion-makers sought a vast economic stimulus that would help create a modern industrial society. The Bureau of Reclamation produced a blueprint for the Colorado River Storage Project. One of the dams was planned for a site just below Echo Park, another in Glen Canyon.[3]

In 1950, however, the columnist, historian, and novelist Bernard DeVoto became alarmed when he learned of the Colorado River plan. In the July issue of the *Saturday Evening Post,* DeVoto denounced the proposal, particularly for dams in Dinosaur National Monument and Glen Canyon. He warned of possible damage to Rainbow Bridge National Monument. DeVoto depicted Dinosaur National Monument and Rainbow Bridge as places where urban dwellers could access wild nature. Those areas, he wrote, "were set aside to the sole end that they should be preserved as they are, that there should always be places where Americans could have the inestimable experience of untouched wilderness, unspoiled natural beauty and unmarred natural spectacle." When the article was reprinted in *Reader's Digest*, it publicized the controversy to a wider audience. DeVoto's writing also served to alert the members of wilderness preservation organizations.[4]

Meanwhile, the Sierra Club made "perhaps the most important organizational change" in its sixty-year history. In 1952 club officers created the post of executive director and named David Brower to fill it. Brower had been appointed to his first Sierra Club committee in 1933 and for years had served as publications editor. Since its founding in 1892 by John Muir and others, the club had been a rather elite group of volunteers whose ethos was a conservation based largely on shared recreation in the outdoors. The club's focus had been protecting recreational and scenic areas in California while accommodating industrial development. The naming of Brower as executive director as the controversy began to brew over Echo Park proved a critical moment in the history of the club and the wilderness movement in the United States.[5]

The controversy over the Echo Park Dam in Dinosaur National Monument in some ways mirrored another of the formative experiences of the Sierra Club's early years, the unsuccessful fight from 1908 to 1913 to prevent the city of San Francisco from building a dam in the Hetch Hetchy Valley of Yosemite National Park. Then, as in the Echo Park controversy some fifty years later, the club launched a national publicity campaign against the dam that attracted considerable interest. In 1916, Congress created the National Park Service to oversee and protect the nation's parks and monuments.[6]

One of the visions that contested Hetch Hetchy was that of a scientific, professional ethos of rational planning to efficiently use resources for economic development. Its proponents were professional men, a group that expanded in number in the late nineteenth century with industrialization and urbanization. The other vision was that of the preservation of wild nature, or places largely untouched by the human hand and set aside for protection. Each ethos was a product of

nineteenth- and twentieth-century modernization and the organization of the economy for efficient industrial production, a main component of which was urbanization. Indeed, in this context, nature was
a product of industrialization and urbanization; the word "nature" is a
changing motif of how we think and talk about the world.[7]

Historians in recent years have shifted the understanding of what
we mean when we use the word. Nature, as in energy, climate, and
ecological processes, still guides and limits the capacity of societies to
prosper through resource exploitation. However, when we talk about
nature, write about it, picture it, use it for certain ends and not others,
and legislate preserves of it, we do so in ways that are bound within a
cultural and historical context.[8] In this vein, American national parks,
monuments, and wilderness areas are not simply preserves of wild,
nonhuman nature but spaces produced by the urban industrial world.

The urban experience has been the foremost engine for the production of this nature. When the United States was largely a country of
family farms, most people tended animals and grew crops. But with the
switch to a modern market economy in the early nineteenth century,
many people moved to cities and had little contact with environments
that weren't built. Nature was no longer a place of work, production,
and consumption, as on a farm, but rather was (from a city dweller's
point of view) a romantic, pastoral space that contrasted with the city.
In one of the first factory towns, Lowell, Massachusetts, the editor
of a local publication that printed writings of young women who
worked in the factories was asked why such works were almost inevitably about nature. She answered, "Why is it that the desert-traveller
looks forward upon the burning, boundless waste, and sees pictured
before his aching eyes, some verdant oasis? When you answer this, then
I will tell why the factory girl . . . thinks not of the crowded tenement
which is her home, nor of the thronged and busy street which she may
sometimes tread, but of . . . still and lovely scenes."[9]

Residents of the new industrial spaces invented "nature" as landscape. The landscape of nature became an aesthetic ideal separate, or
so it might appear, from industrialism. As the English literary critic
Raymond Williams has pointed out, "A working country is hardly
ever a landscape. The very idea of landscape implies separation and
observation."[10]

At the end of the nineteenth century, Anglo-Americans' mythic space migrated from the pastoral family farms that Thomas Jefferson had proclaimed incubators of American democracy to wilderness. Cities provided the material means to romanticize wilderness. Modernization supplied the lifestyle options, the level of comfort, and the technologies to spread the words and images of wild nature. As industrialization and urbanization accelerated, nature was seen and spoken of as the nonhuman world and a space for recreation and aesthetic enjoyment or of relief from the pollution and burdens of the modern world. The philosopher Henri Lefebvre suggests that this view of nature is created by a modern capitalist society in which the constant production of an urban world makes it a scarce commodity and imparts the impulse to consume nature for its supposed rustic or wild characteristics. Because of the absence of the urban-industrial productive apparatus, this nature seems to be "counter-space," or in other words not modern, and rapidly disappearing. Modern nature therefore lends itself, in Lefebvre's words, "to the ideological posture of nostalgic regret for a space that is no longer."[11]

Here is the nature of the modern wilderness movement, seen as primitive because it is supposedly untouched by the hand of modernization. This is nostalgia for a nature seemingly of the past, of an American land that was pure before the arrival of the Europeans or before industrialization.[12] In national parks, monuments, and wilderness areas, the wilderness preservation movement sought to protect the remnants of these lands of the past in their pure form. This politics of nostalgia sought to preserve something from the past that could be experienced as real and authentic in the present, in contrast to modern development and to contemporary lives in cities. This nature is, therefore, but a remnant of an imagined past, a nostalgia for something not remembered, like Zane Grey's desert as "the storehouse of unlived years," a feeling of uneasy desire for the memory of a nature long alienated from the modern present.[13]

The quest for an authentic present was a product of modernization, and the wild spaces it created were thoroughly modern. Indeed, because of the absence of the productive processes that made modern human life possible, the lands finally enshrined in the Wilderness

Act of 1964 were thoroughly abstract space, seemingly separate from the spaces of industrial production and everyday life. Wilderness was a place not to live or work but to visit for a therapeutic or aesthetic experience. A modern sensibility produced a place abstracted from the means of production necessary to sustain life and then called adventures in that environment authentic experiences. In its abstraction from daily life and work, this wilderness became, perhaps, the most modern space of all.[14]

Before 1850, the American landscape was little known for spectacular scenery, particularly when compared with Europe. A noted exception was Niagara Falls, which had been surrounded by commercial exploitation that brought widespread condemnation. Europe, in contrast, had spectacular mountains and a tradition of art and literature that grounded its identities and made envious those Americans searching for their own. By mid-century, the eastern United States had gone through a first round of industrialization and embraced a market economy, and all of the West had become part of the nation. Looking west, Easterners saw much land still untrammeled, an America like the wilds from which the mythical nation had been born. That is, not yet modern. Writes historian Simon Schama, "The presumption was that the wilderness was out there, somewhere in the western heart of America, awaiting discovery, and that it would be the antidote for the poisons of industrial society." Westward movement, according to environmental historian Robert Gottlieb, "elevated wilderness as a key issue, both in terms of the scenic impact of the West's natural wonders and the ambiguities associated with the expansion and the closing of the frontier."[15]

In the idea of wilderness, American popular culture and the continent's nature merged. Aldo Leopold, one of the intellectual pillars of wilderness literature, promoted the cause of preservation in 1925 using the mythic image of the covered wagon of America's frontier past.[16] Meanwhile, Zane Grey was lamenting the destruction of his American West by forces of urban industrialization. In addition to his romanticized Westerns, Grey wrote dozens of articles on the wastefulness of sportsmen and developers.[17] His West of unspoiled desert and few people was by 1920 overrun with autos and tourists. "Time is cruel," he wrote about a 1919 visit to Kayenta, Arizona. "The years are tragic. The pioneer could not stay the approach of deadly civilization." In 1922, Grey called for "two million Boy Scouts to save some of our green, fragrant, untrammeled land for the boys to come."[18]

Nature in the American West also was understood as monumental, in keeping with Romantic notions of the sublime of nineteenth-century Europe and America. It was a space to which American nationalist pride could point, even if the nation lacked the cultural achievements of Europe. It was in the West that the national park as an institution was first imagined. Historian Alfred Runte comments that "although the grandeur of the Far West inspired the national park idea, eastern men invented and shaped it." In 1864, the federal government granted the Yosemite Valley to California as a park, creating a significant precedent. In 1872, Yellowstone became the first national park.[19] The Antiquities Act of 1906 allowed the president to create national monuments that could preserve examples of spectacular nature.

Zane Grey wrote in 1930 that the Utah-Arizona border country "has been ruined by motorists."[20] With the rapid spread of automobiles and road networks, activists who formed the Wilderness Society began in the 1930s to venerate a nature more primitive than that on display in the national parks, which were inundated with tourists in cars. The society founders saw wilderness as a space for recreation and aesthetic enjoyment, uninhabited, and generally free from the forces of the market economy. Historian Paul Sutter writes, however, that modern American wilderness "was certainly the product of an emergent consumer society." Yet the birth of the wilderness movement in the 1930s served as a critique of mass consumption, he notes, particularly that of the spread of automobile tourism. Sutter labels it a paradox that the Wilderness Society was created while its founders were on a trip in a car, the very product against which they sought to protect areas of untouched nature.[21] The situation was not so contradictory, however, if you accept the notion that it was the specific conditions of modernization that produced that car, provided lifestyle options to the occupants of it, *and* created the idea of wilderness areas as primitive nature. It was industrialization that provided the means and choices that permitted Wilderness Society founders to speak of unpeopled, untrammeled wilderness and provoked their desire to do so at the same time that it made wild nature ever more scarce.[22] So it was this space called nature and wilderness that David Brower and members of the Sierra Club received at the beginning of the 1950s as they discovered the canyons and mesas of the Colorado River and transformed themselves into a national political force.

Brower's appointment as the first paid staff member of the Sierra Club anticipated a growing disenchantment of some middle-class Americans during the post–World War II economic boom. The post-war United States underwent massive and accelerated change. Writes historian Samuel Hays, "Seldom, if ever, in American history had so much been altered within a single lifetime."[23] The acceleration of economic growth saw increased use of chemicals in manufacturing and agriculture, a proliferation of energy-producing projects, an expansion of automobile use and of the highways to serve them—all creating environmental and aesthetic pollution.

These changes also produced unprecedented prosperity in the United States. Federal highway and housing programs drew millions of mostly Anglo-Americans out of the cities and into car-dependent homes in the suburbs. The expanded Anglo, college-educated middle class moved to suburbs, then sought out amenities that included outdoor recreation, clean air and water, health, security, and a greater emphasis on the natural world in the form of parks, wilderness areas, and access to other nonurban areas. This emphasis on the wild was part of the new postwar affluence and the ability of the American middle class to consume goods and lifestyles. Hays sees postwar environmentalism as a consumer movement. Suburbs themselves, with their sprawl and destruction of open spaces, played a key role in awakening the postwar environmental consciousness.

The origins of the growth of the postwar environmental movement lay in the twin phenomena of affluence and discontent. Affluence provided lifestyle options that included the consumption of nature for recreation, regeneration, and aesthetic enjoyment; discontent came from the rapid changes spawned by the affluence. It also provided the money to finance conservationist activism. From 20,000 members in 1959, the Sierra Club grew to 113,000 by 1970.[24]

In 1953, with the Echo Park Dam on the drawing board, the Sierra Club sponsored raft trips through Dinosaur National Monument that acquainted members with its beauties. Through a film made during the river trips, *Wilderness River Trail,* the first such project by the Sierra Club, preservationists around the country became acquainted with the canyons inside the monument. Brower decided to capitalize on the success of the movie with a book. In 1955, *This Is Dinosaur* was the first book to publicize a threat to a national park or wilderness.[25] "Dinosaur National Monument is one of the last almost 'unspoiled' wildernesses—which means it is relatively unmarked by man," wrote Wallace Stegner, who edited the book shortly after he finished writing a biography of John Wesley Powell.

Stegner framed Dinosaur as a place of refuge from modern life yet one within the rhythms of that life: time only for a short vacation in which to reinvigorate oneself for reinsertion into the rat race. Yet it was only a refuge he sought, an island or remnant of the nature that was rapidly disappearing. Stegner's nature was thus the product of modernization and a modern sensibility, nature as a retreat to help cope with modern life but also thoroughly in accord with that life, abstracted from the forces that sustain humans but in step with the rhythms of industrial production.

> *How much wilderness do the wilderness-lovers want?* ask those who would mine and dig and cut and dam in such sanctuary spots as these. The answer is easy: *Enough so that there will be in the years ahead a little relief, a little quiet, a little relaxation, for any of our increasing millions who need and want it.* That means we need as much wilderness as can still be saved. There isn't much left, and there is no more where the old open spaces came from.[26]

In response to the threat to Dinosaur National Monument, the Sierra Club, the Wilderness Society, and other groups joined to oppose the dam.

The debate over Dinosaur took place within the context of the entire Colorado River Storage Project, including the relationship among the various proposed dams. Brower took the lead in challenging the Bureau of Reclamation and its data on storage capacity and evaporation. Focused on saving the national monument, Brower calculated that a "high dam" at the Glen Canyon site could make the Echo Park project upstream unnecessary.

The bureau, seeking to discredit the analysis, pointed out that such a dam would threaten Rainbow Bridge, an issue DeVoto also had raised. The bureau's reaction prompted the preservationists to demand that Rainbow Bridge, a national monument like Dinosaur, also be protected.[27] With cooperation from eastern interests and farmers and members of Congress from California who viewed the upper Colorado project as a threat to their claim to the water, and helped by an effective public relations campaign, the groups stalled congressional approval of the entire project. With some dam proponents realizing that the Echo Park Dam had to be dropped in order to get the rest through Congress, project backers met in Denver in November 1955. The Council of Conservationists, a coalition of top leaders of preservationist groups, placed an advertisement in the *Denver Post* declaring opposition to the Colorado River Storage Project as long as it threatened any national park or monument. The council also warned in a press release of political retaliation against those supporting Echo Park. Project supporters finally conceded and agreed to remove the dam.[28]

Later that year, Howard Zahniser of the Wilderness Society, representing the Council of Conservationists, met with Utah Congressman William A. Dawson. The two negotiated an agreement to insert language into the Colorado River Project bill to preclude Congress from reviving the Echo Park dam and to protect Rainbow Bridge National Monument. Dawson expressed fear that Brower, in particular, would continue to oppose the Glen Canyon Dam. Indeed, Brower and others had made intensive studies of the project and concluded it was unnecessary because it duplicated Hoover Dam. The board of directors of the Sierra Club refused, however, to oppose the Glen Canyon Dam, focused as they were on the main goal of protecting the national park system.[29]

Zahniser assured Dawson that Brower would not oppose Glen Canyon, but he said, according to a transcript he produced soon after the meeting, "We want to have a provision put in the authorization of the Glen Canyon project that will say that the Glen Canyon project shall be so constructed as to include the safeguards for the Rainbow Bridge

National Monument." Zahniser was politically pragmatic about the Colorado River project, willing to give up Glen Canyon because it was not a national park. The preservation groups, he said, "are sorry to see any piece of fine scenery destroyed as scenery, of course, but as I told you earlier, we're working on a project that includes all kinds of development and if the areas that are set aside for preservation can be protected as such we're not objecting to development that is necessary elsewhere." The groups promised to withdraw opposition to the Colorado River project as soon as the protections were in place in the authorizing legislation.[30]

With the provisions protecting parks and monuments inserted into the Colorado River Storage Project Act, the U.S. House of Representatives debated the measure in March 1956. When a question arose over whether the Sierra Club had withdrawn its opposition, Colorado Representative Wayne Aspinall found Brower in the House gallery, and Brower confirmed that the group had indeed signed off on the project. It was approved.[31]

The battle over Dinosaur National Monument in the 1950s, according to historian Mark Harvey, helped make "national parks" and "wilderness" nearly interchangeable terms. After the defeat of the Echo Park Dam, Zahniser drafted a plan for a national wilderness system. Seventy-eight national organizations had joined the fight against the Echo Park Dam, and their success gave impetus to the wilderness bill that became law in 1964.[32] The national debate over Dinosaur also made the Sierra Club and other groups aware of the Colorado Plateau. Its canyons, rivers, mesas, and deserts became places for wilderness lovers and, in Mark Harvey's words, the Colorado River Plateau was "destined to become a focal point of conservation activity in the decades ahead."[33]

The advocates of preserving wild spaces believed that they had made a wise choice in the clause inserted into the law that protected national parks and monuments. But in the late 1950s and early 1960s, Sierra Club members who rafted the Colorado River through Glen Canyon were dazzled by its beauties. Glen Canyon had, of course, been known before the Sierra Club trips. Powell rode boats through it, twice. In 1923, guide David Rust began taking the first commercial boat trips through Glen Canyon.[34]

In the mid-twentieth century, various commercial raft companies took vacationers down the canyon, many Boy Scouts among them. Wallace Stegner rafted through the canyon in 1947.[35] Ken Sleight rafted through it in 1955 and then built up a commercial guide business catering to Boy Scouts and tourists. He and other river runners formed a group called Friends of Glen Canyon to oppose the dam. They were few in number, and the group also lacked a critical component to save the canyon: "There were no articulate people out there who knew it."[36] Friends of Glen Canyon did not yet have a Sierra Club or a David Brower, someone of influence to widely circulate words and images of the canyon and make a case for its preservation. But during the Sierra Club ventures into the canyon, Brower and others began to talk about Glen Canyon as a place of unmatched wild nature, thus beginning the process of making it a place in modern America.

In Glen Canyon, the triad of components for making such a place were the physical presence of Sierra Club members, the words and images about nature that they had in their possession, and their ability to circulate these discourses to a wider audience.[37] Brower had to bring with him food and other supplies. He also used a guide and rafts. So his presence at Glen Canyon was possible only through the intervention of money and the transportation, supplies, and services that money enabled him to buy. As Sierra Club executive director, Brower depended on donations and dues, both of which came primarily from people living in cities who had disposable income. In other words, Brower's encounter with wild nature in Glen Canyon was possible only through the affluence of modern American society. His presence there was an extension of that society and its economic system. Money connected the urban world and the wild nature of Glen Canyon and made them parts of a single complex.[38]

Brower purchased a 16mm Bolex motion picture camera and took it on canyon trips with his family. The group flew from Page, Arizona, where Glen Canyon Dam was being built, to Hite, Utah, where they were ferried across the river and then launched on raft trips guided by Richard Norgaard. Brower took three miles of film in Glen Canyon during these outings. In 1997, portions of the film were made into a videotape. "I went down Glen Canyon after my proposal of a higher Glen Canyon [dam] caused a lot of static among the people who had

David Brower, the executive director of the Sierra Club from 1952 to 1969, took a small movie camera with him on a "farewell trip" through Glen Canyon before it was covered by the waters backed up by a huge dam on the Colorado River. (Reproduced with permission of Northern Arizona University, Cline Library, Tad Nichols Collection.)

been down Glen Canyon, which I hadn't," Brower says on the videotape. "And they were asking, 'What the hell was I up to. Did I know anything about what I was doing,' which I didn't."[39]

In Brower's hands, the camera became an instrument for seeing Glen Canyon in certain ways. "Whenever I film anything I talk to myself, sometimes audibly, saying what it means to me. And I was continually going through that: 'We have no right to trash this. This is beautiful. Look at that. Why would we let anybody mess it up.'"[40] Brower, like many others, saw Glen Canyon through the lens of certain discourses, those strings of words and images through which we talk about, picture, and therefore create our understanding of the world. Those discourses were part of the dialogue of what some scholars term "the gaze," the ways people look at things and experience what they see. Looking, one of the fundamental activities within modern nature, is never neutral. Instead, it involves the emphasis placed on sight by a culture and the meanings chosen to narrate what is seen. Raymond Williams commented on such a process: "From a whole possible area of past and present, certain meanings and practices are chosen for emphasis [and] certain other meanings and practices are neglected or excluded."[41] Brower narrated what he saw through modern American notions of wild nature.

The side canyons of Glen Canyon were the objects of Brower's most fervent comment. In an alcove of sheer rock walls and overhead light called "Cathedral of the Desert," Brower found "the ultimate magical place in Glen Canyon." He writes, "When you walked into that it was so much like a cathedral that you thought you should be quiet there. And we were." For Brower, the side canyons were "*the* special place on earth."[42]

In 1963, Brower and photographer Eliot Porter produced *The Place No One Knew,* a Sierra Club coffee-table book of pictures and text extolling the virtues of Glen Canyon modeled on *This Is Dinosaur.* "Glen Canyon died in 1963 and I was partly responsible for its needless death," Brower wrote in the foreword. "So were you. Neither you nor I, nor anyone else, knew it well enough to insist that at all costs it should endure."[43] *The Place No One Knew* juxtaposes snippets of text, usually only a short paragraph, that appears on the left half on the open book, with photographs of Glen Canyon on the right. The text is an eclectic blend of discourses from more than a century of American commentary on nature, from the high culture of Thoreau to the popular culture of the Wild West. The use of text from Owen Wister, author of *The Virginian,* the first modern Western novel, connects Glen Canyon to the masculine "Old West" of popular culture and its ideal of wilderness.[44]

A quotation from Henry David Thoreau places Glen Canyon within the Romanticism of the nineteenth century and its attempt to contrast nature with the burgeoning modern values of market capitalism and the city. Nationalism is evoked in lamenting the loss of an American dream, the notion of an exceptional nation that has fallen under the crush of progress that ruined European nature (in contrast to those mid-nineteenth-century Americans who honor European nature because of its validation by culture and history). Brower writes: "The wilderness is there, however, to recall the dream." Brower in another passage evokes the wistfulness of time, as he makes Glen Canyon a space where the linear time of the clock can be exchanged for the cyclical time of nature: "There must be room enough for time—where the sun can calibrate the day, not the wristwatch, for days or weeks of unordered time, time enough to forget the feel of the pavement and to get the feel of the earth, and of what is natural and right."[45] The photographs contain no images of human presence except ancient petroglyphs. This nonhuman canyon is a place abstracted from every-day human life and the forces that support and sustain it. It is a modern space seemingly alienated from the present yet thoroughly within the sensibilities and rhythms of industrial society.

To produce a place in modern America, Brower and the others had to translate what they had seen into photographs, film, texts, or political speech. The dues that Sierra Club members paid gave Brower the ability to circulate these depictions. Yet what is said and pictured also had to appeal to a wider audience. So Brower narrated Glen Canyon through classic American and modern discourses already connected to a large body of cultural products with which Americans were familiar, from the Boy Scouts and Westerns of popular culture to Thoreau and the story of a nation sprung from raw nature.[46]

Consistent with the new policy of protecting the national park system written into the Colorado River Storage Project Act, the Bureau of Reclamation studied possible sites for a secondary dam that would keep the waters behind the Glen Canyon Dam from flooding Rainbow Bridge National Monument. The bureau settled on one site, which also would require a small diversion dam. Congress, however, would not allocate money for the project. Utah Senator Frank Moss told colleagues the $25 million requested to protect Rainbow Bridge "would be an unnecessary expenditure and represents a nonsensical and indefensible waste of taxpayers' money."

Arizona Congressman Stewart Udall traveled to Rainbow Bridge to gain firsthand knowledge of the controversy. Udall and a Pennsylvania congressman who accompanied him concluded that a secondary dam to hold back Lake Powell would itself despoil the area.[47] The *New York Times* saw the failure to appropriate the money as troubling and cast the controversy as symbolic of contemporary threats to the integrity of national parks. The *Times* editorialized that it was "difficult to believe the Eighty-Seventh Congress, or any congress, would wish to be responsible for marring this natural wonder or for setting a precedent permitting artificially impounded waters to flood into an established component of the national park system."[48]

When Udall became secretary of the Interior in 1961 after the election of President John F. Kennedy, he proposed a compromise that would allow the waters to flow under Rainbow Bridge but would enlarge the area of the monument and make it a national park. Udall proposed a "primitive park" of 775 square miles that would include Navajo Mountain and the canyons surrounding Rainbow Bridge, to be called Navajo Rainbow National Park. The northern and western boundaries would be the high-water mark of Lake Powell, thereby absolving the dam from violating the terms of the Colorado River Storage Project Act that were designed to protect Rainbow Bridge National Monument. The secretary sought to trade land that would be included in the park for Navajo Nation land. Udall argued that the Navajo land was "uninhabitable and unproductive."

Tribal Chairman Paul Jones vehemently disagreed, however, and he was "deeply incensed" that Udall had not consulted the tribe before he announced the proposal. Five years earlier, when the tribe had ceded land for Lake Powell, it had prohibited use of those parcels for "park, recreational, scenic or waterfront protective purposes." The tribe wanted water and electricity, not tourists. Udall subsequently dropped the park proposal, saying Navajo leaders "have a very inadequate appreciation of the significance of the national park system."[49]

Udall's was not the first attempt to create a national park in the area, nor the first to run into opposition from the Navajos. In 1931, two Californians took a raft trip with guide John Wetherill to promote creation of a Rainbow Bridge national park. Also in the 1930s,

National Park Service Director Horace Albright proposed an Escalante National Park. A 1933 bill in Congress dubbed Albright's proposal Navajo National Park and included 1.3 million acres containing Monument Valley, Glen Canyon, Rainbow Bridge, Navajo Mountain, Natural Bridges National Monument, and Navajo National Monument. The proposal was backed by Utah and Arizona and was supported by numerous congressmen and by President Franklin Roosevelt. The plan fell apart, however, when the Navajo Tribal Council became worried that a park would mean fencing out livestock. The chairman of the council, Tom Dodge, warned that the Park Service coveted Navajo Mountain and Monument Valley and that tourists would not want to see sheep and goats, the basis of the Navajo economy. Instead, in 1934, the Navajo Tribal Council voted to develop its own park system.[50]

The two unsuccessful attempts to create national parks on Navajo lands illustrate how the production of places such as national parks is culturally bound. Navajo opposition to the first park proposal stemmed in part from a U.S. livestock reduction program that began in 1933 on the reservation with the stated objective of halting overgrazing and improving herds. The program required the slaughter of thousands of animals. Livestock were intimately tied to the Navajo economy, culture, and psychology. The slaughter of thousands of animals in the 1930s was, historian Robert McPherson has written, one of the "major tragedies in the Navajos' tribal memory."[51] To strip the lands of that ability to produce, to modernize it as a space outside of production in the form of a park, was to abstract it from the Navajo means of survival and its cultural context.[52]

By 1961, it was clear that Congress and the Bureau of Reclamation had no intention of honoring the protections outlined in the Colorado River Storage Project Act. Brower called the impending flooding of Rainbow Bridge National Monument "the greatest welsh in the history of conservation."[53] As the construction of Glen Canyon Dam neared completion in 1962, Brower warned that Rainbow Bridge was in danger. Brower accused the Bureau of Reclamation of secretly lobbying against appropriations for the secondary dams.[54]

In August, the Sierra Club and other groups sued in U.S. District Court in Washington, D.C., seeking an injunction to prevent Udall from closing the gates of the Glen Canyon Dam. They asked the judge to order the government to comply with the Colorado River Storage Project Act. Judge Alexander Holtzoff dismissed the lawsuit, however, ruling that the preservationists did not have a sufficient claim of potential personal harm. But the judge also stated that the provisions of the act, including the clause on national parks and monuments, remained in effect.[55]

On January 21, 1963, workers closed the gates of the Glen Canyon Dam, and the reservoir started to fill. On that same day, Brower was in Washington, D.C., hoping for an audience with Udall. The secretary, however, already had scheduled a press conference. So Brower sat in the back of the room and listened as Udall made a pitch for construction of several dams in the Grand Canyon, with revenue from the sale of electricity to pay for a massive water development plan for the Southwest. The dams were to be in adjoining canyons just outside the boundaries of Grand Canyon National Park. With the waters of Glen Canyon rising and plans moving ahead for more dams, Rainbow Bridge became the representative place of the threats to nature by modernization in the American West. "The arch, which is situated in Utah," the *New York Times* said in July 1963, "has become the symbol of the fight over the future of the country's natural wonders and outdoor beauty."[56]

In 1964, Phil Pennington and Chuck Washburn produced a slide show from photographs taken while kayaking through the Glen Canyon of the Colorado River in southeastern Utah. The show was, however, no simple remembrance of excursions into wild nature. Since January of the previous year a massive concrete dam had been backing up the river that winds its way through five states in the arid American West before crossing into Mexico. The slide show became a Sierra Club presentation about the canyon vanishing beneath the waters backed by the Glen Canyon Dam. For the club, the rising waters represented a political betrayal and a bitter reminder of the deal that permitted congressional approval of the Colorado River Storage Project Act. The Glen Canyon slide show was an expression of nostalgia and regret for a place soon to be no more. The presentation ended in a black screen with only the lonely sound of a bird's call to remember the nature found in Glen Canyon.

The slides were made into a 16mm film titled *Glen Canyon*. Later, David Brower, by then the former executive director of the Sierra

Club, had his copy transferred to a videocassette, but he noted a problem: "The studio making the transfer thought the film was over when the screen went dark, and somehow lost the last notes of the canyon wren. I've got to find them."[57]

As the waters of the Colorado River continued to fill Lake Powell, Brower swung into action to fight the dams proposed for the Grand Canyon. The Sierra Club placed newspaper advertisements that declared, "Now Only You Can Save Grand Canyon from Being Flooded . . . For Profit." Those ads framed the canyon as a place outside the capitalist economy, while another linked it to a great cultural treasure of Western civilization: "Should We Also Flood the Sistine Chapel So Tourists Can Get Nearer the Ceiling?" The advertisements made clear that wildernesses were special places rapidly disappearing and that it fell to the wilds advocates to ensure "that something untrammeled and free remains in the American earth."

The ads and articles on the controversy prompted one of the largest public reactions in the history of the wilderness movement. Thousands of letters flooded Congress. On February 1, 1967, Udall announced that the plan to construct dams in the Grand Canyon would be scrapped. Even more than the fight over the Echo Park Dam, the battle over the soul of the Grand Canyon had placed the Sierra Club in the national spotlight and reinvigorated its commitment to protect the Colorado Plateau. It proved the environmental movement's coming of age. Brower, however, was forced to resign in 1969 over questions of his brash leadership style and poor financial management.[58]

By November 1970, the waters of Lake Powell were just six feet in elevation below and a quarter-mile downstream from the boundary of Rainbow Bridge National Monument. On November 4, Friends of the Earth, a group Brower formed after leaving the Sierra Club, filed another lawsuit in U.S. District Court in Washington, D.C., to prohibit the Interior Department from allowing the waters to reach the monument. Recruited to the lawsuit to meet the standard for showing potential personal harm were the Wasatch Mountain Club, a Salt Lake City–based conservation organization that took members on outings to Rainbow Bridge; and Ken Sleight, the commercial river runner who guided tourists through Glen Canyon.[59]

The complaint claimed that damage would occur to the arch, surrounding rocks, and plants because of fluctuating water levels. The lawsuit cited the language of the Colorado River Storage Project Act, which clearly expressed the intent to protect Rainbow Bridge. As an offering of its cultural value, the lawsuit included a 1961 National Park Service bulletin that linked the arch to American nationalism by comparing it in size to the U.S. Capitol. Federal attorneys moved to transfer the lawsuit from Washington, D.C., to the United States District Court for Utah in Salt Lake City.[60] The case came under the jurisdiction of U.S. District Judge Willis Ritter, known for his cranky antagonism to established power. The states of Utah, Colorado, and Wyoming, as well as several water districts, successfully intervened in the lawsuit as defendants.

The Department of the Interior and the other defendants argued that Congress, after the approval of the Colorado River Storage Project Act, repeatedly refused to appropriate money for a secondary dam to keep the waters out of the national monument. In declining to allocate funds, they argued, Congress had implicitly repealed the provision of the act that had prohibited dams or their waters in a national park or monument.[61] As a result of the lawsuit, the bridge also became the object of scientific study. Engineers and geologists measured it and made drawings that detailed the stresses on it. Two reports concluded that the waters would not structurally impair Rainbow Bridge. In a report commissioned by the National Park Service, one engineer found the effects of the fluctuating waters of Lake Powell would be only aesthetic.[62]

As the case proceeded, it was clear that for Brower and Friends of the Earth, Rainbow Bridge was not in and of itself a place of great importance. Asked during a court hearing to state the "worth of Rainbow Bridge," Brower, in a rather uninspired response, said, "It seems to me that places like Rainbow Bridge are worth every bit of what it would cost to build a separate but equal Rainbow Bridge if you lost that one. I think it would be a rather high cost. . . . And you can't replace it." For the preservationists, Rainbow Bridge was a representative space, a last glimmer of the lost Glen Canyon, a fragment of a nature rapidly receding into the past under the waters of the dam. Glen Canyon, Brower asserted, "would have qualified for several national parks, really with respect to its scenery, extraordinarily qualified, qualities which are now gone." However, he continued, "one of the finest remaining parts of that system was, by great foresight, set aside in that small little national monument portion, one of the extraordinary features of the Earth, Rainbow Bridge, and we can see a promise kept."[63]

For Brower and others, the changing circumstances of Rainbow Bridge through the twentieth century also symbolized loss of the ability to have an authentic experience in a "primitive" landscape. For pre-dam visitors, the emotion of the sight of Rainbow Bridge prior to the Glen Canyon Dam was heightened by the task of reaching it on horseback or foot over difficult terrain, a reenactment of the mythology of Anglo pioneers in the American "wilderness." The trek also was a chance for the modern male to escape from the confinements of his office and home.

Zane Grey, forty years before Brower, thought the sight of Rainbow Bridge should be earned by the modern body toiling through the desert to reach it. "It was not for many eyes to see," Grey wrote about the arch he called Nonnezoshe, based on a Navajo word. "The tourist, the leisurely traveler, the comfort loving motorist would never behold it. Only by toil, sweat, endurance and pain could any man ever look at Nonnezoshe."[64] Neil Judd, who in 1909 was with the parties that first publicized Rainbow Bridge as an Anglo-American discovery, also lamented the arrival of the waters rising as Lake Powell: "With one of the world's greatest wonders to be seen almost without effort I detect, or thought I detected, a noticeable lack of appreciation. The average visitor, if I saw correctly, appears content to scramble up the path from the boat landing, take a picture to prove he was really there, and scramble back again."[65] So it was with Brower, who commented on pending arrival of motor boats at Rainbow Bridge: "The experience of discovery, of doing something on one's own two good feet, would vanish. You could 'put' him under there in a motor boat and drop a beer can or two and 'put' back out, but the experience could not be there any more."[66]

Thus, while the loss of Glen Canyon, was the true lament of Brower and others in the wilderness movement, Rainbow Bridge was its representative space where one more remnant of the nature of the past

was being breached. Yet, this nature, this loss of an authentic experience, was itself based on thoroughly modern ways of looking at and
experiencing the world. Glen Canyon was gone, like the last notes of
the canyon wren lost when Brower's movie screen went black. Now,
only Rainbow Bridge remained.

Judge Ritter took an unusual interest in the Rainbow Bridge case.
His papers show that he made a personal effort to gather historical
evidence and to recruit Navajos to join the lawsuit. Ritter feared a
decision to prohibit waters in the monument could be overturned on
the grounds the plaintiffs did not have sufficient showing of potential
personal harm to meet the legal requirements to bring suit. He also
wanted to strengthen the lawsuit with Navajo claims of a religious
connection to the bridge that would be affected by the waters of Lake
Powell. Ritter wrote letters to scholars and others, and affidavits were
gathered from Navajos at the judge's request. However, a clerk warned
in a memo that much of the information probably was not admissible
as evidence. Ritter also had wanted to convene the court somewhere
outside of Salt Lake City to hear new evidence. The clerk, Craig S.
Smay, noted, "The procedure appears to be a novel one." Smay also
reported that it was unlikely the Navajos could enter the case at that late
date and introduce new arguments. He suggested a separate lawsuit.[67]

In May 1972, the Shonto Chapter of the Navajo Nation and several individual Navajos described as medicine men filed a motion
seeking to enter the case on behalf of Friends of the Earth and the
other plaintiffs. They argued that the bridge had deep religious meaning and played an important role in the mythological history of the
Navajo people. The motion said that having waters enter the Rainbow Bridge area would cause the Navajos "much suffering, anguish
and humiliations" and violate their statutory and constitutional rights.
"Plaintiffs-intervenors believe that if man alters the earth in the area
of Rainbow Bridge their prayers and ceremonies will be ineffective to
prevent evil and disease, and the good life ('the Beauty Way') will be in
jeopardy." Ritter denied the motion, saying it would delay proceedings
that already had advanced to the final stage of arguments for summary
judgment, and he appeared ready to rule for the plaintiffs.[68]

Shortly thereafter, on February 27, 1973, Ritter found in favor of
Friends of the Earth and the other plaintiffs. Ritter declared valid the

provision of the Colorado River Storage Project Act of 1956 that pro-
hibited the dams or their waters in units of the National Park Service.
Ritter ordered the Bureau of Reclamation to halt the rise of Lake
Powell and to remove its waters from the monument.[69] However, the
10th Circuit Court of Appeals in Denver stayed Ritter's order, then on
May 1, 1973, overturned it.

The U.S. Supreme Court refused a request to intervene, and Friends
of the Earth, the Wasatch Mountain Club, Ken Sleight, and twelve
preservationist groups that had joined the suit requested that the full
panel of judges from the 10th Circuit overturn the earlier decision
of the court. A brief submitted by the Sierra Club and other groups
had little in the way of legal arguments. Instead, it appealed to the
American nationalist mythology that connected Rainbow Bridge to
the emergence myth of America, a nation and people sprung from the
European interaction with wilderness:

> Thus a nation founded upon the conquest of wilderness and
> almost uninhabited lands has nevertheless seen fit to pre-
> serve for all time climax portions of its natural and wilderness
> heritage—beautiful lakes, streams, sea shores, primeval forests,
> magnificent mountains, colorful deserts, inspiring canyons and
> geological formations. A nation endowed with natural and hu-
> man resources enabling it to stand alone in the first rank of
> power and affluence has preserved for all time the greatest
> examples of what it has been and from what it came in order
> that its people may enjoy and be inspired by the best nature
> has provided.[70]

On August 2, 1973, the full court ruled that Congress had indeed
repealed by implication the protections for parks and monuments. The
Supreme Court declined to hear the case. On May 16, 1974, waters
rose under Rainbow Bridge.[71]

On June 22, 1980, Lake Powell was full, and water was forty-six
feet deep under Rainbow Bridge. The solitude of the arch that Zane
Grey had written about was gone, and so was Glen Canyon, to the
lasting lament of Brower and other wilderness advocates. Zane Grey
had made the bridge a place to hold off the social changes of the

first two decades of the twentieth century. In the 1970s, Rainbow Bridge became another type of symbolic space, a remnant of primitive American wilderness lost to modernization. The politics of nostalgia began with the river trips by Brower and other Sierra Club members as the dam was under construction and they realized what was being lost was the place no one knew. Theirs was nostalgia for something not remembered, like Zane Grey's desert as the storehouse of unlived years, a faint feeling of unease for a nature of the distant past now alienated from their modern present. The quest for authenticity in this unremembered nature was the product of modernization, and the spaces produced thoroughly modern. This nostalgia was not, therefore, a politics that offered a powerful alternative to or even a sustained critique of the ravages of modernization. Rather, it sought to produce symbolic places that were but remnants of a nature fast receding, a product of modernization. Rainbow Bridge was thus.[72]

In 1995, the 83-year-old David Brower, again a member of the Sierra Club board of directors, proposed partially draining Lake Powell so that Americans could see some of nature's wonders in Glen Canyon. The Sierra Club board's decision in the 1950s not to oppose the Glen Canyon Dam was made, he said, before members realized that the canyon "happened to be possibly the most beautiful canyon on the planet, or any other planet we can think of." The next year the Glen Canyon Institute was formed to promote draining Lake Powell and received the backing of the Sierra Club board.[73] Though the institute's goal was nowhere near realization by 2003, a five-year drought left Lake Powell at a record low. Revealed for the first time in years was the Cathedral of the Desert that had enthralled Brower in the early 1960s.

Richard Ingebretsen, founder and president of the Glen Canyon Institute, told a reporter that entering the area produced a "sense of spirituality, a sacred oneness with nature." The Glen Canyon Institute sells books and videotapes about the canyon, keeping alive the sense of place that Brower had begun constructing years before.

In 1974, Tom Turner of Friends of the Earth wrote to other parties who again were appealing the Rainbow Bridge case to the Supreme Court to say the Shonto Chapter of the Navajo Nation and individual Navajos had asked to join the lawsuit. "Our attorneys agree that it was a mistake not to have had the Navajos in the case all along (Judge Ritter refused to let them in originally, but we could have sought their aid in appealing to the Supreme Court). The Navajos' brief to the Supreme Court scolds us (the plaintiffs) for excluding them previously but seeks the same ruling we do." Indeed, the Navajos' request to file a friend of the court brief with the Supreme Court complained that "not only does no party on this case represent the interests of movants [Navajos], but in fact those interests have been completely ignored by all parties, including the environmentalists who initiated the action."[74] The remarks pointed to the racial aspects of Rainbow Bridge as a space produced by Brower and other preservationists. The Navajos sought to intervene in the case on behalf of the Rainbow Bridge of their own making.

The Navajos' interest in Rainbow Bridge was decidedly a local one; tribal headquarters did not join the legal proceedings. The Shonto Chapter of the Navajo Nation, located in the area of Rainbow Bridge, voted to retain a lawyer to pursue its interests. The affidavits of the individual Navajos submitted to bolster their case linked the bridge to tribal mythology and noted that it was a site used for various ceremonies and prayers. But the affidavits also made it clear that the mythology and the bridge were connected to the Navajo desire for good rains, necessary for grazing and agriculture. The Shonto Chapter's resolution noted: "The Rainbow Bridge's similarity to the meteorological phenomenon of a Rainbow has long made it the site of Navajo religious ceremonies for rain." Paul Goodman, an elderly man who described himself as a medicine man, said if the waters of Lake Powell were not withdrawn, "The Diné [Navajo] would no longer be able to stand under the Rainbow Bridge and offer prayers for the good life, the livestock and for rain."[75]

In contrast to Brower and the preservationists, local Navajos saw Rainbow Bridge not simply as a beautiful natural phenomenon that inspired a spiritual attachment, but as a part of a whole in which spirituality was inseparable from those aspects of economic production that sustained them and their culture. The Navajos, although by the 1970s thoroughly connected to the national economy by way of consumption of mass-produced goods, still used land for grazing and growing crops for a family or local economy, seeing those practices as necessary to their health, as they also were intertwined with their spirituality. They narrated Rainbow Bridge through adaptations of the tribal emergence myth and local historical factors. They circulated that knowledge about the place within the local Navajo culture until the threat led some to divulge aspects of it for legal purposes. One Navajo, Jimmy Goodman, connected Rainbow Bridge to the "death of God" in the modern world. "We want to have this, our Holy Shrine, let alone by the whiteman. If they destroy this it would be killing our God. Just because they have killed their own God and Jesus, they should not kill ours."[76]

The space-making by Brower and other preservationists and the Navajos differed, then, in aspects of history, culture, economic modes of production, and questions of power. For Brower, the Sierra Club, and then Friends of the Earth and other preservationists, Rainbow Bridge was a symbolic space of nature, abstracted from the components of everyday modern existence. For the Navajo, it was connected through ceremony and song to daily life. The preservationists and the Navajos had sought the same end, the withdrawal of the waters of Lake Powell, but to preserve different places.

After their unsuccessful intervention in the preservationists' lawsuit, three chapters of the Navajo Nation and eight individual Navajos filed a lawsuit in September 1974 in U.S. District Court for Utah seeking their own legal solution to rid Rainbow Bridge of the waters backed up behind Glen Canyon Dam. Under the law and legal precedents, the Navajos had to show a monetary interest in the bridge, assert a claim of damages from the waters, and prove their connection to Rainbow Bridge. In shaping the Navajo lawsuit in this way, the U.S. legal system demonstrated that it operated on the basis of assumptions pegged to Anglo-American history and culture. Thus, Betty Holiday asserted that her monetary interest exceeded $10,000: "The sacred area—it's invaluable, therefore it's greater than any monetary price." Holiday said that she was a medicine woman but that there was no recognition of such a position by tribal authorities. Instead, in keeping with Navajo traditions, she named those who had trained her as a medicine woman and said she was recognized as such by local people. "I am known to the people that know me for my religious occupation." Holiday said she had personally conducted ceremonies at Rainbow Bridge three times since 1965.[77]

Several other Navajos who participated in the case asserted that Navajos had never ceded Rainbow Bridge to Anglo-America. They noted it as a place of refuge for Navajos. Said Paul Goodman in 1976: "The Navajos never gave up the bridge to the white man; this is not his land. Why does the white man claim everything? We must still retain control over the area to save ourselves."

Navajos argued that the flooding of Rainbow Bridge National Monument had destroyed or desecrated Navajo gods and sacred areas and violated their right to exercise their religious beliefs under the First Amendment of the Constitution of the United States; that the government was violating the provisions of the Colorado River Storage Project Act that require protection of the monument; and that Glen Canyon Dam and Lake Powell fell under the National Environmental Policy Act and, therefore, required an impact statement.

U.S. District Judge Aldon Anderson ruled, however, that Rainbow Bridge National Monument had never been part of the Navajo reservation. "Any aboriginal proprietary interest that the Navajos may have held in this land would have been extinguished by the entry of the white man in earlier years," the judge wrote, referring apparently to the Cummings-Douglass "discovery" of 1909 and the subsequent declaration of it as a national monument. Since the Navajos had no "property interest" in the land, they had no ability to seek First Amendment religious protections. Anderson likened the Navajos' claim to someone who entered the Lincoln Memorial, had a religious experience, and then claimed it was a sacred shrine. That person could not expect others to be kept out of the memorial, the judge said, dismissing the Navajos' historical claim to the bridge.

Anderson also emphatically refuted Navajos' claims about the religious significance of Rainbow Bridge. He wrote that the Navajo medicine men who were plaintiffs in the suit were not recognized by the tribe and their training was not overseen by the tribal government. He noted that since 1965, the individual Navajos who brought the suit had held only nine ceremonies within the boundaries of the monument, and infrequently prior to that. The judge wrote:

> Taking the information supplied by the plaintiffs as true, there
> is nothing to indicate that at the present time the Rainbow

Bridge National Monument and its environs has anything approaching deep, religious significance to any organized group, or has in recent decades been intimately related to the daily living of any group or individual.

Further, the judge ruled the Navajos did not have a consistent history of use of the area, despite their explanations that ceremonies at the bridge took place only when requested by an individual or a family. Anderson allowed Glen Canyon reservoir to continue filling. In upholding Anderson's decision, the 10th Circuit Court of Appeals ruled that, contrary to his findings, the Navajos did have a religious claim to Rainbow Bridge. But the judges said the government's interest in operating Glen Canyon Dam overrode the religious significance of Rainbow Bridge to the Navajos.[78]

After the 1974 lawsuit, the National Park Service responded with the Native American Relationships Policy, which was designed to be sensitive to the multicultural aspects of the land. After consultation with the Navajos and other local tribes in the area, the Park Service created a management plan designed to minimize the effects of tourists, including asking visitors not to walk under the bridge.[79]

Still, by 1992, visits by tourists to Rainbow Bridge numbered more than 250,000 a year. Conflicts erupted with Navajos and the hordes of tourists who arrived almost entirely by boat for two reasons: the failure of Navajos to profit from the tourist trade on what they viewed as their land, and the insensitivity of tourists and the National Park Service to the sacred nature of the arch. In 1995, a group of Navajos calling themselves Protectors of the Rainbow shut down the tourist trade for four days to hold a cleansing ceremony. Among them were Bonnie and Wally Brown, whom the Park Service earlier had turned down for concession to bring tourists to the bridge because a company called Aramark held the exclusive concession. A newspaper quoted Wally Brown as saying that Aramark "makes millions of dollars on this lake every year and no money ever goes to the Navajo Nation or to the City of Page. This is not a political statement, but then again I guess everything is political."[80]

Responding to the closure and the Park Service's policies to try to persuade tourists to respect the local Navajo belief in the sacredness of Rainbow Bridge, a group of natural arch enthusiasts, the Natural Bridge and Arch Society, filed suit in 2000 arguing that the agency violated the religious establishment clause of the U.S. Constitution. The suit was dismissed two years later, and that decision was affirmed on appeal.[81]

In 2001, Aramark was still taking tourists to the bridge by boat for a tour billed as the "Rainbow Bridge Cruise Adventure" to "the world's largest natural stone bridge." Its brochure proclaimed the structure as "quite likely the most photographed geological wonder in the American West" and touted early visitors Zane Grey and Theodore Roosevelt. On the two-hour trip to the monument on October 18, 2001, the boat operator and tour guide gave tourists a short Anglo-American history of the monument, including the first Anglo men to discover the bridge in 1909. As the boat neared the dock, the guide reminded everyone to stay on the trail and, because there were no garbage receptacles, to return all trash to the boat. "It's all totally natural," he said.[82]

CHAPTER SIX

Salting the Scenery

Modern Tourists in the Modern Landscape

Louisa Wade Wetherill observed a change in the use of the land of the Utah-Arizona border country about 1913, the year her husband, John, guided Zane Grey and then Theodore Roosevelt to Rainbow Bridge from the couple's trading post at Kayenta, Arizona. Louisa Wade and John Wetherill had grown up in families that migrated to southwestern Colorado and turned to ranching. Early in their marriage, Louisa and John left ranching to manage a trading post and to guide artifact collectors, archaeologists, and anthropologists on the Navajo Indian Reservation in New Mexico. In 1906, the Wetherills moved by horse-drawn wagon to Oljato, Utah, and set up a trading post in the Monument Valley area. In addition to exchanging goods with Navajos and Paiutes for wool, sheep, and labor, they provided accommodations and guide services to Anglo-Americans, activities they continued after they moved to Kayenta in 1910. Louisa saw in the couple's history stages of developments related to the land. First came prospectors, traders, and settlers—people who wrung a living from the earth or were dependent on those who did. Then arrived scientific explorers, "excavating, surveying, and mapping" the land. Finally, Louisa Wetherill observed, in about 1913 there arrived "the men who came to accept it as their playground."[1]

Wetherill narrated from her experience the creation in the early part of the twentieth century of a landscape of aesthetics, leisure, and recreation in the Utah-Arizona border country, one of the remotest parts of the lower forty-eight states. What drew the tourists and guided their experiences were words and images reproduced in photographs, paintings, books, magazines, and movies. Anglo-Americans wanted to experience the spectacles of natural stone arches, towering rock spires, deep canyons, ruins of ancient civilizations, Old West cowboys, and primitive Natives. They sought an authentic experience in contrast to their everyday world but also in keeping with their roles as modern consumers. Louisa Wetherill's fluency in Navajo and her interest in seeking out and collecting aspects of Navajo society and culture made her an ideal person to help broker the transition to a landscape of consumption. Rainbow Bridge became the preeminent tourist site of the area after John Wetherill in 1909 conducted the first expedition that publicized what then was believed to be the world's largest natural stone arch. It was one of the paramount places of American nature—"truly one of the wonders of the world," in Theodore Roosevelt's words.[2]

Louisa and John Wetherill's early lives had positioned them to open the deserts and American Indians of the Utah-Arizona border country for Anglo-America. Mary Louisa Wade was born in 1877 in Wells, Nevada, where her father worked in mining. Leaving that occupation, Jack Wade and his family passed through Monument Valley on the way to Mancos, Colorado, where they settled in 1880. John Wetherill was born in 1866 in the Midwest. His father had been in mining, ranching, and government service before the family settled in the Mancos Valley in 1880 to ranch. In 1888 one of John's brothers, Richard, and brother-in-law Charlie Mason discovered a huge three-story cliff dwelling at Mesa Verde near the ranch. The Wetherills and Mason dug in the ruins for artifacts. An 1875 discovery of ruins in Mancos Canyon and the subsequent Wetherill find at Mesa Verde were a national sensation. Many Americans of that era were fascinated by the mystery of the antiquity of their nation buried in the ruins. The Wetherills came to offer artifacts for sale and guide services to archaeologists and tourists. Two books quickly publicized the huge ruins. The author of one, *The Cliff Dwellers of Mesa Verde,* hired John Wetherill as a foreman on the dig and cited his notes throughout the book.[3]

Subsequently, the Wetherills roamed the Four Corners region look-ing for artifacts. They excavated items that were shown at the World's Columbian Exposition in Chicago in 1893. At the fair, the Wetherills met the Hyde brothers, Fred and Talbot, wealthy soap manufacturers who became fascinated with the ruins of the Southwest and formed a company to exploit them. The Hydes hired the Wetherills as guides, packers, and excavators. John and Louisa wed in 1896 but sold their ranch after several years of bad crops. In 1900, John went to work man-aging one of the Hydes' trading posts at Ojo Alamo, New Mexico, on the Navajo reservation.[4]

At Ojo Alamo, John helped excavate ruins and served as a guide while Louisa managed the post. Louisa knew no Navajo, but a sub-sequent event shocked her into learning the language. Her younger brother, John Wade, fell ill with pneumonia while staying at the post. Because Louisa could not communicate with Navajos to send for help, she was left to care for her brother alone. Wade recovered, but the experience made Louisa Wetherill resolve to learn Navajo. She appar-ently had an ear for the language and quickly grasped its nuances. The ability to communicate also opened the Navajo world to a curi-ous mind, and Louisa Wetherill began a lifelong study of the Navajo worldview and cultural mores. The two young Wetherill children also learned Navajo as they mastered English.

In a manuscript written in the 1930s but not published as a book until 2007, Louisa Wetherill described how the barren and forbidding New Mexico desert changed for her when a Navajo man invited her to see a sandpainting, whose beauty and meaning astounded her. That moment led her to an interest in the Navajo culture, and she began to study chants and ceremonies. Those encounters fostered a desire to experience Navajos in a state untainted by encroachment of the modern world. Louisa wrote, "After my five-year initiation among the Navajos of New Mexico, I wanted to go where the Indians still lived in their old ways. That is why, in 1906, we decided to move to Oljato, Utah, where the Navajos and the Piutes reigned supreme."[5]

In 1906 John Wetherill, John Wade, and Clyde Colville, who joined them from another Hyde trading post, loaded wagons and set out for Oljato, a spot that Wetherill had seen while on a prospecting trip.

Louisa Wetherill and the children soon joined them, and they set themselves up as traders in the Monument Valley area.[6] The Wetherills were eminently qualified for their new venture, given John's background as an excavator and seller of ancient artifacts and Louisa's immersion in Navajo language and culture. When Anglo-Americans came to the Utah-Arizona border region, the Wetherills served as intermediaries of their experiences. The cultural moment had arrived to remake the space of the desert and canyon.

Historians have traced the development of tourism in the United States to the 1820s. Those early tourists were a population with leisure time and disposable income, and they were accommodated by businesses offering transportation, hotels, services, and various amenities. They brought with them a body of words and images that enticed people to travel and narrated what they saw and experienced as culturally valuable. These early American tourists were a genteel elite, but as the century progressed tourism drew a variety of people with different interests.

Historian Dona Brown argues that class distinctions were exploded and remade in the process: "Tourism played a crucial role in the creation of a coherent middle class out of these diverse groups and in the negotiations that shaped the shifting boundaries of class over the century." The building of the Erie and other canals, followed by the construction of railroads, provided the transportation for a mass tourism, and hotels met other physical and cultural needs. Finally, a body of literature and images narrated the experience. Niagara Falls, for example, was the subject of history, literature, legends, guidebooks, folklore, and art. All of these phenomena were part of commercial and industrial development, most explicitly in the Northeast.[7]

When Europe was not the destination, early nineteenth-century tourism emphasized the grand tour of larger American cities. But by mid-century, American scenery had developed a following. The Romantic language and images of the sublime in the works of writers such as Ralph Waldo Emerson and painters such as those of the Hudson River School produced a romanticized American landscape. The commercialization of this landscape as a tourist destination depended upon its being seen apart from industrial America. Tourists wanted to think of their experiences in nature or quaint locations as separate from the market economy. Such consumption, therefore, required that the involved commercial transactions remain hidden.

By the last quarter of the nineteenth century, Brown notes, New England had become a tourist landscape, propelled by a sentimentalization found in history, journalism, novels, and short stories. This literature, in step with architecture, altered towns and landscapes to fit the new ideal. "Out of these diverse cultural movements emerged a mythic region called Old New England—rural, preindustrial, and ethnically 'pure'—a reverse image of all that was most unsettling in late 19th-century urban life." Brown notes a similar process at work toward the end of the century as American culture produced the "Old South" and "Appalachia."[8]

Notably, the Southwest also became a culturally valued region and tourist destination at this time. Through most of the nineteenth century, the American West had proved difficult for travel, with few quality accommodations. Tourists oriented to European standards had little appreciation for the vastness of the Far West and its aridity. Accounts through the middle part of the nineteenth century spoke of hardship of travel through an inhospitable desert. Those tourists who went West passed over the vast open spaces of the Great Plains and Southwest deserts to reach California, and then compared it to Italy. The Southwest particularly was despised and feared as a wasteland of burning deserts, ugly land forms, and oftentimes dangerous Indians.[9]

By the 1890s, however, the Southwest had become a destination, a space to see and experience. The second industrial revolution of the late nineteenth century created larger working and middle classes able to afford tourist experiences. Hotels, restaurants, railroads, and, later, automobiles provided comfort and transportation. Once-hostile Natives had been subdued. Then, too, a body of texts and images arose to lure tourists and define their experiences. Writers such as Charles Lummis promoted spectacular nature, Indians, and Mexicans of the Southwest as an antidote to the overcivilized East. Archaeologists provided a usable past from the cliff houses and ruins of the region.

Anthropologists and photographers wrote about and took photos of "primitive" Natives who served as relics of an authentic past available for consumption as a tourist experience or through purchase of Native crafts such as rugs, pottery, and jewelry. The Fred Harvey Company, in association with the Atchison, Topeka & Santa Fe Railroad, created advertisements and guidebooks and commissioned Anglo artists and photographers to romanticize the landscape and its American Indian inhabitants. Literature, art, and advertising helped create a region of primitive nature and exotic peoples.[10]

This quest to find authenticity lay at the core of modernism. The sociologist Dean MacCannell argued that the search for authenticity is the prime motivation of modern heritage- or ecotourism.[11] Modernism's drive to constantly produce something new, a process of creative destruction that eliminates the old to manufacture new places, fashions, and goods, encouraged the feeling that modern life was inauthentic.[12] In turn, Americans desiring to touch something real and authentic sought out landscapes and cultures believed to be untainted by modernization and its values and practices. It was in this historical context that Americans began producing and consuming the American Southwest. It became a region of primitive Indians untouched by Anglo-American progress, ruins that spoke of a long historical past, exposed rocks that measured a vast geological time, spectacular and untouched wilderness, and an Old West of popular culture where cowboys and Indians still roamed.[13]

The Wetherills, after receiving permission to open a trading post from the Bureau of Indian Affairs, in 1906 occupied an old mining claim at Oljato surrounded by reservation land. Upon arrival, John Wetherill met resistance from local Navajos, but he provided coffee, sugar, and bread for a rabbit feast that helped overcome opposition. The Wetherills built a house and a store.[14]

If Louisa Wetherill wanted to move to Oljato because the Navajos were still living traditional ways, the arrival of the Wetherill trading post marked an end of some of those ways. For local Navajos, the Wetherill's post provided access to food and goods that were not readily available. Trading posts were not merely Anglo-American institutions, recent scholarship has shown, but rather ran on rules that came from both cultures bound together by a debt system. Navajo women became pivotal to a family's ability to acquire food and manufactured goods from the posts. Women produced prized textiles that were a main source of trade.[15]

Once at Oljato, Louisa Wetherill began a relationship with the local Navajos that not only profited the trading business but also greatly enhanced the couple's ability to act as hosts for tourists. Her fluent command of the language, appreciation of Navajo culture, and friendships with Navajos led area residents to adopt Louisa and her children into a clan. At the same time, however, Louisa Wetherill's interest in the Navajo was mediated by her own Anglo culture. Louisa displayed the interests and attitudes and shared some of the methods of anthropologists and archaeologists. In collecting cultural information, Louisa Wetherill sought out traditional Navajos, duplicating the salvage operation of anthropology to record Native life before it disappeared.

Louisa took notes of her observations of Native cultural practices. "I found the Indians as they had always been except for the loss of a few chants." About the time of her arrival at Oljato, she began to gather plants that Navajos used as medicines and in rituals. Louisa Wetherill persuaded Navajos to identity the plants, their names and uses, and then to help her find them. At the time of her death in 1945, Wetherill's collection numbered about three hundred plants. One of her chief informants was a Navajo named Wolfkiller. This man, elderly by the time the Wetherills arrived, provided Louisa with descriptions of Navajo cultural systems and other aspects of life. Along with stories and myths, recipes interested Louisa, and she wrote everything down.

Louisa also worked to persuade Navajo men to create sandpaintings, which are used in ceremonies and then destroyed because of their dangerous powers. "I asked several medicine men to give me the copies of paintings but they all said the same thing, that it would not do to let them stay on paper or it would cause some very bad things to befall them." After two years at Oljato, she persuaded one of them to make sandpaintings but only after promising not to let other Navajos know that he had done so or that she even possessed them. As with some anthropologists, Louisa's ability to compile information depended in part upon her persuading Navajos to break tribal taboos.[16]

Louisa Wetherill's curiosity and knowledge of language and culture allowed her to mediate between Anglo-American society and Navajo culture. She passed on to scientists and tourists who came to the Wetherill and Colville trading post information she had gleaned

With the curiosity and sensibilities of an anthropologist and a command of the Navajo language, Louisa Wetherill was instrumental to the success of her family's trading post and guide service, first in Oljato, Utah, and then at Kayenta, Arizona. (Reproduced with permission of Northern Arizona University, Cline Library, Stuart M. Young Collection.)

about Navajo life, ceremonies, mythology, and customs. Sandpaintings that she gathered later went to a museum.

In 1909, Louisa Wetherill was responsible for two Anglo-American discoveries, the most significant of which put the Wetherills on the map. While she was accompanying a University of Utah party led by archaeologist Byron Cummings, a local Navajo told her of the area called Betatakin. Cummings and others hurriedly "discovered" the spectacular ruin, which became part of Navajo National Monument. The previous year, in a conversation about why Anglos were in the country looking at rock arches, a Navajo told her about Rainbow Bridge. She relayed the information to Cummings, who returned in 1909. It was then that he, with government surveyor William Boone Douglass in tow, found Rainbow Bridge and commenced the production of a new place in America—what they believed was the world's longest natural stone bridge. This "discovery" was possible only through Louisa Wetherill's command of the Navajo language and relationships with Natives.[17]

After arriving in Oljato in 1908, Cummings found in the Wetherills a couple readily able to expedite his mission of archaeological exploration. And in Byron Cummings, the Wetherills found someone with commercial and institutional connections whose interests in promoting tourism matched theirs. Though dedicated to education and scientific knowledge, Cummings also acted as a cultural entrepreneur. Historian Don Fowler has called Cummings one of the three great scholar entrepreneurs of the Southwest.[18] Cummings's trips to southeastern Utah had been paid for in part by a mining magnate who was interested in the development of Utah, and his 1909 expedition to Rainbow Bridge also depended upon a state government allocation.[19]

In return, Cummings wrote a newspaper article in which he promoted the area's attractions. Sunshine, mild winters, and pure air offered regeneration for the modern body—"health and peace to a man with a weary brain." The ruins of ancient civilizations and the eroded rocks and canyons were a "treasure house" of archaeology and geology. "The great natural beauties and wonders, as the natural bridges and Monument Valley, make it a veritable playground for the nation."

Also, there was the Navajo, a primitive child of nature who "hoes his corn, eats his squashes and watermelons before they are ripe and craveth not at all of the dress and customs of the white man. He leads the simple life and is happy." Ignoring American Indians' physical and cultural claims to the area, Cummings concluded, "This region surely deserves to be set aside as a national park and these great beauties kept unharmed and accessible to all."[20]

Other publications revealed a vocabulary of exploitation for gain. Cummings referred to archaeological objects as "treasure" and "plunder." The language suggests that his motivation in these early expeditions was entrepreneurial in lockstep with science. In that regard, Cummings reflected the practice of archaeology of that era. Historians have noted that professional archaeology rose in tandem with the consumer economy that began to take shape in the late nineteenth century. Alice Beck Kehoe has even pointed to the similarities with advertisements for consumer goods: "The same attributes of surface, shape, size, and material that advertisements emphasized were noted by archaeologists for the ancient artifact." William Leach has remarked on the parallels between the displays of artifacts at museums and those of consumer goods in department stores. Both served as attractions to a new economy of desire.[21]

Archaeologists provided a history that narrated the ruins of the Southwest as part of the national story. For Byron Cummings, southeastern Utah was, therefore, "a mine of wealth and wonder." He wrote of Rainbow Bridge in *National Geographic* in 1910, with accompanying photographs, and he and others touted its existence in newspaper accounts.[22] The Wetherills helped Cummings's cultural entrepreneurship, which through texts and images sanctioned the consumption of space in the Utah-Arizona border country.

Fifteen days after John and Louisa Wetherill aided the Cummings-Douglass party's "discovery" of Rainbow Bridge, John guided the first tourists to the site, New Yorkers Arthur and Helen Townsend. In July of the next year John Wetherill led another group of tourists, and a few days later he packed in another party. The latter was led by Herbert Gregory, a government geologist. Gregory had been to Oljato in July 1909 mapping and carrying out fieldwork. His field books show that he was impressed with Louisa Wetherill's interest in the Navajos: "Mrs. John Wetherill—adopted into tribe has access to all legends &

myths, has many sand paintings is very intelligent—wants to continue work & have it published." Gregory also noted, "Wetherill says big natural bridge near Navajo Mountain." Gregory continued his scheduled work that summer and did not try to reach the arch. However, in January 1910 Gregory wrote John Wetherill to ask about the cost of guide services for two to three months of exploration that summer.

Wetherill responded with a list of prices. They included "American Horses grain fed" at $1.50 a day, "Navajo ponies not grain fed" at $1 a day, guide services at $5 a day. If Gregory did not provide the "grub," the daily charge was $12.50 for one man or $20 for two men, including guide services. "The expense depends on what horse you want, and the number of men you take with you."[23]

Gregory reappeared in the summer of 1910, and John Wetherill guided his party to Navajo Mountain and Rainbow Bridge. Like his shepherding of Byron Cummings to Rainbow Bridge and such ruins as Betatakin, Wetherill acted again as a conductor of scientific discourses and practices, with the backing of the federal government. Like Cummings, Gregory had another agenda: to open the lands for Anglo-American consumption. Gregory was engaged in exploration in the name of science, in his case geology. Geology was another of the scientific discourses that, like anthropology and archaeology, helped to narrate the Southwest as a desirable destination for Anglo-Americans. For late-nineteenth- and early-twentieth-century Americans, geology meant access to a language that told them how to see the eroded rocks and canyons of the desert Southwest. "Geology furnished nature with a history," in the words of one historian.[24] John Wetherill's role was to keep the party moving and fed. Along the trail to Rainbow Bridge, Gregory and his assistant, Joseph Pogue, searched out rocks, while Wetherill shod horses or tended to camp duties. On July 23, Wetherill wrote in his notebook, "The professor and Pogue are not good as helpers, though at times they think they are." When the party reached Rainbow Bridge, Gregory wrote in his notes: "Natural Bridge [rudimentary sketch] Clearly one of the world's wonders."

For Wetherill, however, the trip by now was routine. Wetherill wrote in his notebook: "We reached the bridge about 12:15. They all thought it was worth coming to see we had lunch at the spring under the bridge. Looked around for an hour taking photos & telling how wonderful the bridge is & guess we would not get back that night to camp & telling about our sore places & saddle up & started back at 1/4 after two."[25]

For Gregory, Wetherill's help made possible not just a scientific mission but a modern one. Pogue published an article in *National Geographic* in 1911 that described the trip, the geology of the area, and Rainbow Bridge. In 1916, Gregory published his findings as *The Navajo Country: A Geographic and Hydrologic Reconnaissance of Parts of Arizona, New Mexico, and Utah,* also known as *Water Supply Paper 380.* He noted the hostility of local Navajos to the presence of the party on Navajo Mountain but insisted in the rightness of his task, that of bringing progress. Along with detailed descriptions of the geology and geography of the area, Gregory also offered suggestions to travelers. "A Navajo, preferably a school boy recommended by a superintendent, should be a member of each party, not only to serve as guide and interpret but to obtain advance information regarding water and forage and to establish friendly relations with those Indians who have slight acquaintance with the whites." Gregory recommended Wetherill and Colville as suitable guides for scientists and tourists.[26]

When Cummings, Gregory, and others published their accounts of trips into the Utah-Arizona border area, they always characterized the area as unknown, unmapped, a last wilderness, a final American frontier, a wild untamed land. What those accounts left out—aside from Natives' possession, use, and knowledge of the lands—was that access to these places had required expenditures. There was a direct relationship between the hiding of the financial transactions and the characterization of the area as wilderness.

Like Dona Brown's finding that the tourist sites of New England were sold as if they had no connection to the market economy, accounts of Rainbow Bridge failed to mention the market-oriented nature of the undertakings. For Cummings, Gregory, and the others, to keep Rainbow Bridge as a place apart from contemporary America—to maintain its authenticity as an example of spectacular, unsullied nature and to portray the hardships of the trail as replicating those of the mythological pioneer-explorer trek—required that the monetary transactions remain concealed. To reveal that connection to the consumer economy would have, of course, exposed Rainbow Bridge and Monument Valley for what they were in twentieth-century America: spaces of consumption and part of the market economy.[27]

In the fall of 1910, the Wetherills moved to Kayenta, Arizona, just south of Monument Valley and some thirty miles from Oljato. The move put the couple a day closer to supplies and gave them access to a school for their children and a better water supply.[28] In the spring of 1911, the Wetherills and Colville built a trading post and house out of stones and cedar poles. Louisa Wetherill planted trees and a lawn. John and Colville also began constructing a road through Marsh Pass that would connect to the Red Lake Trading Post and to roads to Tuba City and Flagstaff. Zane Grey soon arrived in Kayenta, after *Heritage of the Desert* had been published and his career as a writer of Westerns was launched. John Wetherill packed Grey through Marsh Pass to Tsegi Canyon and the ruins of Keet Seel and Betatakin in Navajo National Monument. From the experiences of that trip and of two previous forays into the Utah-Arizona border country, Grey wrote *Riders of the Purple Sage.*

In her autobiography, Louisa Wetherill notes a number of geologists, archaeologists, and anthropologists who came to Kayenta (she does not mention Grey). It was, however, the written accounts of Theodore Roosevelt's visit to Kayenta in 1913 that Louisa Wetherill credits with making the couple widely known to the American public. Roosevelt's visit was strictly for pleasure, and, at least in Louisa Wetherill's thinking, that was a marked difference from most Anglo-Americans who had come before. The difference seemed to be whether work was performed. "With the Roosevelt trip," her autobiography observed, "the Wetherills became known to sportsmen as well as to scientists, to those who wanted hard trips in a new country as a stunt and a vacation."[29]

Theodore Roosevelt began planning a trip to the Southwest soon after his defeat in the 1912 presidential election. In the Southwest, he wanted to see the Grand Canyon and hunt mountain lions on its north rim (where Zane Grey had in 1907 and 1908), visit ruins of cliff dwellings and Rainbow Bridge, and observe a Hopi snake dance. Nicholas Roosevelt, the former president's cousin, arrived early to make arrangements. He wrote a trader, "What we intend to do if possible, is to go direct to the Natural Bridge and back to Wetherill's store." Theodore

Roosevelt published two accounts of this trip. He was particularly impressed with Louisa Wetherill and her studies of the Navajo. He noted it was she who had learned of Rainbow Bridge: "Mrs. Wetherill was not only versed in archaeological lore concerning ruins and the like she was also versed in the yet stranger and more interesting archaeology of the Indian's own mind and soul. . . . If Mrs. Wetherill could be persuaded to write on the mythology of the Navajos, and also on their present-day psychology—by which somewhat magniloquent term I mean their present ways and habits of thought—she would render an invaluable service."

Roosevelt described the Wetherills' "delightfully attractive house" in the midst of the "utterly desolate" desert country. "Our new friends were the kindest and most hospitable hosts, and their house was a delight to every sense: clean, comfortable, with its bath and running water, its rugs and books, its desks, cupboards, couches, and chairs and the excellent taste of its Navajo ornamentation." The Wetherills' house melded modern comfort with the modern primitive, an interior that reflected the exterior space into which the Wetherills were conducting guests.[30]

Several later travel accounts also described the interior of the Wetherill home. W. D. Sayle, who also used the Wetherills for a visit to Rainbow Bridge, called the couple's home the "most picturesque and artiest dwelling imaginable. Indian rugs everywhere, covering floors and walls, beautiful examples of Indian weaving, pottery, implements of peace and war, and above all, which showed the true character of our hosts, shelf after shelf filled with interesting historical books." Charles Bernheimer also wrote of the house: "Rare Indian relics give a den-like look to living room, hallway, and bedroom. The dining room has painted friezes along side, replicas of 'sand paintings' of the Navajo."

For visitors, the Wetherills' home of books and plumbing juxtaposed with the Indian relics and objects expressed the relationship of the America of progress and the primitive. The Wetherill home certainly was decorated within the same invented tradition of the arts and crafts movement, which itself dwelled within the antimodern discourses of the era. Adherents valued the handmade over the mechanically reproduced, and they decorated cottages or rustic homes with handcrafted or natural objects from primitives, peasants, or Indians. Gustav Stickley, editor of the *Craftsman* magazine, suggested the use of Navajo blankets to decorate porches.[31]

It was not, however, merely a style prevalent of that era, but rather expressive of a whole series of social relationships and cultural meanings. As Marianna Torgovnick has pointed out, the appropriation of Native artisan objects in the twentieth century was a result of Western nations' attempts to colonize so-called primitive societies. The placing of such objects in a home or museum took them from their social and cultural contexts and gave them different meanings. The primitive objects in the Wetherill home spoke to the desires of the couple and their visitors to connect with the authentic through contact with primitive peoples. These handmade objects were desired because they contrasted with what was seen as the devaluation of workmanship and the vulgarity of modern mass production. While some modern Americans might embrace strands of Oriental and medieval cultures, others experienced the primitive peoples, ruins, artifacts, and the products of American Indian artisans of the American Southwest.[32]

The rugs, sandpaintings, ancient relics, and other objects in the Wetherills' home also encapsulated the market economy of that time. John Wetherill and his brothers had gathered artifacts from Southwest ruins for the 1893 World's Columbian Exhibition, a vast showplace of the modern and the primitive that helped to market the Southwest, its peoples, and its cultural objects to Anglo-Americans. Writes Ronald Freeman Lee, "The desires and needs of growing numbers of collectors and dealers, exhibitors and curators, teachers and students, added to the Native curiosity of cowboys, ranchers, and travelers, created an avid demand for original objects from the cliff dwellings and pueblo ruins of the Southwest." Besides actual artifacts collected from ruins, the products of contemporary Native artisans—Hopi pottery, Navajo silver jewelry and rugs, Pomo baskets, and other goods—were sold. For their part, Indian artisans produced "prehistoric" goods not for their own cultural and social uses, but to meet the demands of tourists and collectors. They altered styles and sizes to fit the requirements of the market.

The Fred Harvey Company, which also helped prepare Southwest exhibits for the World's Columbian Exhibition, was the chief commercial engine driving the market. Writes Leah Dilworth, "The central icon of Fred Harvey's Southwest was the Indian artisan. Images of weaving, pottery making, basket making, silversmithing, and turquoise drilling were prevalent in Harvey publications." Indeed, the Wetherill home resembled Fred Harvey's El Tovar Hotel on the rim of the Grand Canyon: the hotel had conveniences such as running hot and cold water and electric lights, but an interior designed in rustic frontier motifs, with stuffed animal heads and Native American artifacts. So when Theodore Roosevelt and others arrived at the Wetherills' house for guided tours, the style of the home met their desires to reconnect to the primitive through objects and artifacts, in keeping with their consumption of the wild nature and Indians outside the doors.[33]

Roosevelt's accounts of his experiences at the ruins of Navajo National Monument and on the way to Rainbow Bridge were colored by martial rhetoric. He found warnings about national weakness in the ruins of a disappeared civilization. Still, Roosevelt described Rainbow Bridge as a monument to American nationalism: "It is a triumphal arch rather than a bridge, and spans the torrent bed in a majesty never shared by any arch ever rendered by the mightiest conquerors among the nations of mankind."[34]

Zane Grey also wrote nonfiction accounts about his trip with John Wetherill to Rainbow Bridge in a 1915 magazine article and 1922 book. In *The Rainbow Trail,* the fictional sequel to *Riders of the Purple Sage,* Grey included the couple as the traders named Withers. The character Shefford arrives at Kayenta and is greeted by the Withers: "The room Shefford entered was large, with logs smoldering in a huge open fireplace, blankets covering every foot of floor space, and Indian baskets and silver ornaments everywhere, and strong Indian designs painted upon the whitewashed walls." Grey had discussions with Louisa Wetherill about the Navajos and their beliefs, and she later entered into a contract with him to provide "legends, paintings and Indian materials" for use in stories in return for half of the profits of publication. When Grey returned in 1914, John Wetherill arranged for him to attend a Navajo ceremony, the one where he met the Byron Cummings party (see chapter 2).[35]

Louisa and John Wetherill also provided services for movie companies. Zane Grey had required that early movies based on his books be filmed at the actual locations where he had set them. In 1918, a Flag-staff newspaper noted the arrival of movie companies, including one to film in Marsh Pass near Kayenta. In 1924, John Wetherill sent Grey a telegram with a desperate tone complaining that the movie producer Jesse Lasky had failed to pay and had left them "in a bad hole." Grey lent the Wetherills $1,000 and said he would ask Lasky to advance the Wetherills for their services for the filming of *The Vanishing American* in the spring of 1925. The studios regularly used the Wetherills when filming in the Kayenta area. John Wetherill established prices for their services, which included wages and meals for packers and camp attendants, with differences in wages between white and Indian labor-ers. The *Coconino Sun* recognized the role of movies in bringing the region to the notice of Anglo-Americans with the headline, "Filming of Famous Grey Novels to Carry Fame of Our Scenery over World," and the newspaper excitedly declared, "Now we have started on that road on a bigger scale than we ever imagined possible."[36]

Louisa Wetherill's dating of the change in the use of land that took place in 1913—from a land of production to one of play—points to the convergence of factors that created the Utah-Arizona border region as a space available for consumption. The Wetherills' Kayenta lodgings offered comfortable quarters decorated in a way that would appeal to Americans seeking the trappings of authenticity through primitive objects. The road John Wetherill and Clyde Colville built to Kayenta provided easier automobile access. Louisa Wetherill's abil-ity to interpret Navajo language and culture allowed her to pass on aspects of Navajo life to Americans looking to investigate or experi-ence untainted authenticity or to scientists wanting to "salvage" Native life before it disappeared. The publications of Cummings, Gregory, Roosevelt, Grey, and others produced the area as a space of American history and romantic ruins and examples of untouched, remote, and spectacular nature—as well as a setting for Grey's famous Westerns. More Americans began to consume the space, aided by the material comforts and drawn by modern discourses contained in the burgeon-ing mechanical reproduction of words and images.

Perhaps the ultimate tourist attracted to the area by the texts and images of American culture was Charles Bernheimer, a wealthy New York clothing manufacturer. His presence and subsequent publications exemplified, if in an exaggerated manner, the production of a space of consumption that the Wetherills had helped fashion. In 1919, Bernheimer went to Natural Bridges National Monument, then returned the next summer and hired John Wetherill and Blanding, Utah, guide Zeke Johnson to guide him to Rainbow Bridge. In May 1920, Bernheimer wrote his wife and lamented not being able to communicate with her daily, then reminded her, "But as you aptly said, 'Charlie, go and see the Rainbow Bridge as soon as possible. You won't rest until you have done it.'"

In his field notes, letters, and publications, Bernheimer was explicit about why he had so desired to see Rainbow Bridge. Bernheimer traced his "boyhood dream" to the Leatherstocking tales of James Fenimore Cooper and stories of the West and Southwest that "fixed Arizona as the land of mystery to be penetrated only by the most hardy and brave and laid the foundation for a wish." Explorers such as Robert E. Peary "fired my imagination" and "kept it alive." Still later, "the romances and exquisite descriptions of Zane Grey contributed their share . . . which finally led me to turn my vacations into something more substantial to do in a small way what our big explorers and discoverers were permitted to do on a heroic scale." Bernheimer read books and articles on the Rainbow Bridge country "but none influenced me more in my final determination than Prof. Herbert Gregory's treatise on the Navajo country printed by the United States Geological Survey. It gave me something definite on which to plan. I believed him to be a safe pilot."[37]

Having been drawn to visit the area by various texts, Bernheimer on the actual trail to Rainbow Bridge narrated what he saw and experienced through them. On May 21, 1920, arriving at Surprise Valley: "I am here in this marvelous little oasis which Zane Grey so cleverly described, and, I may say, accurately." And then, "one reaches the places which Grey described in pursuit by Shadd at the end of Rainbow Trail." On May 23: "I forgot to mention that the 'Purple Sage' is not a poetic myth." May 25: "We took lunch at a spring . . . There Roosevelt and his sons and nephew lunched." Little wonder, then, that Bernheimer, immersed in the Anglo-American culture of exploration, scientific study, and popular culture texts and images, found in Rainbow

Bridge "one of the most inspiring marvels of the ages . . . an open textbook of creation."[38]

In the 1920s, various travel accounts, increasingly by automobile tourists, noted the Wetherills trading post and their guide services to Rainbow Bridge. John Wetherill gave his customers what they wanted: to Zane Grey, the naming of an area along the trail to Rainbow Bridge; to Charles Bernheimer, the "discovery" of a stone arch, which he named after his wife, Clara.[39] So thoroughly were tourist expectations of the region standardized that by 1929 the routine of visiting the Utah-Arizona border country was open to satire.

Writer Wilbur Hall gave a tongue-in-cheek account in *Sunset* magazine of a trip he took with John Wetherill and Colville. The article exposed not just how the two guides played to tourists' expectations, but how America had accumulated a storehouse of texts and images that "salted" the scenery. That is, the discourses produced the landscape that drew tourists, who then experienced it through the expectations created by what they had read and seen. "Colville leads you out to the point and watches you while this stage setting knocks you cold," Hall wrote. "Wetherill prefers to sit back and let you find the view for yourself and then look with mild surprise and say: 'Oh, that little thing? Yes, it is sort of neat. But nothing to get all heated up over.' As you read along, if you do, you will discover that it is, after all, John Wetherill who makes the biggest fool out of you. Because he lets you work your own undoing and hoax yourself."

Hall's group attended a Hopi snake dance and observed Navajos. From Kayenta, they traveled to the Betatakin ruins and Rainbow Bridge—"a thundering big natural bridge with all the colors its name implies, but nothing compared to the scenery that lies carelessly scattered about, as though scenery were plentiful and easy to get in wholesale lots, on the journey to and from the bridge." Concluded Hall, "The scenery is all salted."[40]

In 1922 John Wetherill, accompanied by Charles Bernheimer, used dynamite to blast a new trail to Rainbow Bridge that considerably cut travel time. Wetherill guided his first tourist party over the new route the next year. Within a few years, however, the new trail was no longer in use. Despite resistance from local Navajos, two brothers, S. I. and

Hubert Richardson, built a road and a lodge on Navajo Mountain. Rainbow Lodge in 1925 offered horseback trips at a cost less than what John Wetherill charged for the much longer route from Kayenta. A pamphlet priced a two-day trip to Rainbow Bridge at $50 a person. By 1939, the Fred Harvey Company had established a hired car service from Flagstaff to Rainbow Lodge.[41]

With the ability to use an automobile to get to Rainbow Lodge and the considerably shorter time on horseback or even hiking to Rainbow Bridge, the massive stone arch lost some of its allure and primitive characteristics. A traveler there, Richard Frothingam, in an echo of Zane Grey, wrote in the 1920s of Rainbow Bridge, "If this sublime illustration of the forces of Nature were accessible by a Pullman sleeper or motor car, its name would be on all men's tongues." Grey also had seen the physical toil it took to get to the arch as the natural bulwark that resisted the incursions of soft city dwellers and preserved it out of time and space from the modern world.[42] With the lodge on the slopes of Navajo Mountain accessible by car and tourists able to get to Rainbow Bridge and back in two days, "physical toil" was minimal, and the arch was no longer remote from the modern world. By the early 1930s, with the nation in the Depression, the Wetherills suffered financial losses and sought to turn over part of their business to a creditor.

John Wetherill was in his late sixties, and his son, Ben Wetherill, did not do well managing the business. In 1941, John wrote Louisa: "Things about the same. No future . . . Ben has many ideas but no way of carrying them out . . . . Everything he do [sic] he loses money. . . . Ben has plenty of ambissioin [sic] but not strength to carry it out. Too much wine."[43]

The same year that Rainbow Lodge began offering horseback trips to Rainbow Bridge, a new pair of traders motored into Monument Valley. Harry and Leona Goulding would become the conduits for Anglo-America to Monument Valley to the 1960s as it replaced Rainbow Bridge as the premier tourist destination of the area and became an iconic site of modern America.

In 1921 Harry, then a sheep rancher in Colorado, had learned of Monument Valley from residents of Bluff, Utah. He and a friend took time off and traveled by horseback into the area. Goulding found the views infatuating. After the Posey War in 1923, the Paiute band living in the Monument Valley area was moved. As Goulding saw it, that left room for a trading post. In late 1925, Harry and "Mike" (Harry's nickname for Leona) sold their ranch and set up shop in Monument Valley. The Gouldings' intention was to trade with the local Navajos and remaining Paiutes. The Gouldings did not possess the Wetherills' knowledge of archaeology or Louisa Wetherill's command of Navajo; nor did they have her desire to collect beliefs and cultural customs. But the couple became for Monument Valley what the Wetherills were to Rainbow Bridge; the Gouldings mediated the experience of the landscape for Anglo visitors, whether writers, photographers, movie-makers, or tourists.[44]

Before the Gouldings, Monument Valley long had been known to Navajos, Paiutes, and some Anglo-Americans. In 1859, Captain John N. Macomb, chief federal topographical officer in New Mexico, mounted an expedition in what is now called the Four Corners area, where the corners of Utah, Arizona, Colorado, and New Mexico meet. In a report published in 1876, a member of Macomb's party, geologist John Strong Newberry, described the land largely through the rather dull language of geology. Yet one day after the expedition left camp above the San Juan River, Newberry paused to write in his notebook:

> The distance between the mesa walls on the north and south is perhaps ten miles, and scattered over the interval are many castle-like buttes and slender towers, none of which can be less than 1,000 feet in height, their sides absolutely perpendicular, their forms wonderful imitations of the structures of human art. Illuminated by the setting sun, the outlines of these singular objects came out sharp and distinct, with such similitude of art, and contrast with nature as usually displayed, that we could hardly resist the conviction that we beheld the walls and towers of some cyclopean city hitherto undiscovered in this far-off region.[45]

By 1873, Monument Valley was known as a local landmark. That year a visitor at Lee's Ferry, a Colorado River crossing run by John Lee for the Mormon Church, scrawled directions and a map in Lee's diary noting "Monumental Valley." In 1903, T. Mitchell Prudden published an account of his summer inventories of ruins in the Four Corners region in which he described Monument Valley as "dwindling remnants of great red buttes standing up in a fantastic array of pinnacles and towers." In 1909, three years after the Wetherills had begun guiding visitors through the area, photographer Stuart Young, who was accompanying Byron Cummings on his expedition to discover Rainbow Bridge, took photographs of Monument Valley that he labeled "Monumental Park."[46]

The Gouldings lived in tents at first, trading foodstuffs and goods to the Navajo for wool and sheep. John Holiday, who grew up in the Monument Valley area, remembered Goulding going hogan-to-hogan with flour, coffee, potatoes, and other foods to trade. A Goulding nephew did the same and became known in Navajo as "I Want Sheep."[47] Sometime in 1927, however, a few local Navajos asked when the Gouldings would leave. Then a group of men appeared, led by Adikai Yazzie, an "agitator" to Harry Goulding because Yazzie believed the land belonged to his family through the traditional Navajo understanding of ownership: by use and mutual agreement with neighbors. Harry Goulding remembered keeping a gun nearby as he talked to the group. He spoke little Navajo but indicated he would leave only when his hair turned white. The group left, and the Gouldings apparently faced no serious challenge to their occupation of the land after that. The couple began work in 1927 on a permanent trading post and home and finished the building the following year.

The Gouldings leased the land, a section given by the federal government to the state of Utah to support schools. In 1937, the Gouldings bought the section from the state, despite objections from federal Indian officials. The Gouldings' physical presence in Monument Valley, therefore, posed a challenge to traditional Navajo culture and was based upon land-use or ownership provisions of federal and state laws that relied on legal descriptions and individual ownership rights obtained through monetary transactions. Even many years later, Fred Yazzie, Adikai's son, wanted compensation for the land the Gouldings occupied.[48]

Harry Goulding conducts business with Navajos at his trading post in Monument Valley. Harry and Leona "Mike" Goulding ran the post in Monument Valley from 1925 until 1963. (Reproduced with permission of Northern Arizona University, Cline Library, Josef Muench Collection.)

The Gouldings had only a few early visitors. Most tourists stayed with the Wetherills in nearby Kayenta because they offered better accommodations. The Gouldings watched as John Wetherill guided Zane Grey through the valley. Even so, the first year, while they were still living in tents, the Gouldings played host to two visitors, described as artists from Oklahoma. More arrived after the Gouldings finished building their trading post, a two-story stone building with a trading and storage area below and living accommodations above, along with a separate rock cabin. Then, remembered Ted Cly, a Navajo who sometimes worked for the Gouldings, "we saw some other white people: '28, '29, '30, '31, pretty soon there was a big corral right down here, and he started pack trips on saddle horses." The couple later built a second cabin. Overflow guests stayed in the Gouldings' own room, which

had a view of the valley.[49] With the new accommodations, the Gouldings could cater to guests with a degree of modern comfort. Mike
Goulding cooked, and Harry provided guide services. Roads passable
in the summer and fall enabled visitors to arrive in Monument Valley
by automobile, though not without some effort.

One of the Gouldings' first visitors was Charles Kelly, a college-
educated Salt Lake City printer, photographer, painter, amateur
archaeologist and geologist, and writer. Kelly recalled a 1924 article in
National Geographic by Neil Judd, a member of the 1909 Cummings-
Douglass expedition to Rainbow Bridge, that first attracted his attention to the area. The article had photographs of the valley that included
a caption that read: "Monument Valley, Playground of the Desert Gods,
Here man is made to feel his comparative insignificance." Judd, still
playing the role of European American explorer of the unknown some
fourteen years after helping to publicize Rainbow Bridge, wrote that
"areas still exist . . . about which little or nothing is definitely known.
They remained in hiding when the 'last frontier' was pushed westward
into the Pacific."

Kelly also saw a movie based on a Zane Grey novel. "Not long
after these pictures appeared," Kelly wrote years later, "a silent movie
called 'The Vanishing American' was made in the valley and proved to
be a photographic masterpiece. After reading Judd's article and seeing the picture I made up my mind to see Monument Valley or bust."
Kelly and companion Bill Campbell arrived at Monument Valley in
the summer of 1928 in their Ford Model T. To their surprise, they
discovered the Gouldings and their newly finished trading post and
accommodations.[50]

Ready to see the land as a picture, Kelly described the trading
post as "the most picturesque spot in America. . . . Behind them the
sun rises each morning, painting the desert with innumerable deli-
cate tints, never twice alike." The Gouldings set Kelly up with Navajo
guide Leon Bradley, who at that time was one of three natives of the
area known to the Gouldings who spoke some English. Kelly experienced the horseback journey through Monument Valley through the
motifs and practices of his own culture. Their first camp was "the most
picturesque, most perfect desert retreat it has ever been my privilege
to enjoy. Encircling us on three sides were perpendicular, smoothed

walls, which sprung directly out of the earth. . . . The silence was pro-
found, unbroken by the song of a bird or chirp of an insect." Ruins
called Bent Cliff were the romantic, nostalgic past: "How many feet
had trod the path to that natural cistern in prehistoric days? . . . In the
half light our imagination peopled the ancient apartment with moving figures."

Kelly and Campbell witnessed a Navajo rain ceremony. They found
the idea fascinating, but missed the point of bringing rain, which was
to produce crops and feed for livestock so that the society could sur-
vive and flourish. Texts and images from his culture prepared Kelly to
narrate a certain moment when Bradley stopped his horse. Kelly rode
up to him to see why he had stopped. "I caught my breath in surprise.
Before us was the view I had especially come to Monument Valley to
photograph! We stood on the brink of a thosand[sic]-foot precipice.
Below us the valley had been eroded away by titanic floods in ancient
times, leaving three magnificent perpendicular monuments standing
in a group outlined against the sky." In the rain ceremony, Navajos had
acted in accord with their own cultural beliefs in reproducing a ritual.
With photography, Kelly ritually replicated the cultural imperatives of
his own America.[51]

Kelly added more texts and images to the storehouse of modern
culture. The year after his visit, *The Illustrated London News* printed
Kelly's photographs. The publication described him as a member of
the Primitive Art Society of Salt Lake City and quoted from his letter:
"You reproduced recently a painting of a fantastic landscape by Franz
Sedlacek, and in the description you spoke of 'a road that leads into the
land that never was.' It struck me peculiarly since, last summer, I visited
the Land That Never Was and obtained photographs."

Monument Valley was certainly the land that was for the Navajos
and Paiutes who had made their home in the area. Through family, clan, and personal experience, and rituals, stories, and connections
made to the tribal emergence myth, local Navajos produced the area
as their own social and cultural space. Kelly's "land that never was"
was a reflection not of the Monument Valley of the Navajo, but of the
seeming weightlessness of contemporary America. It was a product of
Americans' search for authenticity in primitive nature and Natives and
in a history narrated by geology and archaeology, and then consumed

as such through the physical presence of tourists and their photographs and descriptions.

The availability of automobiles made that consumption far easier than ever before and permanently changed the nature of tourism in the American West. Cars provided a break from the work of the industrial world. They allowed American consumers to free themselves from the railroad and its strict timetable and fixed destinations. The West for the automobile tourist represented freedom and a chance to encounter authentic peoples and landscapes that contrasted to the bureaucratized and industrialized cities. Some auto tourists reveled in the open plains and deserts of the West, others in the Rocky Mountains and Yellowstone National Park. Some of these tourists likened their experiences to those of the stagecoach or the covered wagon. They were able to explore and mimic the experience of Anglo-American pioneers from the comfort of their vehicles. Their sense of history from popular culture, guidebooks, slide shows, and museum exhibits led them to a "Wild West" of comforts, adventure, and spectacular nature.[52]

O. C. Hansen was likely the first motorcyclist to arrive in Monument Valley. Photographs from his trip in 1916 label the scenery "Monumental Valley, the land of desolation and deceiving distances." A caption narrated the space as "Nature's Monuments" and of geological wonder: "What Has Time Wrought!"[53] The May 1917 arrival of the first automobile in Monument Valley was part of a promotional effort to demonstrate the feasibility of construction of a "Monumental Highway." As conceived locally, the highway would run from Mesa Verde National Park in southwestern Colorado through Monument Valley and past the Grand Canyon.

The idea came to Dolph Andrus of Bluff, Utah, while he was riding horseback to Kanab, Utah, with tourist guide David Rust. With donations from local people and businesses, Andrus and Dr. W. H. Hopkins of Salt Lake City undertook the trip in a Maxwell. Newspapers outlined the scenic attractions of the route: the cliff ruins of Mesa Verde; a side trip from Bluff to Natural Bridges National Monument; from Bluff to Monument Valley; on to Kayenta, Arizona, with a side trip to Navajo National Monument and Rainbow Bridge guided by John Wetherill; to Tuba City, Arizona, and a "very interesting Hopi Indian village"; then back north to Lee's Ferry and to the North Rim of the

Grand Canyon; from there to St. George, Utah, where the road would meet the "Arrowhead Trail" to Los Angeles.

Hopkins wrote, "A scenic highway through this region would enable people of the world to visit some of the greatest natural scenic wonders in existence that up to the present time have been considered quite inaccessible to the tourist."[54] In 1919, Arnold W. Koehler, Jr., of Mamaroneck, New York, drove the Monumental Highway. The roads were said to "present no great difficulties, the obstacles being chiefly sand in spots that any good touring car can easily overcome."[55]

The Monumental Highway Association was formed in 1925 by Monticello, Utah, businessmen to promote a highway through Monument Valley to Bluff. An engineer claimed if properly advertised, the road could bring two hundred thousand tourists to the area every year. In the 1920s, two Utah governors visited Monument Valley and other areas to look into the feasibility of improving roads for tourist development. One newspaper account stated: "One of the chief purposes of the recent expedition [of Governor George Dern] was to determine in some degree the extent and location of the more readily accessible features and ascertain the feasibility of connecting them by roads or good trails with some artery of travel and with developed attractions West of the Colorado River."

Even Fred Harvey of the Fred Harvey Company, the leading commercial developer of Southwest tourism, toured the Monumental Highway with a representative of the Bureau of Public Roads to propose a highway route through the region. Monument Valley, the *Millard County Chronicle* opined in an article lauding Harry Goulding's contribution to tourism, "will eventually be made more accessible and with access made more convenient it will attract thousands in comparison to the few hundreds who already know its great beauty."[56]

Car manufacturers also had an interest in promoting the creation of spaces for automobile tourism. In the 1930s, the Ford Motor Company used the discourses of modern America to entice motorists to Monument Valley. The company provided trucks and cars for a National Park Service expedition to the area to study a proposal for a national park. The auto manufacturer also sent along a camera crew that produced a short film. *Adventure Bound!* begins with the narrator making a case for American "adventurers" to forgo sailing and flying to other countries because there are "wide open spaces, plenty of opportunities for adventure and exploration right here in America." One of those spaces is the Monument Valley area, where, the narrator says, "you may even drive through parts of Monument Valley never before crossed by an automobile."

The film portrayed Navajos as primitive innocents of a timeless past and melded with the land. "The Navajos," the narrator assures viewers, "lead a simple, carefree existence. . . . As unchanging as the chocolate-colored cliffs are the Navajos." Ford showed its cars and trucks conquering the desert sands and rough terrain to get to Monument Valley, where "vast untold lore is jealously guarded behind jagged skyscraper ramparts battered by the elements through millions of years." Ford Motor Company portrayed its vehicles from within the discourses of Anglo-American exploration and adventure, the narrative of geology, a national past in the ruins of archaeology, and "primitive" Indians.[57]

Road building languished, however, through the Depression and World War II. In the meantime, Harry Goulding brought into being another factor that would make Monument Valley a destination for camera-toting tourists: he persuaded the local Navajos to join the tourist economy by posing for photographs. The enticement was, of course, money and goods.

However, what undoubtedly aided Goulding was the federal stock reduction program that took place through much of the 1930s. The aim was to cut erosion because federal officials believed overgrazing caused silting of the Colorado River and the Hoover Dam, which threatened the development of the entire Southwest. The livestock reduction program, however, undermined the Navajo subsistence economy, helping to transform it from one of dependence on crops and livestock to wage labor and welfare.[58]

Harry Goulding stepped into that void to offer an income of money and goods. Goulding recognized that some Navajos were resistant to the intrusion of tourists into the area: "The old Navajos weren't too happy about photography." Navajos repeatedly resisted being photographed by early photographers for cultural reasons, such as the belief that it would bring bad luck or even lead to death. Later, some simply resented the appropriation of their images by Anglos. To overcome that reluctance, Goulding used food and water, enticements that easily worked with children herding sheep. "We'd take pictures of them and then we'd all chip in, all the guests, whatever we had and pay them. Then I'd give them the candy and stuff." The first family to agree to be photographed were the Clys, who lived a short distance from the Goulding trading post. "Hosteen Cly was the first one," Goulding told an interviewer. "I'd go down and take the folks into his place and we'd get the whole ticket, fry bread, and hair-doing, and weaving. I had quite a rigamarole." Goulding later paid some Navajos to make sand-paintings for tourists.[59]

The Cly family became a staple of tourist and professional photographers. "Especially for those of Monument Valley, such as Happy and Willie Cly and their family, photographers must have visited almost daily," according to James C. Faris in *Navajo and Photography.* By persuading the Clys and then others to pose, Goulding assisted tourists whose photographs amounted to a ritual replication of stereotypical scenes. Faris found that images of Navajos over time established the limits and boundaries of how photographers saw and pictured them. One of those motifs was of the "vanishing race," its most influential proponent photographer Edward Curtis.

Curtis's was a salvage project, intended to preserve the images of "primitives" who were thought to be on the brink of extinction. By the early twentieth century, Navajos were established in a series of stereotypical images, photographs that time and again pictured them herding sheep, combing hair with grass brushes, making jewelry, weaving, attending festivals, or peering out of a covered wagon. Photographs of Navajos therefore "saved" them from extinction as "primitives" and made them objects of consumption by modern Americans. For tourists in Monument Valley, Harry Goulding produced the images they expected to photograph.[60]

The Gouldings had arrived in Monument Valley without a camera, but Harry soon learned to pose Navajos for photographs. Professional photographer Josef Muench first arrived in Monument Valley in 1936, and his pictures from there would become ubiquitous in later years. Muench told an interviewer he allowed Harry Goulding to interact with the Navajos before he photographed them. "There was always a conversation going on between them, and he was always bringing the Indians in a natural way into the best position for me to take pictures.

I never had to teach him how to pose himself in a picture or with his Indian friends. We had a sort of unconscious teamwork going between us."[61]

For Navajos, posing for photographs was an opportunity to participate in the modern economy. A snapshot of one of the Cly women weaving brought money or goods to the family while not interfering with her creation (or possibly even prompting it) of a textile that could be exchanged at a trading post. By the 1940s, Navajo women were dependent upon trading posts to feed their families, and their labor was crucial for these exchanges.[62]

Of course, the biggest photographic influence in making the image of Monument Valley widely known was the arrival in late 1938 of John Ford to film *Stagecoach*. Harry Goulding claimed in many interviews through the years that he had carried photographs to California and refused to leave the offices of United Artists until Ford had received him and agreed to film the movie there. Goulding said he rushed back to Monument Valley to prepare for the production by building a barracks to house the crew. In light of accounts by Ford, John Wayne, and others that do not assign Goulding the same role in luring the moviemakers to Monument Valley, Goulding's *Stagecoach* story can be placed within a long pattern of self-promotion in which Goulding put himself at the center of nearly all developments related to Monument Valley. Goulding told interviewer Samuel Moon and many others that he was responsible for major highways through the region and for the first major uranium discovery, and that he played a large role in the establishment of a Navajo tribal park.

Stagecoach production documents show that Goulding approached the movie industry through the Wetherills of Kayenta, where Ford and other principals stayed during the filming. The Wetherills arranged for extras and logistics. Some thirty people also bunked in a Civilian Conservation Corps barracks, with another twenty-six at the Gouldings' at $3 a night per room. In the six subsequent Ford films, the Gouldings played a larger role in housing and feeding cast and crew members.[63]

The World War II years proved lean for Monument Valley tourism. The allocation of human and material resources to the war effort left little for tourism. The postwar period, however, proved a boon for the

Gouldings. Ford returned six more times to film movies, in the process making Monument Valley the iconic landscape of the West and a sacred space of American nationalism.

Text begat text. The movies of Monument Valley became artifacts of its importance as a cultural site. Writing in *Travel* magazine in 1945, Arthur Crawford noted that the maps of Utah still showed a "great blank area" west of the Colorado River and north of Arizona, a "terra incognita" of no roads, no trails, and no topographical features, a "savage hinterland." This primitive wasteland was modern Hollywood's dream setting. "In these arroyos Buffalo Bill battled with Yellow Hand and the U.S. Cavalry charged the Cheyennes."[64]

Writing as World War II ended, Jack Breed's article in *National Geographic* was accompanied by photographs of the stereotypical scenes of Navajos and quotations from Zane Grey. Breed insisted the experience was still primitive. "Monument Valley is not a national park or a national monument. As a part of Navajoland, it is still remote and unspoiled. The Indians want it to remain that way; it is their last frontier."

The Cold War that followed World War II created a demand for uranium to make bombs. Roads were built throughout the Four Corners region to accommodate the mining and transportation of uranium ores. The United States entered an economic boom, and the federal government poured millions of dollars into highways after the war. In 1949, the Gouldings bought two four-wheel-drive Jeeps. In 1953, they tore down their two stone cabins and built a motel. By 1956, they had acquired a bus. Said Mike Goulding: "We were starting to get quite a few more people in the fifties."[65]

In 1963, the year John Ford filmed his last movie in Monument Valley, the Gouldings retired and donated their property to Knox College of Tennessee. The trading post is now a museum. In it, movie memorabilia refer to the discourses that the couple shepherded through Monument Valley for much of the twentieth century. With the museum, the couple themselves became a tourist attraction. As the Gouldings helped make Monument Valley a space of consumption for modern America, the public memory of them became a new object of consumption. The motel's owners in the early 2000s described the museum this way: "Housed in the original 1920's Trading Post, upstairs lived Harry and his wife 'Mike' Goulding. They were lifelong friends of the Navajo. Harry brought director John Ford out to see the landscape and the rest is film-making history." The gift shop peddles Navajo handiwork, videos of John Ford movies, and books about the Gouldings.[66]

It was, of course, modern automobiles that allowed the consumption of this space by large masses of Anglo-Americans. And the Gouldings encouraged that consumption by acting as brokers of the discourses of modern America, conductors of tourists who saw and experienced Monument Valley through the words and images of Anglo-American culture. Those made Monument Valley a space of consumption of a certain primitivism that came from the modern experience. Monument Valley was consumed as not-urban space; as a place of raw, spectacular geology; as the home of "primitive" Natives; as the site of famous movies depicting a Wild West; and as itself primitive space.

For Navajos, the Monument Valley area remained their cultural and social space. The Navajo Nation, in fact, took direct control and supervised Monument Valley's use by tourists and commercial and film producers. In 1957, the Navajo Tribal Council established the Tribal Parks Commission. At the time, the council commented on the increase in improved roads and visitors. "Unless measures are taken to regulate picnicking, camping, and sightseeing, points of interest on the Navajo Reservation will be littered, damaged, desecrated, or destroyed." The tribe also did not want the National Park Service to control scenic sites on the reservation. That sentiment was based on the Navajos' experience with the establishment of the Canyon de Chelly National Monument. In July 1930, the council approved a resolution authorizing the monument under control of the Park Service after the agency agreed that Navajos living in the area would not lose rights to land use and could provide concessions and services. In the 1930s, the federal government's livestock-reduction program raised fears that establishment of national parks might lead to restrictions on grazing and other traditional activities. The council passed a resolution in 1934 requiring the Park Service to "relinquish any rights that they may have acquired to any of our areas."

In 1957, the council moved to take control of scenic areas. The resolution that established the Tribal Parks Commission stated, "The Navajos have a greater love for their country and its beauties than any other people can possibly have, and wish to guard against any changes that may make any part of their country less beautiful."[67] In creating the Parks Commission, the Tribal Council placed limits on the establishment of parks and denied the commission the authority to prohibit mining or traditional uses of such areas. In 1958, the tribe created Monument Valley Tribal Park, the first tribal park in the United States. The council later allocated funds for improvements and took the opportunity to criticize the National Park Service for "attempting for many years to take over this area and make it a national park not under control of the Navajo Tribe." In 1960, the tribe opened a park headquarters and visitors center, and Navajos began to form tour companies, now a major source of income for area residents.[68]

If, as historian Hal Rothman has argued, tourism is the "most colonial of colonial economies," for Navajos, promoting economic development through tourism was an attempt to balance cultural and social priorities.[69] Navajos use the terms "traditional" and "modern" to define what it means to be Navajo. Historian Colleen O'Neill cautions that Navajos don't view those categories as mutually exclusive. They negotiated wage labor and other modern forms of work as pathways for maintaining traditions even as those practices evolved to meet economic conditions.[70] Tribal officials invoked modern Anglo-American discourses to entice visitors, while they also strove to maintain the Navajo cultural and social space.

A 1960 "Navajoland" brochure had a message from Council Chairman Paul Jones and Vice Chairman Scott Preston, who were shown dressed in business suits with an American flag behind them. In Navajoland, the tribal leaders wrote, "You will see a land of great contrasts—not only between towering cliffs and yawning canyons—but also between the cliff dwelling life of the ancients and the great strides forward which are being made by the Navajo people in their March of Progress." The brochure pictured a girl overlooking Monument Valley, "a magnificent grouping of Nature's handiwork." Navajoland, the brochure promised, was truly "the last frontier." Yet while working within the modern American discourses of primitive, magnificent nature, and the popular culture frontier, Navajos also placed restrictions on tourists in Monument Valley Tribal Park. Another brochure admonished: "DO NOT enter Hogans (Navajo dwellings) without a proper interpreter and guide, who will first obtain permission. Watch your camera manners. DO NOT photograph Navajos without their permission. A small gratuity is usually requested." And in the mythical American landscape of the West, where John Wayne rode stagecoaches and fought Indians, the tribe prohibited the possession of firearms.[71]

While some of the Navajos welcomed tourists and the movies for the jobs they provided, conflicts also arose, particularly between area residents and distant tribal officials. Longtime Navajo resident John Holliday complains in an autobiography, "Today our land is over-crowded with tourists, and the movie outfits secretly do their filming in the area guarded by police to keep out complainers, even those who live a few feet away." Monument Valley residents complained that when *Back to the Future: Part II* was filmed there, Michael J. Fox's Delorian car made a path on the earth that was still visible a few years later. Those kinds of complaints led the Navajo Nation to institute a policy in which every family with customary land rights to an area being used for filming must give permission.[72]

But the Navajo Nation also has moved aggressively to boost tourism to the Monument Valley area and increase its own revenues. In 2003, it turned the Monument Valley visitors center gift shop and restaurant over to a non-Navajo company based in Gallup, New Mexico, saying it had promised to increase employment and revenues. The former operator, Leroy Sacato, disputed the new arrangements when he was forced out after decades. But to no avail. The company, Artsco, also had permission to construct a $10 million hotel at the Monument Valley visitors center. The proposal was supported by Navajo tour operators as a way to increase tourism, but they wanted it located so that it didn't obstruct the view of the monuments from the visitor center.[73]

In April 1995, a group of three Americans and three Germans engaged one of the Navajo companies that offer tours from the Monument Valley visitors center. As the tour van descended toward the valley floor, Navajo guide Tom J. Phillips intoned humorously, "Welcome to Marlboro Country." A German tourist shot back, "It's the Wild, Wild West." The tour wound up to John Ford Point, the site of a scene in *The Searchers* in which John Wayne lowered another actor over a cliff. Then it was on past two corrals made of aged, twisted boards and branches. Phillips explained that a crew that had photographed a

Marlboro advertisement built one of the corrals because the existing one was not big enough. Still, as the tour wound deeper into Monument Valley, Phillips left the Old West behind. He explained Navajos' traditional uses of hogans and the proper conduct inside. Phillips cut twigs off a branch of a plant and explained the plant's traditional use as a medicine. In those ways, Phillips reminded the tourists that the space they were in was still Navajo.[74]

Contrast Phillips's use of the plant with a 1963 account in which guide Harry Goulding plucked a flower and told a visitor, "This is the purple sage Zane Grey wrote about."[75] Goulding connected the sage and, thereby, the space to the Old West of Anglo-American popular culture. Phillips and Goulding provided examples of how different spaces are constructed. With Goulding's reference to Zane Grey, a whole set of associations to texts and images in Anglo-American culture took place. Monument Valley, in that telling, became the site of the Old West for tourists who arrived for a short visit, then returned to the city to resume their day-to-day lives. Phillips, on the other hand, used another plant to explain a connection to the Navajos who still inhabit the space. Still, Phillips also spoke to tourists who provided the money from their urban lives that sustained the local Navajo economy. Navajos in Monument Valley live in and negotiate different spaces, that of the Navajo culture, modernity, and that which lingers from America in the twentieth century. Thus the Utah-Arizona border country.

Artifacts in the Museum
of a Modern American Space

Well, there's something about the American Southwest that's enchanting. It's magical. And it's the correspondent of the Mideast, and it's almost biblical, the landscape is.

James Lee Burke, 2009

In 1999, Virgil Bedonie, the owner of Totem Pole Tours in Monument Valley, told a Navajo tourism conference that when he attended various trade shows in countries such as Russia, France, Germany, and Japan, he always found people who knew the landscape he was promoting. "No matter where I travel, I always see a picture of Monument Valley." But Bedonie lamented that while people he had met throughout the world know the images of Monument Valley, it was because of advertisements and John Wayne movies, not through his own Navajo culture.[1] Indeed, words and images throughout much of the twentieth century produced Monument Valley and the Utah-Arizona border country as a certain space in Anglo-American culture. By the end of the century, area Navajos played off this image in selling guide services to tourists. The Navajos were negotiating between two spaces produced in twentieth-century America, that created by the Native inhabitants and that by Anglo-Americans.

Navajos brought this area into their space in accord with historical circumstances and through their own unique social and cultural requirements. Inhabitants of the Rainbow Bridge area made it a place within local Navajo culture by linking it to the tribe's emergence myth. They connected it to their own social and physical needs by stories and ceremonies. Rainbow Bridge demonstrated an organic relationship to the world and to social and cultural space.

Beginning in the early twentieth century, however, an American Occidentalism—the social and cultural forces that created the modern "Old West"—constructed the Utah-Arizona border country as, in Zane Grey's phrase, "the storehouse of unlived years." The storehouse held the feeling that modern lives were inauthentic, and that, in turn, led anxiety-ridden middle-class urban Anglo-Americans to create "primitive" spaces and peoples and then seek out real approximations of their creations. In the American West, this Occidentalism produced the Utah-Arizona border region as a modern space through antimodern discourses and practices. Within it were "authentic" places of unblemished nature, the "Old West," the deep time of geology, a story of progress told in the remnants of ancient cultures, and "primitive" Native Americans with handmade wares for sale. The conductors of this American Occidentalism were Anglo-Americans who largely ignored Navajo and other tribes' spaces and carved out their own places.

Modern culture propelled Byron Cummings into archaeology and the role of explorer. In the field, Cummings used the script of words and images from his own culture and role models of Euro-American explorers and scientists. Cummings brushed aside confrontations with Navajos and other American Indians using the institutional power he worked within and the imperatives of science, and he acted out the legacy of the Old West, the national origin myth of Europeans who battled Indians and wilderness. In doing so, Cummings projected himself and other members of his parties as the latest in a line of scientists and explorers who for centuries had been "discovering" the world and bringing it into the space of the European Occident.

Within the stories of American popular culture, Cummings was a pioneer, his aim not to make a family farm but to extend science into those "blank" spaces on the national map. In the role of archaeologist, Cummings made the ruins of older civilizations into a history of the nation, one that defined a story of linear progress from the primitive to the modern. Cummings and government surveyor William Boone

Douglass circulated their "discovery" of Rainbow Bridge as a certain form of modern knowledge, a geological wonder of nature, and they promoted themselves as hero explorers. The tens of thousands of annual visitors to Navajo and Rainbow Bridge national monuments continue to testify to the appeal of the place that was produced.

Zane Grey's legacy is his role in the creation of the modern Western. His characters, plots, and settings placed the Utah-Arizona border country at the heart of that Old West. Yet the meanings Zane Grey projected upon Rainbow Bridge and other locations spoke of his masculine identity and his angst over changes in gender roles in the first decades of the twentieth century. Grey depicted Rainbow Bridge as a place where the prerogatives of his masculinity and spiritual longing produced by a seemingly vacuous modernity found expression and fulfillment. Grey may not be known to many now, but the space itself has become a culturally sedimented image of the Old West through the decades of movie Westerns that followed his formulas and stereotypes.

With the Utah-Arizona border country already a modern space, John Ford made Monument Valley a shrine of American nationalism. Ford used the genre of the Western and its embodiment of the national emergence myth to comment upon the historical challenges to the United States in the twentieth century of the Depression, World War II, the Cold War, and the confrontation of that mythology with the rising voices asserting the role of racism in the nation's past. The vertical mesas and spires were the space through which Ford ran linear stories that probed questions of nationalism, ethnicity, race, and class. The juxtaposition of stories of American nationalism through a vertical landscape of rock towers and mesas gave Ford's movies a mythical quality. As the century progressed, and questions about the role of race in American history and contemporary life gained currency, Ford used the Western and Monument Valley to expose and comment upon racism toward blacks and, finally, Native Americans. Ford's last Western displayed his diminishing powers as a filmmaker, but finally also the inability of the Western to contain a more complicated national story that took account of race and gender. By century's end, the Western genre was all but dead. Yet, Monument Valley remained an iconic

The set from John Ford's film *My Darling Clementine* still sits in Monument Valley in this photo taken sometime after the film was shot there. (Reproduced with permission of Northern Arizona University, Cline Library, Josef Muench Collection.)

American space. There, the artifacts of Ford's images and discourses linger still in the clear sunshine of the high desert.

By the 1970s, the canyon country of the Utah-Arizona border also became the symbolic space of disappearing American nature. This nature was modern, but still cast in opposition to the modernization of American life, particularly with the post–World War II economic boom and the pollution and destruction it caused. U.S. capitalism provided many people with great material bounty and lifestyle and consumer choices. One of those choices was the consumption of raw nature seemingly untouched by the destructive forces of that modernization. Rainbow Bridge, the huge stone arch that Zane Grey constructed as a place to hold off changes in society in the 1920s, became by the 1970s the symbolic remnant of that nature being lost to the crush of modernization. There, David Brower and others wished to preserve the last vestiges of Glen Canyon, that Cathedral of Lost Nature, that America of the past lost to the modernization of the twentieth century. They sought to make Rainbow Bridge a place set aside to preserve an artifact of the drowned canyon where one might still find a remnant of nature imagined as untainted by modernization.

A tourist economy wound together the various strands of this American Occidentalism and produced spaces for consumption by modern America. Through nearly all of the twentieth century, the Utah-Arizona border region was consumed by tourists who were attracted by the texts and images from their culture. They saw and experienced the area as that culture dictated. First, Louisa and John Wetherill and then Harry and "Mike" Goulding brokered this space for a swirl of archaeologists, anthropologists, photographers, writers, movie crews, and tourists. Tourists sought out nature, ruins, "primitive" peoples and their blankets, pots, and baskets while on vacations that were part of the regimentation of time by the industrial economy.

The arrival of motorists at Rainbow Lodge and the lessening of the time it took to travel to Rainbow Bridge began a process that undermined the arch as primitive space. Rainbow Bridge faded from the popular imagination. Monument Valley replaced Rainbow Bridge as the spectacular site of nature in the area as the automobile and the demand for easy access helped to make it a quick visit for busy tourists. Working- and middle-class tourists used the new roads of postwar America for a short stay during which they could find spectacular nature, the Old West, primitive Natives, and even the sites where famous Western movies were filmed. Monument Valley was "camera ready." With the snapshot, tourists ritually reenacted the stereotypical scenes such as Navajos combing hair with grass brushes or riding a horse while dressed in colorful clothes.

So these are the artifacts of the American Occidentalism that made the Utah-Arizona border country a twentieth-century space. An archaeology of this space reveals that the driving force of its production was modernization and modernism. Modernization provided the material means and the choices that allowed the Anglo-American body to be present in the space and to make use of it. Modernism supplied the discourses that made this a primitive space, an authentic place in contrast to the ever-changing urban world of industrial

America. Here, then, was the heart of the Old West: a masculine space to hold off the evolving gender roles of the twentieth century; the last refuge of wild nature; a place for white men to discover or experience spectacular examples of American nature; rocks that spoke of a long, deep history; ancient ruins that supplied a nostalgic national past. This was the nation sprung in myth from the European encounter with the wilderness. Here it remained, an artifact of a mythical past. But, then, so did the Navajo who had made this country into their own through their own stories, names, and myths that reflected the social relations of their own culture. There, Navajos still dwell. There, still, is Navajo space.

Thousands of tourists flock each year to Rainbow Bridge, where the tour boat waits about forty-five minutes for them to walk a short distance and snap a few photos. Monument Valley attracts thousands more, for many of the same reasons. A writer in the *Orange County Register* wrote in 1997, "When it came time to plan the family trip, the West shouted at us—the West where tall, rugged brick-red spires rise to meet the skies of 'She Wore a Yellow Ribbon' starring John Wayne. We wanted Monument Valley." As her children cried, "'Look, Indians,' and as the soundtrack to *The Magnificent Seven* filled the car, Monument Valley came into view." Or take a *Salt Lake Tribune* account in 2001: "We stop at a viewpoint called John Ford's Point. . . . A Navajo man, standing by for the purpose, rides off on a horse to pose for us. He even sports a red shirt to enliven our snapshots. Cameras click. He rides back and offers us the chance to sit on his horse. The Frenchman and the Japanese man bite. More cameras click. A little cash changes hands."[2]

Movie director George Lucas paid homage to John Ford and his Westerns in filming parts of his Star Wars movies in Monument Valley or with digital look-alikes. In the 1977 *Star Wars,* Lucas shot a scene similar to one in Ford's *The Searchers* in which Ethan Edwards returns to find his brother and sister-in-law massacred. In *The Phantom Menace,* a race takes place through a digital Monument Valley, and the landscape shows up again in *Attack of the Clones.*

Many people who know the sights of the Utah-Arizona border country do so not through movies or as tourists but rather as an image of advertising. In the last decades of the twentieth century, Monument Valley was photographed for commercials and advertisements for such products as Estée Lauder perfume, Guinness beer, IBM typewriters, Norfolk Southern Railroad, and Come 'N Get It dog food. Arnold Palmer drove a golf ball from the top of a butte. Taco Bell placed one of its restaurants in front of Monument Valley in a 1997 advertising campaign. Globalization spread American culture, including the image of Monument Valley, throughout the world. "Indeed," commented one writer, "the iconography of America has become international. Italian blue jean manufacturers now advertise their wares in Germany on posters depicting Monument Valley. The German cigarette brand West mounted an international advertising campaign whose central metaphors revolved around the American West." The numerous uses of such images led one commentator to write, "An empty, sprawling landscape like Monument Valley is the ideal frame for an effective billboard."[3]

By the end of the twentieth century, the most widespread use of Monument Valley and its desert environs appeared to be for automobile advertisements. Hanging in Goulding's Museum and Trading Post in recent years was a poster advertising a 1963 Ford Galaxie in which a well-dressed couple watch cowboys ride horses toward them with the red rock mesas and spires in the background. In 1972 a *Life* magazine advertisement showed that some of the modern meanings attached to the image through much of the twentieth century had begun to fade. That ad had a drawing of various cars parked in front of Monument Valley, with the occupants loitering about, presumably enjoying the scenery. There was no reference to movies and the Old West, or to the Navajo. The message, it seemed, was simply one of access. Monument Valley had become a free-floating image in a world of hyperconsumption, of what scholars label the postmodern era.

In Madison Avenue's imagination, at least, that space held such wide recognition that the image makers turned to it again and again. As the twentieth century gave way to the twenty-first, the most widely depicted automobile in Monument Valley was the sport utility vehicle, the four-wheel-drive cars/trucks that purport to be for off-road and street use. In a 2001 print advertisement, the luxurious inside of the Jeep Grand Cherokee is shown in a golden light, the sunset colors of

Monument Valley visible through the windows. "How spacious is it?" the ad asks, ambiguous whether "it" refers to the inside of the vehicle or to Monument Valley. "Let's just say there are a thousand miles between you and the next person." The advertisement wants to promise solitude in a crowded world through the consumption of the SUV that framed the image of Monument Valley through its windows. Also in 2001, a print advertisement for the Honda CR-V pictured it alone on a small hill facing the monuments. "You stand there doing nothing," read the text. "Now how long have you waited to do that?"[4]

The SUV advertisements represent another level of abstraction of the space depicted. Unlike the Ford Motor Company's promotional film *Adventure Bound!* from the 1930s, many of the vehicles are not shown driving or even on a road. Sometimes one can't even see a road. The message obscures the relationship between the environment and the SUVS, while at the same time asserting that the issue is access to pristine nature, a refuge from the workaday world through consumption. Megan Shaw and Rick Prelinger commented on such advertisements: "The landscape contains no streets or freeways, and the SUV is united with the wilderness in a manner reminiscent of the pre-roadway horse-and-wagon experience. The vision that is being sold in these commercials ignores all implications of the environmental impact on millions of two-ton vehicles let loose on roadless spaces, and instead invites the viewer to imagine a personal freedom to explore uncharted territories—a freedom that doesn't exist anymore in well-mapped North America." Acquiring the image through purchase of the vehicle seemed to be the main message. That is, the vehicles promised a sort of freedom to consume such a space, and any other meanings it might hold are left to the purchaser.[5]

Travel advertisements used this same device, the juxtaposition of Monument Valley with another image to demonstrate how easily one could be transported to a new experience. British Airways even put an image of London's Big Ben Tower into the middle of the monuments. A Ford ad from 1994 showed an Explorer in the foreground, and across a stretch of a melded image of desert/water the towers of Monument Valley were displayed next to those of Manhattan. "In each of us, there's a dreamer and a realist," read the text. "But now they can share a ride." The message was that the Ford Explorer offered access

JEEP GRAND CHEROKEE LIMITED Talk about a lot of leg room. But while Jeep Grand Cherokee lets you leave the confines of civilization behind,

Always use seat belts. Remember a backseat is the safest place for children 12 and under. Jeep is

In the late twentieth century, Monument Valley became a favorite backdrop for advertisers, especially those marketing SUVs. (Reproduced with permission of Chrysler Group LLC, courtesy *The New Yorker* magazine.)

to Monument Valley and Manhattan: "The world's just too big to be left unexplored." The towers of Manhattan and those of Monument Valley were blending; two iconic images of America shared meanings.[6] Somehow from the discourses of the early twentieth century that had positioned nature such as that found in Monument Valley in opposition to the city, the two had melded into a postmodern collage.

In the 1981 science fiction novel *Hello America,* British writer J. G. Ballard made fun of the American emergence tale of Europeans' encounter with the wilderness of the New World that had, at least in myth, re-created them as Americans. As Ballard depicted it, the end result of this encounter was environmental catastrophe. In the story, the economies of the Western world collapsed at the end of the twentieth century. Soon, hordes of refugees made their way to Europe. To feed the influx, European scientists instituted climate controls, the effect of which was to dry up the Mississippi River and leave much of the United States as a parched wasteland. Then at the end of the twenty-first century, enthralled by the mythical American dream, a group of Europeans goes on a daring mission to return to the land of their ancestors. They arrive in New York and send out a reconnaissance party. That group pauses on the George Washington Bridge and looks out over the dried-up Hudson. "Beyond the Jersey shore Wayne could see the rectangular profiles of isolated buildings, their sunset façades like mesas in Monument Valley. Already they had arrived at an authentic replica of Utah or Arizona."[7]

Like Ballard, several French intellectuals embraced the image of Monument Valley. In a tour by car of parts of the United States, Jean Baudrillard described a postmodern combination of images and discourses. "Monument Valley is the geology of the earth, the mausoleum of the Indians, and the camera of John Ford. It is erosion and it is extermination, but it is also the tracking shot, the movies. All three are mingled in the vision we have of it. And each phase subtly terminates the preceding one." Baudrillard continued the erasure of the Navajos from that space, postmodern though it now be. The French military theorist Paul Virilio used the idea of Monument Valley to construct an image of the postmodern city: "Neo-geological, the 'Monument Valley' of some pseudolithic era, today's metropolis is a phantom landscape, the fossil of past societies whose technologies were intimately aligned with the visible transformation of matter, a project from which the sciences have increasingly turned away." Those types of character-izations of America led the art critic Robert Hughes to complain that for French intellectuals, the United States dwindled to two vertical images: Manhattan and Monument Valley.[8] Just like that Ford Explorer advertisement, it would seem.

Yet, for all of the postmodern jargon, those images of Monument Valley are the artifacts of modern meanings. Baudrillard was capti-vated by John Ford movies, and for him that's what Monument Valley became. Virilio's contemporary cities were like some Western movie town, while a sport utility vehicle advertisement too hinted that the Ford Explorer was ideal for excursions into the wilds of Monument Valley and Manhattan. That is, these postmodern images of French intellectuals and advertisements are the remnants of twentieth-century culture as it fades into the welter of images that now flood the world. Meanings give way just as Monument Valley at sunset dissolves into shadow, and yet the sight lingers in the eye.

Notes

INTRODUCTION: AN AMERICAN OCCIDENTALISM

1. Kluckhohn, *To the Foot of the Rainbow,* 8–9, 34, 48, 224; Kluckhohn, *Beyond the Rainbow;* Parsons and Vogt, "Clyde Kay Maben Kluckhohn 1905–1960."

2. For a more complete explanation of the theoretical basis of this book, see my dissertation, Thomas J. Harvey, "The Storehouse of Unlived Years." Major works consulted were: Lefebvre, *The Production of Space;* David Harvey, *Justice, Nature, and the Geography of Difference;* Soja, *Postmodern Geographies* and *Thirdspace;* Massey, *Space, Place, and Gender;* and Rose, *Feminism and Geography.*

3. See Stuart Hall, "The Work of Representation."

4. See Said, *Orientalism* and *Culture and Imperialism.* Quotation from Said, "Invention, Memory, and Place," 181.

5. Fowler, *A Laboratory for Anthropology,* viii; Babcock, "A New Mexican Rebecca," 406; Weigle, "Southwest Lures," 535; Gutiérrez, "Charles Fletcher Lummis."

6. Schumpeter, *Capitalism, Socialism, and Democracy,* 83; David Harvey, *Condition of Postmodernity,* 16–37.

7. Brenner, *The Domestication of Desire,* 13. Brenner also quotes Peter Osborne, *The Politics of Time: Modernity and the Avant-Garde* (New York: W. W. Norton, 1995), xii; Berman, *All That Is Solid Melts into Air,* 5–18, 21.

8. Howe, "The Market Revolution," 266. See also Sellers, *The Market Revolution.*

9. Lasch, *The True and Only Heaven,* 84. Jean-François Lyotard says one of the essences of modernism is the metanarrative of emancipation of humanity by progress. Cited by Ellwood, *The Politics of Myth,* 16–17.

10. Lears, *No Place of Grace,* xiii–xiv; Berman, *All That Is Solid,* 5–6.

11. Benjamin, "The Work of Art in the Age of Mechanical Reproduction."

12. Lefebvre, *Production of Space,* 122; Dilworth, *Imagining Indians in the Southwest,* 4; McClintock, *Imperial Leather;* Torgovnick, *Gone Primitive.*

13. Lasch, *True and Only Heaven,* 94–95; Clifford and Marcus, *Writing Culture,* 113.

14. Deloria, *Playing Indian,* 100–101.

15. Pomeroy, *In Search of the Golden West;* Hyde, *An American Vision.*

16. Lears, *No Place of Grace.* Philip Deloria, *Playing Indian,* 101, writes that antimodernism and modernism "were, in effect, sides of the same coin." MacCannell, *The Tourist,* 3.

17. O'Neill, *Working the Navajo Way,* 28–29, 61–75.

CHAPTER 1. SEND OUT A RAINBOW

1. Luckert, *Navajo Mountain and Rainbow Bridge Religion,* 9–10; Gillmor and Wetherill, *Traders to the Navajo,* 130. For a discussion of pre-Navajo occupation of the area of Rainbow Bridge, see Sproul, "A Bridge between Cultures."

2. See the introduction to this book.

3. Gillmor and Wetherill, *Traders,* 239–41. A slightly different version of this is found in Louisa Wade Wetherill, interpretation, undated, Willis W. Ritter Papers.

4. Sproul, "Bridge between Cultures." Even before the Navajos, other humans likely had known the bridge, perhaps for thousands of years. Archaeological evidence places humans in the area as early as 6000–4000 B.C., and shows that the area of the bridge was used at least a thousand years ago.

5. Towner, *The Archaeology of Navajo Origins,* 3–18.

6. Copeland and Rogers, "In the Shadow of the Holy People," 213; Gary M. Brown, "The Protohistoric Transition in the Northern San Juan Region," 68; Gilpin, "Early Navajo Occupation West of the Chuska Mountains," 173; and Towner, *Defending the Dinétah,* 2003.

7. Curtis Schaafsma, on the other hand, disputes the existence of a Dinétah, arguing that Navajos took part in a late migration from the Great Plains. See Schaafsma, *Apaches De Navajo;* Jarrold Levy, *In the Beginning: The Navajo Genes,* 27–30; and Kelley and Francis, *Navajo Sacred Places,* 188.

8. Jarrold Levy, *In the Beginning,* 62–81.

9. Ibid. Levy says Giant Spruce Mountain is also called Huerfano; Linford, *Navajo Places,* 215, says it is Gobernador Knob and, on p. 153, that Blanca Peak rather than Levy's Mount Baldy is likely the mountain of the east, but there are other possible candidates.

10. Pinxten, vanDooren, and Frank Harvey, *The Anthropology of Space,* 34.

11. Walters, *New Perspective on Navajo Prehistory,* 18.

12. Wyman, *Navajo Beautyway,* 1, 36; Walters, *New Perspective,* 15, 17, 18; Gilpin, "Early Navajo Occupation West of the Chuska Mountains," 173.

13. Wyman quoted in Editha L. Watson, lecture, March 17, 1968, Doris Duke Oral History Project.

14. Watson, *Navajo Sacred Places,* 5; Linford, *Navajo Places,* 22.

15. Kelley and Francis, *Navajo Sacred Places,* 43.

16. Naol Nishi, interview, February 4, 1961, Doris Duke Oral History Collection. The boundaries of the reservation were set by the U.S. government 1868 treaty with the Navajo people and have been adjusted since then.

17. Linford, *Navajo Places,* 153–54.

18. Basso, *Wisdom Sits in Places,* 156 n. 11.

19. Watson, *Navajo Sacred Places,* 5; Kelley and Francis, *Navajo Sacred Places,* 5; Lamphere, "Symbolic Elements in Navajo Ritual," 280.

20. Jarrold Levy, *In the Beginning*, 24–35.

21. Wyman, *Navajo Beautyway*, 10.

22. Harrison, "Women in Navajo Myth," 50, 81, 120–23, 202.

23. Towner and Dean, "Questions and Problems in Pre-Fort Sumner Navajo Archaeology," 5; Brugge, "The Navajo Exodus," 1.

24. Correll, "Navajo Frontiers in Utah and Troublous Times in Monument Valley"; Begay and Roberts, "The Early Navajo Occupation of the Grand Canyon Region," 197–99; Gilpin, "Early Navajo Occupation West of the Chuska Mountains," 173–74; Shepardson and Hammon, *The Navajo Mountain Community*, 28; Isabel T. Kelly, *Southern Paiute Ethnography*, map facing page 1, 167; McPherson, *Northern Navajo Frontier*. One account has Navajos in the Black Mesa area in the 1600s; see Johnson, "Significance of Rainbow Bridge," 57.

25. Dunlay, *Kit Carson and the Indians*, 251–324; Kluckhohn and Leighton, *The Navaho*, 41.

26. Correll, "Navajo Frontiers," 151; Hoskaninni Begay, interview, 1938, Charles Kelly Papers; Charles Kelly, "Chief Hoskaninni," 219–26; Cummings, *Indians I Have Known*, 2–4; Gillmor and Wetherill, *Traders to the Navajo*, 152.

27. See the affidavits of Paul Goodman, Lemar Bedoni, Teddy Holiday, Jessie Yazzie Black, Jimmy Goodman, and Bitsinnie Begay in the lawsuit *Friends of the Earth v. Ellis L. Armstrong*, Willis W. Ritter Papers.

28. Sproul, "Bridge between Cultures."

29. Fishler, *In the Beginning*, 45; Wyman, *Windways of the Navaho*, 144–45.

30. Gillmor and Wetherill, *Traders to the Navajo*, 241; Louisa Wade Wetherill, Rainbow Bridge Documents, n.d., Willis W. Ritter Papers.

31. McPherson, *Sacred Land Sacred View*, 77–121.

32. Wyman, *Blessingway*, 10.

33. See McPherson, *Sacred Land*, 23–26. Some Navajos worked for archaeologists or gathered and sold Anasazi objects to traders or scientists; see John Wetherill to Prof. Byron Cummings, November 6, 1910, Byron Cummings Papers.

CHAPTER 2. "DISCOVERING" RAINBOW BRIDGE
FOR MODERN AMERICA

1. Byron Cummings, "Dr. Byron Cummings' Expedition of 1909," Byron Cummings Papers; Cummings, *The Discovery of Rainbow Bridge*.

2. William B. Douglass, "The Discovery of Rainbow Natural Bridge," *Our Public Lands* (Washington, D.C.: Bureau of Land Management, 1955), 8–15. This article is derived from Douglass's field notes.

3. "Discover Bridge of Great Height," *Deseret Evening News*, September 3, 1909, 1.

4. "The Greatest Natural Bridge," *Cortez Herald*, September 23, 1909, 1.

5. William Franklyn Williams, statement, Rainbow Bridge National Monument Collection; Hassell, *Rainbow Bridge*, 60–64; Richardson, *Navajo Trader*, 61–62; Gregory Crampton, *Standing Up Country*; Neil Judd, "The Discovery of Rainbow Bridge," *National Parks Bulletin*, November 1927, 15; James W. Black, statements of James W. Black, Rainbow Bridge National Monument Collection; Weldon Fairbanks Heald, "Who Discovered Rainbow Bridge?" *Sierra Club Bulletin*, October 1955, 24–28; Jett, "The Great Race to Discover Rainbow Natural Bridge," 42; Johnson, "The Significance of Rainbow

Bridge"; Byron Cummings, "The Great Natural Bridges of Utah," *National Geographic,* February 1910, 165; Douglass, "Rainbow Natural Bridge," 14; Knipmeyer, "Did Prospectors See Rainbow Bridge before 1909?" It became a national monument on May 30, 1910.

6. "Bluff City," *Montezuma Journal,* September 2, 1909, 1; "Cook, American Explorer, Reaches the North Pole," *Salt Lake Tribune,* September 2, 1909, 1; "America Once More Is Victor in Quest of Pole," *Salt Lake Tribune,* September 7, 1909, 1; "Peary Tries to Discredit Cook," *Salt Lake Tribune,* September 9, 1909, 1. "Frederick A. Cook Stands by Guns," *Salt Lake Tribune,* September 9, 1909, 1.

7. Goetzmann, *New Lands, New Men,* quotation at 454; Pratt, *Imperial Eyes.* See also McClintock, *Imperial Leather,* 34.

8. Writes literary scholar Krista Comer, "It is commonplace of both western history and literary studies to note that the story of western settlement serves as the nation's founding myth" (*Landscapes of the New West,* 5).

9. Byron Cummings, "Trodden Trails," Byron Cummings Papers; Bostwick, "Revisiting the Dean," 76.

10. Cummings, "Trodden Trails."

11. Rydell, *All the World's a Fair.*

12. Ibid., 40; Slotkin, *Gunfighter Nation,* 63–65.

13. Philip Deloria, *Playing Indian,* 17, 93, 105; Torgovnick, *Gone Primitive,* 190–92; McClintock, *Imperial Leather,* 33; Said, *Orientalism;* Rosaldo, "Imperialist Nostalgia"; Singal, "Towards a Definition of Modernism."

14. Janetski, "150 Years of Utah Archaeology"; Chris Wilson, *The Myth of Santa Fe,* 89; Snead, *Ruins and Rivals,* xxiii, 23, 25; McNitt, *Richard Wetherill,* 54–55. Wetherill was the older brother of John Wetherill, the packer and guide on the 1909 Rainbow Bridge expedition. Cummings, "Trodden Trails"; Bostwick, "Revisiting the Dean," 78. Cummings never did earn a Ph.D.

15. Bruce G. Trigger, "Romanticism, Nationalism, and Archaeology," 268–70; Silberman, *Between Past and Present,* 2; Kehoe, "Contextualizing Archaeology," 99. Some writers even question whether it is possible to imagine nationalism without archaeology. See Ascherson's foreword to *Nationalism and Archaeology,* vi–vii; Curtis M. Hinsley, "Revising and Revisioning the History of Archaeology"; Patterson, *Toward a Social History of Archaeology,* 9.

16. Hyde, *An American Vision,* 17–19, 203, 12–13; Runte, *National Parks,* 7; Philip Deloria, *Playing Indian,* 101; Snead, "Lessons from the Ages"; Rothman, *Devil's Bargains,* 84.

17. Turner, *The Frontier in American History,* 1.

18. White, "Frederick Jackson Turner and Buffalo Bill," 13, 21; Berkhofer, "Space, Time, Culture, and the New Frontier," 22. Thomas Jefferson at age eighty mused about the extent of his Louisiana Purchase, "Let a philosophic observer commence a journey from the savages of the Rocky Mountains eastwardly towards our seacoast. . . . This, in fact, is equivalent to a survey, in time, of the progress of man from infancy of creation to the present day." Quoted in Simmon, *The Invention of the Western Film,* 179.

19. Slotkin, *Regeneration through Violence,* 6.

20. Smith, *Virgin Land;* Slotkin, *Regeneration,* 6; Cronon, "Revisiting the Vanishing Frontier, 158; White, "Turner and Buffalo Bill," 4; Slotkin, *Gunfighter Nation,* 30.

21. Kasson, *Buffalo Bill's Wild West,* 93; White, "Turner and Buffalo Bill," 27–28.

22. Kasson, *Buffalo Bill's Wild West*, 120; White, "Turner and Buffalo Bill," 35.

23. Judd, "Byron Cummings, Archeologist and Explorer," 407; Chauvenet, *Hewett and Friends;* Thomas, "Promoting the Southwest; "Edgar L. Hewett: Anthropology, Archeology, and the Santa Fe Style"; Cummings, "Early Days in Utah," 119; Cummings, "Cummings Describes Natural Wonders and Scientific Treasures of San Juan Region," *Salt Lake Herald*, November 1, 1908, Magazine Section 12; Snead, *Ruins and Rivals,* 69; Kerr, "Byron Cummings"; Clara Lee Tanner, "Byron Cummings, 1860–1954," 303; Cummings, "Trodden Trails"; Judd, "Pioneering in Southwestern Archeology."

24. Cummings, "Early Days in Utah," 119; Snead, *Ruins and Rivals,* 82; Bostwick, "Revisiting the Dean," 100, 102.

25. Steen, "The Natural Bridges of White Canyon; Cummings, "The Great Natural Bridges of Utah," 30; Ezekiel Johnson. autobiography, Utah State Historical Society; W. W. Dyar, "The Colossal Bridge of Utah: A Recent Discovery of Natural Wonders," *Century,* November 1904, 505; H. L. A. Culmer, "The Great Stone Bridges of San Juan County," H. L. A. Culmer Papers; "Exploration of the Wild of Southeastern Utah," *Deseret Evening News,* April 1, 1905, 24, 25; Col. Edwin F. Holmes, "The Great Natural Bridges of Utah," *National Geographic,* March 1907, 199–204. *National Geographic* also published an article on the bridges in 1904, based on the account in *Century* "Colossal Natural Bridges of Utah," *National Geographic,* September 1904, 367–69.

26. Shepard, "The Cross Valley Syndrome," 4–8.

27. Gould, *Time's Arrow, Time's Cycle.*

28. "State News," *Vernal Express,* February 9, 1907, 1; Cummings, "The Great Natural Bridges of Utah"; Cummings, *Discovery of Rainbow Bridge;* Judd, *Men Met along the Trail,* 10–11, 17.

29. Kehoe, *Land of Prehistory,* 91; Hearing before the Subcommittee of the Committee on Public Lands, *Preservation of Historic and Prehistoric Ruins, Etc.,* 58th Cong., April 22, 1904.

30. Ronald Freeman Lee, "The Antiquities Act of 1906," 39–42, 236; Raymond Harris Thompson, "Edgar Lee Hewett and the Political Process," 278–79; Hewett, *Circular relating to Historic and Prehistoric Ruins of the Southwest and Their Preservation;* David Hurst Thomas, *Skull Wars* (New York: Basic Books, 2000), 144, quoted in Sandweiss, *Print the Legend,* 264.

31. Cummings, "Cummings Describes Natural Wonders"; Bryon Cummings. Field Notes, 1908, Byron Cummings Collection; Gordon R. Willey, *Portraits in American Archaeology,* 66; "Trip Was a Grand Success," *Grand Valley Times,* September 4, 1908, 1.

32. Judd, "Pioneering," 11.

33. Judd, *Men Met along the Trail,* 24; Thomas, "Promoting the Southwest," 90; Kasson, *Buffalo Bill's Wild West,* 116–17; Slotkin, *Gunfighter Nation,* 42–54; Willey, *Portraits in American Archaeology,* 4.

34. Judd, "Pioneering," 22–25.

35. Judd *Men Met along the Trail,* 22–25; Cummings, "Trodden Trails"; Judd, "Pioneering," 20–21.

36. Cummings, *Indians I Have Known,* xi, xii; Judd, *Men Met along the Trail.*

37. Cummings, *Indians I Have Known,* 46–47; Cummings, "Trodden Trails"; Judd, *Men Met along the Trail,* 16, 20.

38. Judd, *Men Met along the Trail,* 26, 32; Gillmor and Wetherill, *Traders to the Navajo,*

130. This book was first copyrighted in 1934, many years after the events took place. The quotations should be taken as memories of events, not transcriptions of conversations. Judd, *Men Met along the Trail,* 32, says Blind Salt Clansman had heard of Cummings's work in the canyon and inquired about it before relating the story to Louisa Wetherill.

39. Douglass, "The Discovery of the World's Greatest Natural Bridge, the Rainbow Bridge," undated, William Boone Douglass Papers; Douglass to commissioner, General Land Office, October 7, 1908 Rainbow Bridge National Monument Collection; Douglass, "Rainbow Natural Bridge," 8; General Land Office commissioner to Douglass, Dolores, Colorado, October 20, 1908, in Rainbow Bridge National Monument Collection.

40. Douglass, "Discovery of the World's Greatest Natural Bridge"; Douglass, preliminary report by William Boone Douglass to the General Land Office, March 3, 1909, Rainbow Bridge National Monument Collection.

41. Statement of Ben Wetherill, June 13, 1946, Gary Topping Papers; Johnson, "Significance of Rainbow Bridge," 101–108; Jett, "Great Race," 42.

42. Douglass to Dr. Walter Hough, U.S. National Museum, August 4, 1909, Rainbow Bridge National Monument Collection; General Land Office Commissioner W. B. Douglass, November 16, 1909, William Boone Douglass Papers; Douglass, "Rainbow Natural Bridge," 8; William B. Douglass to Honorable Commissioner, General Land Office, March 30, 1909, William Boone Douglass file, private collection of Stan Jones.

43. Douglass to Dr. Walter Hough, U.S. National Museum, September 13, 1908; S.V. Proudfit to Mr. Wm. B. Douglass, July 3, 1908, Douglass Papers; W. H. Holmes to Wm. B. Douglass, August 19, 1909, William Boone Douglass Papers. Rothman, in "Ruins, Reputations, and Regulation," argues that Douglass was trying to preserve the ruins for scientific study according to professional standards, whereas Cummings was interested largely in stripping them of their artifacts for the University of Utah museum with little regard for archaeological conventions. While Cummings did little more than mine the ruins for artifacts, and his methods were, in the view of today's practices, hardly better than those of pothunters, Rothman's interpretation relies too much on his high opinion of Douglass's motivations. It is clear from the various sources that Douglass was egotistical, was not above self-aggrandizement, and was himself interested in the prestige of being the discoverer of Rainbow Bridge and Southwest ruins. See also Judd, *Men Met along the Trail,* 36; Douglass, "Discovery of the World's Greatest Natural Bridge"; Douglass, "Rainbow Natural Bridge," 9; and Jett, "Great Race," 17.

44. Cummings, *Indians I Have Known,* 26–27; Cummings, "Expedition of 1909"; Judd, *Men Met along the Trail,* 32.

45. Gero, "Gender Bias in Archaeology," 55; Turgeon, "The Tale of the Kettle"; Trigger, *A History of Archaeological Thought,* 13; Vine Deloria, *Red Earth, White Lies,* 37–38; Silberman, "Promised Lands and Chosen Peoples," 250.

46. Young, "Statement of Stuart M. Young," 14; John Wetherill, "Notes on the Discovery of Betatakin," 44–45; Judd, *Men Met along the Trail,* 40; John Wetherill, "Betata Kin," June 1934, Gary Topping Papers; Judd, "Pioneering," 24; Cummings, "Expedition of 1909"; Jett, "Great Race," 15; Gillmor and Wetherill, *Traders to the Navajo,* 167. The different accounts vary in details.

47. Donald Beauregard, "Important Archaeological Discoveries by Utah Explorers," *Deseret Evening News,* August 28, 1909, section 2, p. 1.

48. Cummings, "Expedition of 1909"; Stuart Young, diary, Stuart Young Collection;

Douglass, "Discovery of the World's Greatest Natural Bridge"; Judd, "Return to Rainbow Bridge," 33; Cummings, "Trodden Trails"; Judd, "Discovery of Rainbow Bridge," 10, 12–13; Douglass, "Rainbow Natural Bridge," 8–9.

49. Judd, "Discovery of Rainbow Bridge," 11. See also Neil M. Judd, "How W. B. Douglass, U.S. Examiner of Surveys, 'Discovered' the Big Bridge," *Deseret Evening News,* October 2, 1909, pt. 2, 1; Douglass, "Rainbow Natural Bridge," 14; Cummings, "Trodden Trails"; Cummings, "Expedition of 1909."

50. "Bluff City," 1; "Discover Bridge of Great Height"; "The Greatest Natural Bridge," 1; "Jealousy Besets Gov't Official," *Grand Valley Times,* October 1, 1909, 1; Cummings to John and Louisa Wetherill, October 8, 1909, Gary Topping Collection.

51. Judd to W. B. Douglass, October 2, 1909, Douglass Papers; Judd, "How W. B. Douglass"; Douglass to John Wetherill, 1909, Gary Topping Papers; S.V. Proudfit to Mr. Wm. B. Douglass; Douglass to Dr. Walter Hough, U.S. National Museum, Rainbow Bridge National Monument Collection.

52. Cummings, "Trodden Trails."

CHAPTER 3. THE STOREHOUSE OF UNLIVED YEARS

1. "A Tale of the Desert," *New York Times,* October 8, 1910, BR10.

2. The quotation is from Mitchell, *Westerns: Making the Man in Fiction and Film,* 123. On Zane Grey's success as a writer and influence on the twentieth-century Western, see Cawelti, *The Six-Gun Mystique,* 2; Kevin S. Blake, "Zane Grey and Images of the American West"; Tuska, *The Filming of the West,* 5–28; Farley, *The Many Faces of Zane Grey,* 147. Frantz and Choate, *The American Cowboy,* 173–74, quoted in Candace C. Kant, *Zane Grey's Arizona,* 161; Nash, *The American West in the Twentieth Century,* 53; Wheeler, "Zane Grey's Impact on American Life and Letters," 350. See Pauly's explanation of best-sellers during the early twentieth century in *Zane Grey: His Life,* 112, 254.

3. Zane Grey, diary, October 25, 1917, Zane Grey Collection; Timmerman. "Special Feature #4: From G-R-A-Y to G-R-E-Y."

4. Pauly, *Zane Grey: His Life,* 31; Gruber, *Zane Grey,* 18–29.

5. Grey, "My Own Life," 8; Gruber, *Zane Grey,* 43; May, *Maverick Heart,* 19.

6. Lasch, *The True and Only Heaven,* 84–94.

7. Mitchell, *Witness to a Vanishing America,* xv–63; Roderick Nash, *Wilderness and the American Mind,* 96–102.

8. Philip Deloria, *Playing Indian;* Price, *Flight Maps;* Rotundo, *American Manhood;* Higham, "The Reorientation of American Culture in the 1890s," 27–28; Slotkin, *Gunfighter Nation,* 42–54; Lears, *No Place of Grace;* MacCannell, *The Tourist,* 3.

9. Runte, *National Parks,* 7.

10. Zane Grey, *Captives of the Desert,* 23.

11. Pauly, *Zane Grey: His Life,* 43, 48, 54.

12. Ibid., 10, 43, 58.

13. Ibid., 53, 60; Gruber, *Zane Grey,* 45–55.

14. Pauly, *Zane Grey: His Life,* 1, 320 n. 16.

15. Grey, diary.

16. Trachtenberg, *The Incorporation of America;* Hays, *The Response to Industrialism 1885–1914;* Bederman, *Manliness and Civilization,* 14–15; Lears, *No Place of Grace,* 50; Kas-

son, *Houdini, Tarzan, and the Perfect Man;* Zane Grey, manuscript fragment, undated, Zane Grey Collection, Harold B. Lee Library.

17. Grey, "My Own Life," 1–3; Grey, "Breaking Through," 11; Gruber, *Zane Grey,* 2, 50, 68, 156; Pauly, *Zane Grey: His Life,* 70. Grey wrote that the trip used up all of Dolly's inheritance, but Pauly, 69, doubts that was the case.

18. Zane Grey to Dolly Grey, March 20, 1907, Zane Grey Collection, Cline Library. Here, Grey is working within a modern discourse that identified with parts of medieval and other earlier cultures in which martial and erotic masculinity seemed unbounded by modern strictures. See Lears, *No Place of Grace,* 160–81.

19. Rider and Paulsen, *The Roll Away Saloon;* Zane Grey to David Dexter Rust, January 2, 1911, David Dexter Rust Collection, The Church of Jesus Christ of Latter-day Saints.

20. Zane Grey to Dolly Grey, April 8, 1907, Zane Grey Collection, Cline Library. Bederman, *Manliness and Civilization,* 11–12, points out that middle-class Victorian men saw the ability to control passions as a source of strength and power over women and the lower classes. Grey seemed here to be operating under that social dictate.

21. Shepard, "The Cross Valley Syndrome," used the phrase "reminiscent of something not remembered"; Zane Grey, diary, 1907, Zane and Dolly Grey Papers, Ohio Historical Society.

22. Zane Grey, "The Man Who Influenced Me Most," *American Magazine,* July–December 1926, 52–53.

23. Rider and Paulsen, *Roll Away Saloon,* 58n.

24. Pauly, *Zane Grey: His Life,* 71; Zane Grey, *Last of the Plainsmen,* 3–6.

25. Grey, "Man Who Influenced Me Most," 52–53.

26. Ibid., 55–56. Curiously, though, the incident did not show up in Grey's diary of the trip, but its occurrence, though not the details, is confirmed by Rider and Paulsen, *Roll Away Saloon,* 58.

27. Zane Grey to Dan Murphy, June 2, 1907, Edwin Markham Collection.

28. Zane Grey to Dan Murphy, Christmas Day 1907, reproduced in Scott, "Heritage of the Desert," 10.

29. Zane Grey, diary, 1908, Zane Grey Collection, Cline Library; Zane Grey, "Roping Lions in the Grand Canyon."

30. Farley, *Many Faces,* 118; Scott, "Heritage of the Desert," 11.

31. Grey, "My Own Life," 4–5.

32. Farley, *Many Faces,* 118; Scott, "Heritage of the Desert," 11; Grey, "Breaking Through," 11–12; Pauly, *Zane Grey: His Life,* 81, 89–90; Zane Grey, *The Heritage of the Desert.*

33. The passage is very much like an exchange from *The Last of the Plainsmen* in which Jones asked if he would be able to stake out a cougar's hiding place and shoot the animal if necessary. "Are you to be depended on here?" Jones asked. Grey hesitated in answering. "Then because of the pride of a man, or perhaps inherited instincts cropping out at this perilous moment, I looked up and answered quietly: 'Yes. I will kill him!'" (232–33). It also appears similar to an incident that occurred to another member of the party after Grey returned home and that was related to him in a letter.

34. Grey, *Heritage,* 6, 42, 58, 33, 38, 71, 50, 89, 35, 138, 40.

35. Ibid., 5, 10–11, 13, 60, 62, 81, 90, 79, 169, 229, 307.

36. Zane Grey to David Dexter Rust, December 1910 and January 2, February 15, March 5, March 26, April 4, and April 20, 1911, David Dexter Rust Collection, The Church of Jesus Christ of Latter-day Saints; "Popular Author Visits Flagstaff," *Flagstaff Coconino Sun,* April 21, 1911, 1.

37. David Harvey, *Justice, Nature, and the Geography of Difference,* 232–42; Michael Denning, *Mechanic Accents.*

38. Zane Grey, *Nonnezoshe,* 2–3; Zane Grey, "Down into the Desert," *Ladies' Home Journal,* January 1924, 43; May, *Maverick Heart,* 60; Pauly, *Zane Grey: His Life,* 101, 104; Wheeler, "Zane Grey's Impact," 156; Folsom, *The Western,* 173; Mitchell, *Westerns,* 123.

39. Ibid., 59. Torgovnick, *Gone Primitive,* 68, notes this quality in Tarzan books. The first *Tarzan of the Apes* came out the same year as *Riders.* They share a kind of primitivism/modernism dichotomy in which women were subjected to possible sexual exploitation only to be saved by white middle- or upper-class males.

40. Grey, *Riders,* 193. Mitchell, *Westerns,* 123, says Grey may have used the polygamous Mormons of *Riders* to air anxieties about a supposed global conspiracy to abduct females. Tatum, in "The Problem of the 'Popular' in the New Western History," argues that the collective Mormon society in *Riders* may serve as a mirror of the U.S. economy increasingly dominated by corporations at the expense of individuals and entrepreneurship. He makes this point in the context of arguing that popular-culture Westerns raise issues of social significance.

41. Grey, diary; Grey, "Down into the Desert," 43; Pfeiffer, *The Surprise Valleys of Zane.*

42. Grey, *Riders,* 148, 257; Goodman, *Translating Southwestern Landscapes,* 58.

43. Grey, *Riders,* 72, 240–41, 316–17, 71–72; Pauly, *Zane Grey: His Life,* 83–84, 113.

44. Grey, "Breaking Through," 78; May, *Maverick Heart,* 60; Pauly, *Zane Grey: His Life,* 83–84, 111, 13.

45. "Famous Author Makes Trip with Famous Guide," *Flagstaff Coconino Sun,* May 13, 1913, 1; Ashworth, *Arizona Triptych,* 180–97; Pauly, *Zane Grey: His Life,* 118–23; Dolly Grey to Zane Grey, April 11, 1913, Zane Grey Collection, Cline Library.

46. Zane Grey, "Nonnezoshe," in *Tales of Lonely Trails,* 1–4. This is a reprint of a story published in *Recreation* magazine in February 1915.

47. Ibid., 1; Zane Grey, "Surprise Valley," *Outdoor America* 3, 1 (1924): 6; Hank Hassell, *Rainbow,* 65.

48. Grey, "Nonnezoshe," 12.

49. Pauly, *Zane Grey: His Life,* 132.

50. Nicholson, *Mountain Gloom and Mountain Glory,* 368–69; Gould, *Time's Arrow, Time's Cycle;* Torgovnick, *Gone Primitive,* 188; Lears, *No Place of Grace.*

51. Zane Grey, *The Rainbow Trail,* 219–20.

52. Ibid., 273–74.

53. This force of creative destruction following modernization's lead in Grey's novels also was pointed out by Goodman, *Translating Southwestern Landscapes.*

54. Grey, diary; Zane Grey to Dolly Grey, September 21, 1916, Zane Grey Collection, Cline Library; Dolly Grey to Zane Grey, February 23, 1922, Zane Grey Collection, Cline Library; Dolly Grey to Zane Grey, January 18, 1924, Zane Grey Collection, Cline Library; Dolly Grey to Bob Davis, January 4, 1935, Robert Hobart Davis Papers.

55. Pauly, *Zane Grey: His Life,* 11, 59, 203.

56. Zane Grey, diary, February 16, 1923, Zane and Dolly Grey Papers, Ohio State Historical Society.

57. This discussion was influenced by Philip Deloria, *Playing Indian,* 95–127; and Klein, *Frontiers of the Historical Imagination,* 257.

58. Grey, *The Vanishing American,* 19.

59. Ibid., 306, 13, 21, 28. Originally, Grey ended the story with the marriage of Nophaie and Marion, but its publication in *Ladies' Home Journal* beginning in November 1922 provoked an outcry over Grey's depiction of missionaries' and government agents' treatment of Indians and over the white-Indian relations of Marian and Nophaie. Grey altered the book ending after Jessie Lasky, the producer who was filming Grey's *The Vanishing American,* got Grey to make story changes for the movie. See Pauly, *Zane Grey: His Life,* 241–42.

CHAPTER 4. JOHN FORD AND MONUMENT VALLEY

1. Linford, *Navajo Places,* 33, 296–97; McPherson, *Sacred Land, Sacred View,* 29–31; Watson, *Navajo Sacred Places,* 9–10, 21; Van Valkenburgh, *Dine Bikeyah,* 53; Alan Wilson, *Navajo Place Names,* 38; McPherson, *History of San Juan County,* 298.

2. Gaberscek, *Il West Di John Ford;* Mitchell, *Westerns: Making the Man in Fiction and Film,* 24.

3. Comer, *Landscapes of the New West,* 5.

4. Buscombe, "Inventing Monument Valley"; Hyde, *An American Vision;* Rothman, *Devil's Bargains,* 14.

5. Buell, *The Environmental Imagination,* 71, describes how Thoreau emptied and filled the landscape.

6. On horizontal and vertical spaces, see Tuan, *Topophilia,* 27; Nicholson, *Mountain Gloom and Mountain Glory,* 3; Lefebvre, *Production of Space,* 225.

7. Kant, *Zane Grey's Arizona,* 48, 145–46; "Zane Grey, Noted Author to Make Movies on the Painted Desert," *Coconino Sun,* February 18, 1916, 1; "L.A. Movie Company Will Film Zane Grey's Famous Books Here," *Coconino Sun,* March 1, 1918; "Farnum, the Famous Movie Star Is Here," *Coconino Sun,* May 17, 1918, 1; "Flagstaff Enjoying New Lasky Picture before It's Produced," *Coconino Sun,* September 14, 1923, 1; "Zane Grey's 'The Water Hole' Will Be Filmed Here Next Month," *Coconino Sun,* June 1, 1928, 1; Tuska, *The Filming of the West,* 123–31, 420; Lasky, *Whatever Happened to Hollywood,* 17; Rich Velotta, "Zane Grey Was 'Doc' to This Sedona Man," April 28, 1977, Gladwell Richard Collection.

8. Also see Riley, "Trapped in the History of Film."

9. Bill Libby, "The Old Wrangler Rides Again," *Cosmopolitan,* March 1964, 18.

10. John Ford interview with Dan Ford, John Ford Collection, Lilly Library; McBride, *Searching for John Ford,* 1–64; Eyman, *Print the Legend,* 27–45.

11. McBride, *Searching for John Ford,* 1–64; Eyman, *Print the Legend,* 27–45.

12. Simmon, *The Invention of the Western Film,* 56–58.

13. Eyman, *Print the Legend,* 45; McBride, *Searching for John* Ford, 2, 1, 72–73, 90; Bill Levy, *John Ford,* 63–138; Davis, *John Ford,* 91.

14. Slotkin, *Gunfighter Nation,* 255–56; Pells, *Radical Visions and American Dreams,* 24, 72; Wrobel, *End of American Exceptionalism,* 125, 29; Kennedy, *Freedom from Fear,* 373–74.

15. Pells, *Radical Visions,* 79–80, 328; Wrobel, *End of American Exceptionalism,* 137–38; Slotkin, *Gunfighter Nation;* Conn, *The American 1930s,* 60–61.

16. McBride, *Searching for John Ford,* 278–79; Ernest Haycox, "Stage to Lordsburg," in *The Old West in Fiction,* 427–39.

17. Eyman, *Print the Legend,* 50, 59, 87–88, 135; McBride, *Searching for John Ford,* 90–94, 173.

18. Walter Wanger Productions, tentative budget, "Stage Coach," 1938, John Ford Collection, Lilly Library, Indiana University; John Ford interview with Dan Ford; Wills, *John Wayne's America;* Bogdanovich, *John Ford,* 69; Dan Ford, *Pappy;* Monument Valley, John Ford interview with Dan Ford, John Ford Collection, Lilly Library.

19. Lefebvre, *Production of Space,* 35, 225, notes that vertical space symbolizes power and that production of monumental space involves a horizontal series that became replaced by vertical hierarchy.

20. McBride, *Searching for John Ford,* 333–415; Eyman, *Print the Legend,* 251–87.

21. McBride, *Searching for John Ford,* 3, 53–54; Tavernier, "Notes of a Press Attache."

22. Tavernier, "Notes of a Press Attache," 68; John Ford, "Clementine," interview with Dan Ford, John Ford Collection, Lilly Library.

23. Samuel G. Engel and Winston Miller, screenplay for *My Darling Clementine,* 87.

24. Eyman, *Print the Legend,* 327; Merian Cooper to Mr. John Ford, Royal Hawaiian Hotel, February 27, 1947, Argosy Pictures Corporation Business Records, Harold B. Lee Library; Fort Apache, John Ford Collection, Lilly Library; Fort Apache Files, Argosy Pictures Corporation Business Records, L. Tom Perry Special Collections, Harold B. Lee Library.

25. "Fort Apache," John Ford Collection, Lilly Library.

26. Ibid.; Argosy Pictures Corporation Shooting Schedule, "War Party," 1947, John Ford Collection, Lilly Library. David Harvey, *Justice, Nature and the Geography of Difference,* 226, points out that women have a long history of confinement to cyclical time, leaving them alienated and outside the world of male-defined, linear time. For this, he relies on Forman and Sowton, *Taking Our Time.*

27. Brevet Major General Owen Thursday, U.S.A., 1947, John Ford Collection, Lilly Library. John Ford Notes on "Massacre" by James Warner Bellah to Cooper, 1947, Argosy Pictures Corporation Business Records, Harold B. Lee Library.

28. Michael Breffni O'Rourke, 1947, John Ford Collection, Lilly Library.

29. Capt. Kirby York, 1947, John Ford Collection, Lilly Library.

30. McBride, *Searching for John Ford,* 462–87.

31. Bogdanovich, *John Ford,* 87; James Warner Bellah, "War Party," *Saturday Evening Post,* June 19, 1948, 22–23, 104, 107, 109–10.

32. Slotkin, *Gunfighter Nation,* 334.

33. Carey, *Company of Heroes,* 109.

34. McBride, *Searching for John Ford,* 30, 48–52, 507, 509; "The Searchers," John Ford Collection, Lilly Library.

35. "The Searchers," Production Documents, Lilly Library.

36. Patrick Ford to John Ford, M. C. Cooper, Frank Nugent, Frank Beetson, February 1, 1955, John Ford Collection, Lilly Library.

37. Daily Production Reports: "The Searchers," 1955, John Ford Collection, Lilly Library.

38. Eckstein, "Darkening Ethan"; "The Searchers," Production Documents, Lilly Library; Courtney, "Looking for (Race and Gender) Trouble in Monument Valley," 109. This discussion was influenced by Tessie Liu's "Race and Gender in the Politics of Group Formation," 155–65.

39. "The Searchers," Production Documents, Lilly Library. Ethan of the movie was named Amos in the book.

40. Interoffice memorandum to John Ford.

41. "Captain Buffalo, 1959," John Ford Collection, Lilly Library. "Captain Buffalo" was the original title of the movie *Sergeant Rutledge.*

42. McBride, *Searching for John Ford,* 646, points out that Ford likely also used material from *The Last Frontier* by the blacklisted writer Howard Fast; Eyman, *Print the Legend,* 501.

43. Slotkin, *Gunfighter Nation,* 629; "Cheyenne Autumn," John Ford Collection, Lilly Library.

44. Davis, *John Ford,* 326; McBride, *Searching for John Ford,* 642.

45. Comer, *Landscapes,* 6; Graham, "Western Movies since 1960," 160.

46. Eyman, *Print the Legend,* 351.

47. Holiday, *A Navajo Legacy.*

48. The adjusted monetary figures here and below are rounded from calculations available at the Bureau of Labor Statistics website.

49. "Fort Apache," John Ford Collection; McPherson, *Navajo Land, Navajo Culture,* 145; Holiday, *A Navajo Legacy.*

50. Bogdanovich, *John Ford,* 18; Moon, *Tall Sheep,* 156.

51. Holiday, *A Navajo Legacy,* 155.

52. Bodie Thoene and Fona Stuck, "Navajo Nation Meets Hollywood," *American West* 20 (September–October 1983), 36, 43; McBride, *Searching for John Ford,* 555; Carey, *Company of Heroes,* 69.

CHAPTER 5. LAST NOTES OF THE CANYON WREN

1. Worster, *A River Running West,* 121–27; Mark Harvey, *A Symbol of Wilderness,* 7–14, 16–21; Reisner, *Cadillac Desert,* 27.

2. "New Application for Colorado Water Filed," *Times-Independent,* November 3, 1921, 2; "Curbing the Colorado," *Times-Independent,* November 16, 1922, 1.

3. Hundley, *Water and the West,* 169–214; Mark Harvey, *Symbol of Wilderness,* 23–49.

4. Bernard DeVoto, "Shall We Let Them Ruin Our National Parks?" *Saturday Evening Post,* July 22, 1950, 17; Mark Harvey, *Symbol of Wilderness,* 95–97.

5. Cohen, *History of the Sierra Club,* 149–50; Rothman, *Greening of a Nation?* xi, 17–31.

6. Cohen, *History of the Sierra Club,* 22–29; Roderick Nash, *Wilderness and the American Mind,* 161–81; Sutter, *Driven Wild,* 15–16.

7. Hays, *Conservation and the Gospel of Efficiency;* White, "American Environmental History"; Sutter, *Driven Wild;* Rome, *Bulldozer in the Countryside;* Williams, "Ideas of Nature"; Cronon, *Uncommon Ground.*

8. See the introduction to Sutter, *Driven Wild;* Cronon, *Uncommon Ground;* Price, *Flight Maps;* White, *Organic Machine.*

9. Bender, *Toward an Urban Vision,* 90.

10. Williams, *The Country and the City,* 120. See also Williams, "Metropolitan Perceptions and the Emergence of Modernism."

11. Lefebvre, *Production of Space,* 27, 51, 122, 90, 328, 83.

12. Denevan, "The Pristine Myth."

13. The phrase "something not remembered" was used in a different context in Shepard, "The Cross Valley Syndrome." Williams, "Metropolitan Perceptions."

14. This argument also is influenced by White, "'Are You an Environmentalist, or Do You Work for a Living?'"; and Cronon, "The Trouble with Wilderness; or, Getting Back to the Wrong Nature." See also MacCannell, *The Tourist,* 3.

15. Runte, *National Parks,* 7; Cronon, "Trouble with Wilderness"; Schama, *Landscape and Memory,* 7; Gottlieb, *Forcing the Spring,* 27.

16. Sutter, *Driven Wild,* 78–79.

17. Jackson, *Zane Grey,* 129.

18. The "time" quotation comes from a note among the Grey papers: Zane Grey Papers, Ohio Historical Society; Grey, *Roping Lions in the Grand Canyon,* vii–viii.

19. Cronon, "Trouble with Wilderness"; Runte, *National Parks,* 1–31, quotation from 9.

20. Zane Grey and Dolly Grey, "The Letters of Dolly and Zane Grey," 154.

21. Sutter, *Driven Wild,* quotation from 243.

22. This assertion relies on Foucault's insistence that historians should look not just at what was said in the past, but the conditions that made possible the saying of it. See Foucault's *Archaeology of Knowledge.*

23. Hays, *Response to Industrialism,* 2.

24. Berman, *All That Is Solid Melts into Air,* 306–10; Kay, *Asphalt Nation,* 72–73; Sale, *The Green Revolution,* 7, 24; Gottlieb, *Forcing the Spring,* 43; Rothman, *Greening of a Nation?* 8–19; Hays, *Beauty, Health, and Permanence;* Rome, *Bulldozer,* 5–8.

25. Mark Harvey, *Symbol of Wilderness,* 166–67, 257.

26. Stegner, "The Marks of Human Passage," 14–15. Italics in original.

27. Mark Harvey, "Echo Park, Glen Canyon, and the Postwar Wilderness Movement," 60–61.

28. "Council of Conservationists States Position on Upper Colorado Project," November 1, 1955, William A. Dawson Papers, Marriott Library, University of Utah; Mark Harvey, *Symbol of Wilderness,* 276–85.

29. Mark Harvey, *Symbol of Wilderness,* 280–82.

30. Howard Zahniser to the Honorable William A. Dawson, December 15, 1955, William A. Dawson Papers, Marriott Library; Howard Zahniser, "Report on Conference with Representative Dawson—a Telephone Transcript," December 22, 1955, William A. Dawson Papers, Marriott Library; A. Hildebrand to Congressman William A. Dawson, December 30, 1955, William A. Dawson Papers, Marriott Library.

31. Official transcript of hearing, July 6, 1973, *Friends of the Earth v. Ellis Armstrong,* U.S. National Archives and Records Administration, Rocky Mountain Region; Brower, *For Earth's Sake,* 341; Mark Harvey, *Symbol of Wilderness,* 235–85.

32. Roderick Nash, *Wilderness,* 212–21.

33. Mark Harvey, *Symbol of Wilderness,* 165, 239, 58.

34. Fraser, introduction to *Journeys in the Canyon Lands of Utah and Arizona,* xxxi; Swanson, *David Rust.*

35. Jared Farmer, *Glen Canyon Dammed,* 94–104; Music Temple Visitor Register Collection, 1938–1961, June 10, 1947, Marriott Library.

36. Ken Sleight. Interview by Everett L. Cooley, November 6, 7, 1991, Everett L. Cooley Oral History Projects, Marriott Library.

37. This analysis was based on readings of Lefebvre, *Production of Space;* Foucault, *Order of Things* and *Birth of the Clinic;* and Clifford, *The Predicament of Culture,* 264, though I take Clifford's discussion of discourse and knowledge further than he did and place it in the context of the production of space.

38. David Harvey, in *Justice, Nature, and the Geography of Difference* (232–38), writes about the spatiotemporal relations of money.

39. Brower, *Work in Progress,* 55.

40. *Let the River Run,* directed by Lili Schad, Glen Canyon Institute, 1997, videocassette.

41. Williams, *Problems in Materialism and Culture,* 39, quoted in Neumann, "The Commercial Canyon," 196. For the politics of the gaze, see Rose, *Feminism and Geography,* 86–112. Clifford, "Partial Truths," 11, notes that Western culture values sight over other senses. See also Berger, *About Looking.*

42. *Let the River Run;* Brower, *For Earth's Sake,* 154–55.

43. Brower, foreword to *The Place No One Knew,* 8. See also Tad Nichols, *Glen Canyon.*

44. Krista Comer and Annette Kolodny situate this type of space squarely within a traditional American masculine discourse whose aim was to maintain male political and cultural privilege. See Comer, *Landscapes of the New West;* and Annette Kolodny, *Lay of the Land* and *Land before Her.* See also Tompkins, *West of Everything.*

45. Porter and Brower, *The Place No One Knew,* 6.

46. This interpretation was influenced by White, "Are You an Environmentalist"; Williams, "Ideas of Nature," 67–85; David Harvey, *Justice, Nature,* 198–99; Rothman, *Greening of a Nation?*

47. Hassell, *Rainbow Bridge,* 115–18, quotation 25–26.

48. "The Rainbow Bridge Promise," *New York Times,* July 7, 1961, 24.

49. "New National Park in Utah Considered," *New York Times,* March 28, 1961, 21; Pat Munroe, "Udall Proposes Rainbow Park," *Deseret News,* November 2, 1961, 1; Hassell, *Rainbow Bridge,* 125–30; Keller and Turek, *American Indians and National Parks,* 196–99.

50. "Early Trip up the Colorado from Lee's Ferry to Rainbow Bridge, January 1931," *Plateau* 32, 2 (October 1961), 33–49; Keller and Turek, *American Indians,* 200–203; Richardson, "Federal Park Policy in Utah."

51. McPherson, *Navajo Land, Navajo Culture,* 102–20.

52. Recent scholarship on wilderness and national parks also has pointed to the racial implications of a landscape in which Native peoples have been removed or traditional activities prohibited. The wilderness ideal embodied in the national park was sometimes used to force out Native inhabitants or prohibit traditional uses such as hunting. This scholarship argues that modern parks and wilderness that leave Native inhabitants dispossessed is imperialistic. See Keller and Turek, *American Indians;* and Spence, *Dispossessing the Wilderness.* For an international perspective, see Harmon, "Cultural Diversity"; and Guha, "Radical American Environmentalism."

53. Brower, "Rainbow Bridge and the Quicksands of Time," *Sierra Club Bulletin,* June 1961, 2.

54. Brower, "Please Keep Those Glen Canyon Tunnels Open until Rainbow Bridge Protection Is Certain," *Sierra Club Bulletin*, March–April 1962, 2–3.

55. Hassell, *Rainbow Bridge*, 131–32.

56. Ibid., 132–33; Reisner, *Cadillac Desert*, 283; Nash, *Wilderness*, 228; William M. Blair, "Dam in Colorado Irks; Glen Canyon Project Spurs Fight over Use of Public Lands for Water Sites," *New York Times*, July 24, 1963, 33.

57. Brower, *Work in Progress*, 56–57.

58. Roderick Nash, *Wilderness*, 229–31; Reisner, *Cadillac Desert*, 295, 99. Strong, *Dreamers and Defenders*, 211–17. For an account of the fight over the Grand Canyon dams, see Pearson, *Still the Wild River Runs*.

59. *Friends of the Earth et al., Plaintiffs, v. Ellis L. Armstrong*, 1970, National Archives and Records, Rocky Mountain Region.

60. U.S. District Court Judge William Jones. Official Transcript, May 24, 1971, *Friends of the Earth v. Ellis L. Armstrong*, National Archives and Records, Rocky Mountain Region.

61. This argument is made in many documents and transcripts of court hearings in *Friends of the Earth v. Ellis L. Armstrong*.

62. Wallace R. Hansen, "A Geologic Examination of Rainbow Bridge National Monument to Review Measures to Protect the Monument from Impairment by Glen Canyon Reservoir," 1959, Willis W. Ritter Papers, Marriott Library; Dames & Moore, "Geological and Structural Evaluation of Rainbow Bridge, Rainbow Bridge National Monument, Utah for the Upper Colorado River Commission," 1972, Willis W. Ritter Papers.

63. Brower, transcript of proceedings, July 6, 1973, *Friends of the Earth v. Ellis L. Armstrong*.

64. Grey, "What the Open Means to Me," 48.

65. Hassell, *Rainbow Bridge*, 135; William J. Breed, "Last Chance for Rainbow Bridge," *Outdoor Arizona*, June 1971, 40; Neil M. Judd, "Return to Rainbow Bridge," *Arizona Highways*, August 1967, 39.

66. Brower, transcript, *Friends of the Earth v. Ellis L. Armstrong*.

67. Craig E. Smay, memorandum to Chief Judge Willis W. Ritter, May 18, 1972, Willis W. Ritter Papers; Craig E. Smay, memorandum: Re Motion to Intervene in Rainbow Bridge Matter to Chief Judge Willis W. Ritter, ca. 1972, Willis W. Ritter Papers.

68. Motion to intervene as plaintiffs, May 25, 1972, *Friends of the Earth v. Ellis L. Armstrong*, U.S. District Court for the District of Utah, National Archives and Records, Rocky Mountain Region.

69. *Friends of the Earth v. Ellis L. Armstrong*.

70. *Friends of the Earth, Wasatch Mountain Club, Inc., and Kenneth G. Sleight v. Gilbert R. Stamm*, October 1973, Conservation Collection, Denver Public Library; *Friends of the Earth et al. v. Stamm, Commissioner, Bureau of Reclamation, et al.*, 94 S. Ct. 933 (1974).

71. Frank Hewlett, "High Court Declines Appeal Case in Lake Rift," *Salt Lake Tribune*, January 22, 1974, 13.

72. This interpretation was influenced by David Harvey, *Justice, Nature*; Comer, *Landscapes*; Gottlieb, *Forcing the Spring*; Lasch, *Culture of Narcissism*; Lears, *No Place of Grace*; and Lefebvre, *Production of Space*.

73. Jim Woolf, "Lake Limbo: How Low Should Powell Go?" *Salt Lake Tribune*, November 10, 1995, A1; Matthew Brown, "To Regain Glen Canyon, Sierra Club Wants to Pull Plug on Lake Powell," *Salt Lake Tribune*, December 30, 1996. About the Glen Canyon Institute, see its website at www.glencanyon.org; Christopher Smart, "The Lake Effect,"

Salt Lake Tribune, February 27, 2003, A1; Christopher Smart, "Low Water Reveals Long-Lost Splendor," *Salt Lake Tribune,* May 19, 2003, A1.

74. Tom Turner, Rainbow Bridge Amici, March 20, 1974, Izaak Walton League of America, Conservation Collection, Denver Public Library; Richard W. Hughes, Eric P. Swenson, and C. Benson Hufford, "Motion for Leave to File Brief Amicus Curiae in Support of Petition for Rehearing of Denial of Petition of Writ of Certiorari in the Supreme Court of the United States," *Friends of the Earth v. Gilbert R. Stamm,* 1973, Willis W. Ritter Papers.

75. Paul Goodman, affidavit of Nakai Ditl'oi, aka Paul Goodman, *Friends of the Earth v. Ellis L. Armstrong,* U.S. District Court, in and for the District of Utah, March 17, 1972, Willis W. Ritter Papers.

76. Resolution, Shonto Chapter, April 8, 1972, Willis W. Ritter Papers. See affidavits by Nakai Ditl'oi, aka Paul Goodman, March 17, 1972; Lamar Badoni, March 17, 1972; Teddy Holiday, February 14, 1974; Jessie Yazzie Black, February 13, 1974; Jimmy Goodman, February 13, 1974; and Begay Bitsinnie, February 13, 1974. Photocopies can be found in the Willis W. Ritter Papers.

77. Betty Holiday, answers to interrogatories, November 1, 1976, *Nakai Ditl'oi et al. v. Gilbert V. Stamm et al.* C-74-275, U.S. District Court for the District of Utah, National Archives and Records, Rocky Mountain Region. See also other affidavits in the case, which became *Badoni v. Higginson* after Nakai Ditl'oi died.

78. *Badoni v. Higginson,* 1977 U.S. Dist. LEXIS 12115 (U.S. District Court for the District of Utah, Central Division, 1977); *Badoni v. Higginson,* 1980 U.S. App. LEXIS 12661 (U.S. Court of Appeals, 10th Circuit 1980).

79. Christopher Smith, "Tribal Spiritualism and Tourism Collide When Visitors Venture . . . Under the Rainbow," *Salt Lake Tribune,* July 28, 1996; Sproul, "Bridge between Cultures"; "Navajo Group Closes Rainbow Bridge," *Lake Powell Chronicle,* August 16, 1995, 1.

80. "Navajo Group Closes Rainbow Bridge," 1.

81. Tom Harvey, "S. Utah Hikers Lose Suit," *Salt Lake Tribune,* March 25, 2004, C3; Robert Gehrke, "Park Rules on Rainbow Bridge Stand," *Salt Lake Tribune,* February 23, 2005, C8.

82. "Lake Powell," brochure produced by Aramark, ca. 2001, in my possession. The final quotation is from notes I took on a tour to Rainbow Bridge.

CHAPTER 6. SALTING THE SCENERY

1. Gillmor and Wetherill, *Traders to the Navajo,* quotation from 194.

2. Rainbow Bridge is now considered to be the eighth-largest natural arch in the world. See www.naturalarches.org.

3. Comfort, *Rainbow to Yesterday,* 9–25; Benjamin Alfred Wetherill, *The Wetherills of the Mesa Verde,* 129, 80; Goetzmann, *New Lands, New Men,* 365; Nordenskiöld, *Cliff Dwellers of the Mesa Verde.*

4. Comfort, *Rainbow to Yesterday,* 31–34.

5. Louisa Wade Wetherill and Leake, *Wolfkiller,* xii.

6. Gillmor and Wetherill, *Traders to the Navajo,* 36–39.

7. Dona Brown, *Inventing New England,* quotation from 12; Sears, *Sacred Places.*

8. Dona Brown, *Inventing New England,* 5–11.

9. Runte, *National Parks,* 7; Hyde, *An American Vision,* 5, 12, 25, 39–51; Smith, *Virgin Land,* 175–83; Pomeroy, *In Search of the Golden West,* 31–48.

10. Fowler, *Laboratory for Anthropology,* 247–54; Howard and Pardue, *Inventing the Southwest;* Mark Thompson, *American Character;* Thomas, "Promoting the Southwest," 48–49; Chauvenet, *Hewett and Friends;* Padget, "Travel, Exoticism, and the Writing of Region"; Dilworth, *Imagining Indians in the Southwest;* Hinsley, "Authoring Authenticity"; Babcock, "A New Mexican Rebecca." Liza Nicholas writes that "through the tourist trade, westerners themselves became the perpetrators of the power and knowledge of what the authentic West was and should be" (*Becoming Western,* xvii).

11. MacCannell, *The Tourist.* See also Rothman, *Devil's Bargains.*

12. David Harvey, *Condition of Postmodernity,* 16–37.

13. On the making of an economy of consumption, see Leach, *Land of Desire.* For antimodernism, see Lears, *No Place of Grace;* Price, *Flight Maps;* Deloria, *Playing Indian.* On the consumption of space, see Lefebvre, *The Production of Space,* particularly 122 for the modern creation of rustic and folk space.

14. McPherson, "Naalyéhé Bá-Hooghan," 65–66; Comfort, *Rainbow to Yesterday,* 39–40; Gillmor and Wetherill, *Traders to the Navajo,* 81–82.

15. O'Neill, *Working the Navajo Way,* 61–73.

16. Gillmor and Wetherill, *Traders to the Navajo,* 107–108; Wyman, *Sandpaintings of the Kayenta Navajo,* quotations from 13–14; John Edwin Hogg, "Big Medicine," *Touring Topics,* 1931, 19–21; Wyman and Harris, *The Ethnobotany of the Kayenta Navajo;* "Notes and News," *Kiva* 2, 3 (March 1946), 35; Louisa Wade Wetherill, "Some Navajo Recipes"; Louisa Wade Wetherill, "The Woman Whose Nose Was Cut Off"; Louisa Wade Wetherill, "Creation of Burro"; Cummings, "Kivas of the San Juan Drainage"; Cummings, "Sand Paintings in State Museum."

17. John Wetherill, "Betata Kin," June 1934, Gary Topping Papers, 1824–1998.

18. Fowler, *Laboratory for Anthropology,* 247.

19. E. A. Wall to Prof. Byron Cummings, July 19, 1908, Byron Cummings Collection; Byron Cummings, "Cummings Describes Natural Wonders and Scientific Treasures of San Juan Region," *Salt Lake Herald,* November 1, 1908, Magazine Section 12. These describe the interest of the Commercial Club of Salt Lake City in developing scenic attractions: H. L. A. Culmer, "The Great Stone Bridges of San Juan County, Utah," May 14, 1905, H. L. A. Culmer Papers; "Will Explore Unknown Utah; Culmer Expedition to Start Soon," *Salt Lake Tribune,* March 21, 1905, 12. On the state allocation for the Cummings expedition, see "Is Satisfied with Work," *Grand Valley Times-Independent,* March 26, 1909, 1; Fowler, *Laboratory for Anthropology,* 247.

20. Cummings, "Cummings Describes Natural Wonders."

21. Kehoe, *The Land of Prehistory,* quotation from 82; Leach, *Land of Desire,* 324. See also Kehoe, "Contextualizing Archaeology," 101; Meskell, introduction to *Archaeology under Fire,* 6; Ronald Freeman Lee, "The Antiquities Act of 1906," shows how archaeologists reacted to the commercialization by artifact hunters and lobbied for the Antiquities Act of 1906 to enforce their own authority over the objects; Torgovnick, *Gone Primitive,* 75; Neumann, *On the Rim,* 37.

22. Cummings, "Cummings Describes Natural Wonders"; Fowler, *Laboratory for Anthropology,* 259; Byron Cummings, "The Great Natural Bridges of Utah," *National Geographic Magazine,* February 1910, 199–202.

23. Hassell, *Rainbow Bridge;* Herbert E. Gregory, "Navajo-Moki Book II," 1909, Gary Topping Papers; John Wetherill to Prof. Byron Cummings, Stegliz Bei Berlin, Germany, November 6, 1910, Byron Cummings Papers; Herbert Gregory to John Wetherill, Oljato, Utah, January 17, 1910, Gary Topping Papers; John Wetherill to Herbert Gregory, February 1910, Gary Topping Papers.

24. Sears, *Sacred Places,* 42. See also Goetzmann, *New Lands,* 406; Worster, *River Running West,* 64–65; Hyde, *An American Vision,* 213; Gould, *Time's Arrow.*

25. John Wetherill, Notebook, 1910, John Wetherill Collection; Herbert E. Gregory, "Moki-Navajo Book II," 1910, Gary Topping Papers. The notebooks differ on which day the party arrived at Rainbow Bridge. Wetherill puts it at July 24, Gregory the next day.

26. Joseph Pogue, "The Great Rainbow Natural Bridge of Southern Utah," *National Geographic,* November 1911, 1048–56; Gregory, *Navajo Country.*

27. Herbert Gregory, Estimate of Expenses for Navajo Investigations 1910–11, 1911, Gary Topping Papers. This argument was influenced by the discussion of money transactions in David Harvey, *Justice, Nature and the Geography of Difference,* 163, 232–38; Cronon, *Nature's Metropolis,* 84, 340.

28. Gillmor and Wetherill, *Traders to the Navajo,* 188; Comfort, *Rainbow to Yesterday,* 100–101.

29. Gillmor and Wetherill, *Traders to the Navajo,* 193–194.

30. Nicholas Roosevelt and James E. Babbitt, "Across the Painted Desert"; Nicholas Roosevelt to Lorenzo Hubbell, August 6, 1912, Gary Topping Papers; Theodore Roosevelt, "Across the Navajo Desert," *Outlook,* October 11, 1913, 309–17; Theodore Roosevelt, *A Book-Lover's Holiday in the Open,* 47–56.

31. Nicholas, "1–800-Sundance," 263–65.

32. Sayle, *A Trip to the Rainbow Arch,* n.p.; Bernheimer, *Rainbow Bridge,* 29; Torgovnick, *Gone Primitive,* 82–83, 125–26; Lears, *No Place of Grace;* Leach, *Land of Desire,* 104–11; MacCannell, *The Tourist.* On the value of mechanically produced art, see Benjamin, "The Work of Art in the Age of Mechanical Reproduction"; and Mullin, *Culture in the Marketplace,* 132.

33. Ronald Freeman Lee, "The Antiquities Act of 1906," 213; Dilworth, *Imagining Indians,* 213; Howard and Pardue, *Inventing the Southwest,* 7; Neumann, "Commercial Canyon," 204; Weigle and Babcock, *Great Southwest;* Babcock, "New Mexican Rebecca," 403; Dixon, *Westward Hoboes,* 263.

34. Theodore Roosevelt, *Book-Lover's Holiday,* 49.

35. Grey, *The Rainbow Trail,* 32; Grey, "Nonnezoshe"; Zane Grey and Mrs. John Wetherill, Agreement, September 1924, Gary Topping Papers; Zane Grey, Draft of Essay Fading Indian Trails, 1929, Zane and Dolly Grey Papers, Ohio Historical Society; Grey, *Blue Feather, and Other Stories;* Grey, *The Secret of Quaking Asp Cabin and Other Stories.*

36. "L.A. Movie Company Will Film Zane Grey's Famous Books Here," *Coconino Sun,* March 1, 1918, 1; "Filming of Famous Grey Novels to Carry Fame of Our Scenery Over World," *Coconino Sun,* September 14, 1923, 1; "Farnum, the Famous Movie Star Is Here," *Coconino Sun,* May 17, 1918, 1; John Wetherill to Zane Grey, Altadena, Calif., December 3, 1924, Gary Topping Papers; Zane Grey to John Wetherill, Tucson, undated, 1924, Gary Topping Papers; John Wetherill. Notebook Accounts, 1930–34, John Wetherill Collection, Museum of Northern Arizona, Flagstaff; Garry Wills, *John Wayne's America,* 87.

37. Bernheimer, *Rainbow Bridge;* Charles L. Bernheimer, Expedition Field Notes, Marriott Library.

38. Bernheimer, Expedition Field Notes; Charles Bernheimer, "Encircling Navajo Mountain with a Pack-Train," *National Geographic,* February 1923, 197–224.

39. Sayle, *Trip to Rainbow Arch;* Robert Frothingham, "Rainbow Bridge," *Country Life,* June 1925, 35–39; Dixon, *Westward Hoboes.* Leona Goulding said she visited the Bernheimer Arch in 1931 before it was "discovered" by Charles Bernheimer and named for his wife. "Mike" Goulding, interview, September 6, 1989, Oral History Program, Utah State Historical Society.

40. Wilbur Hall, "The Scenery Salters," *Sunset,* January 1929, 11–13, 47–48.

41. Hassell, *Rainbow Bridge,* 70–83; pamphlet, undated, Gladwell Richardson Collection, Cline Library; "Southwestern Monuments," monthly report, U.S. Department of Interior, National Park Service, March 1939, Rainbow Bridge National Monument, Cline Library.

42. Frothingham, "Rainbow Bridge," 35; Grey, "What the Open Means to Me," 48.

43. Benjamin W. Wetherill to Mr. Hubbell, Tucson, April 10, 1932, Gary Topping Papers; John Wetherill to Dear Little Girl, July 14, 1941, Gary Topping Papers.

44. Moon, *Tall Sheep,* 7–19.

45. J. S. Newberry, J. N. Macomb, and F. B. Meek, *Report of the Exploring Expedition,* 103–104.

46. John D. Lee, *A Mormon Chronicle,* 315; Prudden, "The Prehistoric Ruins of the San Juan Watershed," 283; Stuart Young, photographs, 1909, Stuart Young Collection, Cline Library.

47. Holiday, *Navajo Legacy,* 83.

48. "Harry Goulding Takes First Car to Arches," *Millard County Chronicle,* June 25, 1926, 5; Moon, *Tall Sheep,* 29, 35–36, 39–42. Harry Goulding claimed other Navajos welcomed his presence.

49. Moon, *Tall Sheep,* 19, 39, 77–78.

50. Neil M. Judd, "Beyond the Clay Hills," *National Geographic,* March 1924, 275–86; Charles Kelly, "Review: Land of Room Enough."

51. Charles Kelly, "Review," 175; Charles Kelly, Monument Valley, ca. 1928, Charles Kelly Papers, Marriott Library.

52. Louter, "Windshield Wilderness"; Belasco, *Americans on the Road,* 3–41; John A. Jakle, "Touring by Automobile in 1932"; Rothman, *Devil's Bargain.*

53. O. C. Hansen, photographs, 1916, Manuscript C526, Utah State Historical Society.

54. Genaro Padilla, "Monumental Highway News," *Washington County News,* May 24, 1917; "Andrus Describes Daring Auto Trip," *Grand Valley Times,* June 29, 1917; "Scenes along Monumental H'y," *Washington County News,* July 19, 1917; W. H. Hopkins, "Bluff to St. George by Auto, 400 Miles of America's Wonders," *Deseret News,* July 23, 1921, Automobile Section 1.

55. "Nature's Wonderland within Reach of Auto Tourist," *Grand Valley Times,* May 9, 1919, 2.

56. "Is Satisfied with Work," 1; Oliver J. Grimes, "Scenic Wonders Southeastern Utah Portrayed," *Times-Independent,* May 24, 1928, 5; "Mabel Plans Another Trip," *Grand Valley Times-Independent,* August 10, 1922, 1; "Southern Utah Civic Clubs to Meet in Delta," *Millard County Chronicle,* November 11, 1934, 1; "Seek to Promote Road through Monument Valley," *Times-Independent,* October 22, 1925, 1; "U.S. Investigates Monumental Highway," *Times-Independent,* May 25, 1928, 1; "Governor and Party Return from San

Juan," *Times-Independent,* May 10, 1927, 1; "Monument Valley Scenic Wonder Spot," *Millard County Chronicle,* May 7, 1936, 4.

57. Elmo R. Richardson, "Federal Park Policy in Utah"; Ansel Franklin Hall, *General Report on the Rainbow Bridge–Monument Valley Expedition of 1933,* 5; "Adventure Bound!"

58. Richard White, *Roots of Dependency,* 212–314; O'Neill, *Working the Navajo Way,* 23.

59. Moon, *Tall Sheep,* 139; Faris, *Navajo and Photography,* 152.

60. Faris, *Navajo and Photography,* 15, 40, 108, 60, 246, quotation from 13; Dilworth, *Imagining Indians,* 79.

61. Moon, *Tall Sheep,* 139.

62. O'Neill, *Working the Navajo Way,* 73.

63. Moon, *Tall Sheep,* 44–51; Wills, *John Wayne's America,* 87; Weatherall's [*sic*] Place, 1938, John Ford Collection, Lilly Library; Ray Heinze to Dan Keefe, October 28, 1938, John Ford Collection; Housing and Feeding, 1938, John Ford Collection. Ford also once said that actor George O'Brien, while filming a Western near Monument Valley—an adaptation of Zane Grey's *The Lone Star Ranger*—obtained photographs from Goulding and later showed them to Ford. John Wayne also claimed discovery. See John Ford interview with Dan Ford, John Ford Collection; John Wayne and Ralph Mahoney, "'Arizona: My Favorite Location,'" *Arizona Days and Ways Magazine,* October 23, 1955; Bogdanovich, *John Ford,* 69; Dan Ford, *Pappy,* 125; Zolotow, *Shooting Star,* 148–49; Moon, *Tall Sheep,* 144–50; Hal Erickson, *The Lone Star Ranger,* All Movie Guide, http://www.allmovie .com.

64. Arthur L. Crawford, "Through Utah's No-Man's Land," *Travel,* February 1945, 10; Neil M. Clark, "Desert Trader," *Saturday Evening Post,* March 29, 1947, 36.

65. On the postwar boom, see Gómez, *Quest for the Golden Circle.* The Gouldings tell of their expansion in Moon, *Tall Sheep,* 99.

66. "Goulding's Museum & Trading Post," Goulding's Lodge, http://www.gouldings .com/english/museum.htm.

67. Jett, *Tourism in the Navajo Country;* Sanders, "Tribal and National Parks on American Indian Lands."

68. Sanders, "Tribal and National Parks," 66–70; Frank Jensen, "Rites Open Park Area," *Salt Lake Tribune,* May 6, 1960; Jack Goodman, "Navajos Open Tribal Park," *New York Times,* May 1, 1960, Section 2, Part II, 1.

69. Rothman, *Devil's Bargain,* 11.

70. O'Neill, *Working the Navajo Way,* 143.

71. McPherson, *Navajo Land,* 139–40; Sanders, "Tribal and National Parks," 117; *Navajoland U.S.A.;* Navajo Tribal Council, *Monument Valley, Navajo Tribal Park, Utah-Arizona.*

72. Holiday, *A Navajo Legacy,* 223; Bill Donovan, "Movie Makers May Now Frown on Navajo Sites," *Navajo Times,* February 8, 1996, A5.

73. Bill Donovan, "Ortegas Ink Deal for New Monument Valley Hotel," *Navajo Times,* February 22, 2007, A10; Cindy Yurth, "Monument Valley Tour Guides Unite for Change," *Navajo Times,* April 13, 2006, A8.

74. I was on this tour and wrote about it in Tom Harvey, "Among Myths and Monuments, Real Life Endures," *Salt Lake Tribune,* June 6, 1995, D1.

75. Robert De Roos, "Mysterious Monument Valley," *Reader's Digest,* June 1963, 136.

CONCLUSION: ARTIFACTS IN THE MUSEUM
OF A MODERN AMERICAN SPACE

Epigraph. Novelist James Lee Burke made the comment that opens this chapter in an interview broadcast on National Public Radio on August 11, 2009.

1. Roberta John, "Old Tourism Group Brought Back to Life," *Navajo Times,* March 25, 1999, A5.

2. Jennifer Lowe, "Old West Lives On in Monument Valley," *Deseret News,* June 1, 1997, T5. Janet Rae Brooks, "Behind the Scenes in Monument Valley," *Salt Lake Tribune,* August 19, 2001, H1, H6.

3. Seth Lubove, "In John Wayne's Footsteps," *Forbes,* July 9, 1990, 72–73; Kroes, "American Empire and Cultural Imperialism," 509–10; "Taco Bell Joins the Industry Shake-up with a Review, and There's Nothing Ordinary About It," *New York Times,* February 4, 1997, C6; "Garage Sale U.S.A.," *Life,* August 11, 1972; Jacobson, *Marketing Madness,* 133.

4. "Jeep," *New Yorker,* June 18, 2001. "Take a Number C 89," *This Old House,* May 2001, 8–9.

5. Shaw and Prelinger, "Freeway Landscapes and Timescapes," 795.

6. Ford Explorer advertisement, *Smithsonian,* April 1994, back cover; Messaris, *Visual Persuasion,* 13, 16.

7. Ballard, *Hello America.*

8. Baudrillard, *America,* 70; Virilio, *The Lost Dimension,* 27; Hughes, *Nothing If Not Critical,* 376–77.

Selected Bibliography

ARCHIVAL COLLECTIONS

Special Collections, Marriott Library, University of Utah, Salt Lake City
    Byron Cummings Papers, 1860–1993
    Charles L. Bernheimer Expedition Notes, 1919–1930
    Charles Kelly Papers, 1889–1971
    Doris Duke Oral History Collection
    Everett L. Cooley Oral History Projects
    William A. Dawson Papers
    Willis W. Ritter Papers
Lilly Library, Indiana University, Bloomington
    John Ford Collection
Utah State Historical Society, Salt Lake City
    Gary Topping Papers, 1824–1998
    H. L. A. Culmer Papers
    Oral History Program
Ohio Historical Society, Columbus
    Zane and Dolly Grey Papers
New York Public Library, New York
    Robert Hobart Davis Papers
Special Collections and Archives, Cline Library, Northern Arizona University, Flagstaff
    Gladwell Richardson Collection
    Harold Osborne Collection
    Rainbow Bridge National Monument Collection
    Stuart Young Collection
    Tuba City Guest Ranch Collection
    Zane Grey Collection

Arizona Historical Society, Tucson
    Byron Cummings Papers
L. Tom Perry Special Collections, Harold B. Lee Library, Brigham Young University, Provo,
    Utah
    Argosy Pictures Corporation Business Records
    Zane Grey Collection
National Archives and Records Division, Rocky Mountain Region, Denver
    Friends of the Earth v. Ellis L. Armstrong, U.S. District Court for the District of Utah,
        Central Division
    Nakai Ditl'oi et al. v. Gilbert V. Stamm et al. C–74–275, U.S. District Court for the Dis-
        trict of Utah
Western History/Genealogy Department, Denver Public Library
    The Conservation Collection
    Izaak Walton League of America
Archives, Zane Grey Museum, National Park Service, Upper Delaware Scenic and Rec-
    reational River, Beach Lake, Pa.
Goulding's Museum and Trading Post, Monument Valley, Utah
Rare Book, Manuscript, and Special Collections Library, Duke University, Durham,
    N.C.
    William Boone Douglass Papers
Private collection of Stan Jones, Page, Ariz.
    William Boone Douglass file
Special Collections, Horrmann Library, Wagner College, Staten Island, N.Y.
    Edwin Markham Collection
Historical Department, The Church of Jesus Christ of Latter–day Saints, Salt Lake City,
    Utah
    David Dexter Rust Collection
Museum of Northern Arizona, Flagstaff
    Byron Cummings Collection
    John Wetherill Collection

NEWSPAPERS AND MAGAZINES

American West
Arizona Days and Ways Magazine
Arizona Highways
Century
Coconino Sun (Flagstaff, Ariz.)
Cortez Herald (Cortez, Colo.)
Cosmopolitan
Country Life
Deseret Evening News (Salt Lake City, Utah)
Forbes
Frontier Times
Grand Valley Times (Moab, Utah)
Ladies' Home Journal
Lake Powell Chronicle (Page, Ariz.)

Life
Millard County Chronicle
Montezuma Journal (Montezuma, Colo.)
National Geographic
National Parks Bulletin
Navajo Times (Shiprock, Ariz.)
New York Times
Our Public Lands
Outdoor Arizona
Outlook
Plateau (Flagstaff, Ariz.)
Reader's Digest
Salt Lake Herald
Salt Lake Tribune
Saturday Evening Post
Sierra Club Bulletin
Smithsonian
Sunset
Times-Independent (Moab, Utah)
Touring Topics
Travel
Vernal Express (Vernal, Utah)
Washington County News (St. George, Utah)

BOOKS AND ARTICLES

Ascherson, Neal. Foreword to *Nationalism and Archaeology,* edited by John A. Atkinson, Iain Banks, and Jerry O'Sullivan. Glasgow, Scotland: Cruithne Press, 1996.

Ashworth, Donna. *Arizona Triptych.* Flagstaff, Ariz.: Small Mountain Books, 1999.

Babcock, Barbara A. "A New Mexican Rebecca: Imaging Pueblo Women." *Journal of the Southwest* 32 (1990): 400–37.

Ballard, J. G. *Hello America.* New York: Carroll and Graf, 1981.

Basso, Keith H. *Wisdom Sits in Places: Landscape and Language among the Western Apache.* Albuquerque: University of New Mexico Press, 1996.

Baudrillard, Jean. *America.* Translated by Chris Turner. New York: Verso, 1988.

Bederman, Gail. *Manliness and Civilization: A Cultural History of Gender and Race in the United States, 1880–1917.* Chicago: University of Chicago Press, 1995.

Begay, Richard M., and Alexandra Roberts. "The Early Navajo Occupation of the Grand Canyon Region." In *Archaeological Concepts of Navajo Origins,* edited by Ronald H. Towner. Salt Lake City: University of Utah Press, 1996.

Belasco, Warren James. *Americans on the Road: From Autocamp to Motel, 1910–1945.* Cambridge, Mass.: MIT Press, 1979.

Bender, Thomas. *Toward an Urban Vision: Ideas and Institutions in Nineteenth Century America.* Baltimore: Johns Hopkins University Press, 1982.

Benjamin, Walter. "The Work of Art in the Age of Mechanical Reproduction." In *Illuminations,* edited by Hannah Arendt, 217–51. New York: Schocken, 1968.

Berger, John. *About Looking.* New York: Pantheon Books, 1980.

Berkhofer, Robert F., Jr. "Space, Time, Culture and the New Frontier." *Agricultural History* 38 (1964).

Berman, Marshall. *All That Is Solid Melts into Air: The Experience of Modernity.* New York: Simon and Schuster, 1982.

Bernheimer, Charles. *Rainbow Bridge: Circling Navajo Mountain and Explorations in the "Bad Lands" of Southern Utah and Northern Arizona.* Garden City, N.Y.: Doubleday, Doran, 1929.

Blake, Kevin Scott. "Zane Grey and Images of the American West." *Geographical Review* 85, no. 2 (1995): 202–16.

———. "Zane Grey's Impact on Images of the American West." M.A. thesis, University of Kansas, 1991.

Bogdanovich, Peter. *John Ford.* Berkeley: University of California Press, 1968.

Bostwick, Todd William. "Revisiting the Dean: Byron Cummings and Southwestern Archaeology, 1893–1954." Ph.D. diss., Arizona State University, 2003.

Brenner, Suzanne April. *The Domestication of Desire: Women, Wealth, and Modernity in Java.* Princeton, N.J.: Princeton University Press, 1998.

Brower, David. *For Earth's Sake: The Life and Times of David Brower.* Salt Lake City, Utah: Peregrine Smith Books, 1990.

———. Foreword to *The Place No One Knew: Glen Canyon on the Colorado,* edited by David Brower, 8–10. San Francisco: Sierra Club Books, Ballantine Books, 1963.

———. *Work in Progress.* Salt Lake City, Utah: Gibbs Smith, 1991.

Brown, Dona. *Inventing New England: Regional Tourism in the Nineteenth Century.* Washington, D.C.: Smithsonian Institution Press, 1995.

Brown, Gary M. "The Protohistoric Transition in the Northern San Juan Region." In *Archaeological Concepts of Navajo Origins,* edited by Ronald H. Towner. Salt Lake City: University of Utah Press, 1996.

Brugge, David M. "The Navajo Exodus." *Archaeological Society of New Mexico Supplement* (1972).

Buell, Lawrence. *The Environmental Imagination: Thoreau, Nature Writing, and the Formation of American Culture.* Cambridge, Mass.: Belknap, 1995.

Buscombe, Edward. "Inventing Monument Valley: Nineteenth-Century Landscape Photography and the Western Film." In *Fugitive Images,* edited by Patricia Petro, 87–107. Bloomington: University of Indiana Press, 1995.

Carey, Harry, Jr. *Company of Heroes: My Life as an Actor in the John Ford Stock Company.* Metuchen, N.J.: Scarecrow Press, 1994.

Cawelti, John G. *The Six-Gun Mystique.* Bowling Green, Ohio: Popular Press, 1971.

Chauvenet, Beatrice. *Hewett and Friends: A Biography of Santa Fe's Vibrant Era.* Santa Fe: Museum of New Mexico Press, 1983.

Clifford, James. "Partial Truths." In *Writing Culture: The Poetics and Politics of Ethnography,* edited by James Clifford and George E. Marcus, 1–26. Berkeley: University of California Press, 1986.

———. *The Predicament of Culture: Twentieth Century Ethnography, Literature, and Art.* Cambridge, Mass.: Harvard University Press, 1988.

Clifford, James, and George E. Marcus, eds. *Writing Culture: The Poetics and Politics of Ethnography.* Berkeley: University of California Press, 1986.

Cohen, Michael P. *The History of the Sierra Club, 1892–1970.* San Francisco: Sierra Club Books, 1988.

Comer, Krista. *Landscapes of the New West: Gender and Geography in Contemporary Women's Writing.* Chapel Hill: University of North Carolina Press, 1999.

Comfort, Mary Apolline. *Rainbow to Yesterday: The John and Louisa Wetherill Story.* New York: Vantage, 1980.

Conn, Peter. *The American 1930s: A Literary History.* Cambridge: Cambridge University Press, 2009.

Copeland, James Matthew, and Hugh C. Rogers. "In the Shadow of the Holy People: Ceremonial Imagery in Dinétah." In *Archaeological Concepts of Navajo Origins,* edited by Ronald H. Towner. Salt Lake City: University of Utah Press, 1996.

Correll, J. Lee. "Navajo Frontiers in Utah and Troublous Times in Monument Valley." *Utah Historical Quarterly* 39 (1971): 141–57.

Courtney, Susan. "Looking for (Race and Gender) Trouble in Monument Valley." *Qui Parle: Literature, Philosophy, Visual Arts, History* 6, no. 2 (1993): 97–130.

Crampton, Gregory. *Standing Up Country.* New York: Alfred A. Knopf, 1964.

Cronon, William. *Nature's Metropolis: Chicago and the Great West.* New York: W. W. Norton, 1991.

———. "Revisiting the Vanishing Frontier: The Legacy of Frederick Jackson Turner." *Western Historical Quarterly* 18 (1987): 157–76.

———. "The Trouble with Wilderness; or, Getting Back to the Wrong Nature." In *Uncommon Ground: Toward Reinventing Nature,* edited by William Cronon, 69–90. New York: W. W. Norton, 1995.

———, ed. *Uncommon Ground: Toward Reinventing Nature.* New York: W. W. Norton, 1995.

Cummings, Byron. *The Discovery of Rainbow Bridge, the Natural Bridges of Utah, and the Discovery of Betatakin.* Tucson, Ariz.: Cummings Publication Council, 1959.

———. "Early Days in Utah." In *So Live the Works of Men: Seventieth Anniversary Volume Honoring Edgar Lee Hewett,* edited by Donald D. Brand and Fred E. Harvey. Albuquerque: University of New Mexico Press, 1939.

———. "The Great Natural Bridges of Utah." In *The Discovery of Rainbow Bridge, the Natural Bridges of Utah, and the Discovery of Betatakin.* Tucson, Ariz.: Cummings Publication Council, 1959. This essay first appeared in *First Archaeological Number, Bulletin of the University of Utah* 3, no. 3 (1910).

———. *Indians I Have Known.* Tucson: Arizona Silhouettes, 1952.

———. "Kivas of the San Juan Drainage." *American Anthropologist* 17, no. 2 (1915): 272–82.

———. "Sand Paintings in State Museum." *Kiva* 1, no. 7 (1936): 2.

Davis, Ronald L. *John Ford: Hollywood's Old Master.* Norman: University of Oklahoma Press, 1995.

Deloria, Philip Joseph. *Playing Indian.* New Haven, Conn.: Yale University Press, 1998.

Deloria, Vine, Jr. *Red Earth, White Lies: Native Americans and the Myth of Scientific Fact.* New York: Scribner, 1995.

Denevan, William M. "The Pristine Myth: The Landscape of the Americas in 1492." *Annals of the Association of American Geographers* 82, no. 3 (1992): 369–85.

Denning, Michael. *Mechanic Accents: Dime Novels and Working-Class Culture in America.* London: Verso, 1987.

Dilworth, Leah. *Imagining Indians in the Southwest: Persistent Visions of a Primitive Past.* Washington, D.C.: Smithsonian Institution Press, 1996.

Dixon, Winifred Hawkridge. *Westward Hoboes: Ups and Downs of Frontier Motorings.* New York: Charles Scribner's Sons, 1923.

Douglass, William Boone. *Outline of the Ancestry and Life of Daniel Boone.* Washington, D.C.: Boone Family Association, 1952.

Dunlay, Tom. *Kit Carson and the Indians.* Lincoln: University of Nebraska Press, 2000.

Eckstein, Arthur M. "Darkening Ethan: John Ford's *The Searchers* (1956) from Novel to Screenplay to Screen." *Cinema Journal* 38, no. 1 (1998): 3–24.

Ellwood, Robert. *The Politics of Myth: A Study of C. G. Jung, Mircea Eliade, and Joseph Campbell.* Albany: State University of New York Press, 1999.

Eyman, Scott. *Print the Legend: The Life and Times of John Ford.* Baltimore: Johns Hopkins University Press, 2001.

Faris, James C. *Navajo and Photography: A Critical History of the Representation of an American People.* Albuquerque: University of New Mexico Press, 1996.

Farley, G. M. *The Many Faces of Zane Grey.* Flagstaff, Ariz.: Silver Springs Publishing, 1993.

Farmer, Jared. *Glen Canyon Dammed: Inventing Lake Powell and the Canyon Country.* Tucson: University of Arizona Press, 1999.

Fishler, Stanley A. *In the Beginning: A Navaho Creation Myth.* Anthropological Papers, No. 13. Salt Lake City: Department of Anthropology, University of Utah, 1953.

Folsom, James K., ed. *The Western: A Collection of Critical Essays.* Englewood Cliffs, N.J.: Prentice-Hall, 1979.

Ford, Dan. *Pappy: The Life of John Ford.* Englewood Cliffs, N.J.: Prentice-Hall, 1979.

Forman, Frieda Johles, and Caoran Sowton. *Taking Our Time: Feminist Perspectives on Temporality.* Oxford, UK: Pergamon Press, 1989.

Foucault, Michel. *The Archaeology of Knowledge and the Discourse on Language.* Translated by S. M. Sheridan Smith. New York: Pantheon Books, 1972.

———. *The Birth of the Clinic.* Translated by S. M. Sheridan Smith. New York: Vintage, 1994.

———. *The Order of Things.* New York: Vintage, 1970.

Fowler, Don D. *A Laboratory for Anthropology: The American Southwest, 1846–1930.* Albuquerque: University of New Mexico Press, 2000.

Frantz, Joe B., and Julian Ernest Choate, Jr. *The American Cowboy: The Myth and the Reality.* Norman: University of Oklahoma Press, 1955.

Fraser, George C. *Journeys in the Canyon Lands of Utah and Arizona, 1914–1916,* edited by Frederick H. Swanson. Tucson: University of Arizona Press, 2005.

Gaberscek, Carlos. *Il West Di John Ford.* Tavagnacco: Arti Grafiche Friulane, 1994.

Gero, Joan M. "Gender Bias in Archaeology: A Cross-Cultural Perspective." In *The Socio-Politics of Archaeology,* edited by Joan M. Gero, David M. Lacy, and Michael L. Blakey, 51–57. Amherst, Mass.: Department of Anthropology, University of Massachusetts, 1983.

Gillmor, Frances, and Louisa Wade Wetherill. *Traders to the Navajo.* Albuquerque: University of New Mexico Press, 1934.

Gilpin, Dennis. "Early Navajo Occupation West of the Chuska Mountains." In *Archaeological Concepts of Navajo Origins,* edited by Ronald H. Towner. Salt Lake City: University of Utah Press, 1996.

Goetzmann, William. *New Lands, New Men: America and the Second Great Age of Discovery.* New York: Penguin, 1986.

Gómez, Arthur R. *Quest for the Golden Circle: The Four Corners and the Metropolitan West, 1945–1970.* Albuquerque: University of New Mexico Press, 1994.

Goodman, Audrey. *Translating Southwestern Landscapes: The Making of an Anglo Literary Region.* Tucson: University of Arizona Press, 2002.

Gottlieb, Robert. *Forcing the Spring: The Transformation of the American Environmental Movement.* Washington, D.C.: Island Press, 1993.

Gould, Stephen. *Time's Arrow, Time's Cycle: Myth and Metaphor in the Discovery of Geological Time.* Cambridge, Mass.: Harvard University Press, 1987.

Graham, Don. "Western Movies since 1960." In *A Literary History of the American West,* edited by J. Golden Taylor, 1256–62. Fort Worth: Texas Christian University Press.

Gregory, Herbert E. *The Navajo Country: A Geographic and Hydrologic Reconnaissance of Parts of Arizona, New Mexico, and Utah.* Vol. 380, Water Supply Papers. Washington, D.C.: Government Printing Office, 1916.

Grey, Zane. *Blue Feather, and Other Stories.* New York: Harper, 1961.

———. "Breaking Through: The Story of My Own Life." *America Magazine,* July 1924, 11–13, 76–78.

———. *Captives of the Desert.* New York: Grosset and Dunlap, 1952.

———. *The Heritage of the Desert.* New York: HarperPaperbacks, 1910.

———. *The Last of the Plainsmen.* 2nd ed. New York: Grosset and Dunlap, 1911.

———. "My Own Life." In *Zane Grey, the Man and His Work,* 1–18. New York: Harper and Brothers, 1928.

———. "Nonnezoshe." In *Tales of Lonely Trails,* 1–17. New York: Harper and Brothers, 1922. Previously published as *Nonnezoshe: The Rainbow Bridge,* Tempe: Arizona Historical Foundation, 1915.

———. *The Rainbow Trail.* New York: Harper Paperbacks, 1990.

———. *Riders of the Purple Sage.* New York: HarperPaperbacks, 1992.

———. *Roping Lions in the Grand Canyon.* Zane Grey Books for Boys. New York: Grosset and Dunlap, 1922. Simultaneously published in *Tales of Lonely Trails,* 61–183. New York: Harper and Brothers, 1922.

———. *The Secret of Quaking Asp Cabin and Other Stories.* New York: Pocket Books, 1983.

———. *Tales of Lonely Trails.* New York: Harper and Brothers, 1922.

———. *The Vanishing American.* New York: HarperPaperbacks, 1991.

———. "What the Open Means to Me." In *Zane Grey, the Man and His Work,* 34–48. New York: Harper and Brothers, 1928.

Grey, Zane, and Dolly Grey. "The Letters of Dolly and Zane Grey." *The Missouri Review* 18, no. 2 (1995): 115–76.

Gruber, Frank. *Zane Grey.* New York: World Publishing, 1970.

Guha, Ramachandra. "Radical American Environmentalism and Wilderness Critique." In *The Great New Wilderness Debate,* edited by J. Baird Callicott and Michael P. Nelson, 231–45. Athens: University of Georgia Press, 1998.

Gutiérrez, David. "Charles Fletcher Lummis and the Orientalization of New Mexico." In *Nuevomexicano Cultural Legacy: Forms, Agency, Discourse,* edited by Francisco Lomeli, Victor Sorrell, and Genaro Padilla. Albuquerque: University of New Mexico Press, 2002.

Hall, Ansel Franklin. *General Report on the Rainbow Bridge—Monument Valley Expedition of 1933.* Berkeley: University of California Press, 1934.

Hall, Stuart. "The Work of Representation." In *Representation: Cultural Representations and Signifying Practices,* edited by Stuart Hall, 13–74. London: Sage, 1997.

Harmon, David. "Cultural Diversity, Human Subsistence, and the National Park Ideal." In *The Great New Wilderness Debate,* edited by J. Baird Callicott and Michael P. Nelson, 217–30. Athens: University of Georgia Press, 1998.

Harrison, Edith S. "Women in Navajo Myth: A Study in the Symbolism of Matriliny." Ph.D. diss., University of Massachusetts, 1973.

Harvey, David. *The Condition of Postmodernity.* Oxford: Basil Blackwell, 1989.

———. *Justice, Nature, and the Geography of Difference.* Malden, Mass.: Blackwell, 1996.

Harvey, Mark. "Echo Park, Glen Canyon, and the Postwar Wilderness Movement." *Pacific Historical Review* (February 1991): 43–67.

———. *A Symbol of Wilderness: Echo Park and the American Conservation Movement.* Albuquerque: University of New Mexico Press, 1994.

Harvey, Thomas J. "The Storehouse of Unlived Years: Producing the Space of the Old West in Modern America." Ph.D. diss., University of Utah, 2004.

Hassell, Hank. *Rainbow Bridge.* Logan: Utah State University Press, 1999.

Haycox, Ernest. "Stage to Lordsburg." In *The Old West in Fiction,* ed. Irvin R. Blacker. New York: Ivan Obolensky, 1937.

Hays, Samuel P. *Beauty, Health, and Permanence: Environmental Politics in the United States, 1955–1985.* New York: Cambridge University Press, 1987.

———. *Conservation and the Gospel of Efficiency.* Cambridge, Mass.: Harvard University Press, 1959.

———. *The Response to Industrialism 1885–1914.* The Chicago History of American Civilization. Chicago: University of Chicago Press, 1969.

Hewett, Edgar L. *Circular Relating to Historic and Prehistoric Ruins of the Southwest and Their Preservation.* Washington, D.C.: Government Printing Office, 1904.

Higham, John. "The Reorientation of American Culture in the 1890's." In *The Origins of Modern Consciousness,* edited by John Weiss, 25–48. Detroit: Wayne State University Press, 1965.

Hinsley, Curtis M. "Authoring Authenticity." *Journal of the Southwest* 32 (1990): 462–73.

———. "Revising and Revisioning the History of Archaeology: Reflection on Region and Context." In *Tracing Archaeology's Past: The Historiography of Archaeology,* edited by Andrews L. Christenson, 79–96. Carbondale: Southern Illinois University, 1989.

Holiday, John. *A Navajo Legacy: The Life and Teachings of John Holiday.* Edited by Robert McPherson. Norman: University of Oklahoma Press, 2005.

Howard, Kathleen L., and Diana F. Pardue. *Inventing the Southwest: The Fred Harvey Company and Native American Art.* Flagstaff, Ariz.: Northland Publishing, 1996.

Howe, Daniel Walker. "The Market Revolution and the Shaping of Identity in Whig-Jacksonian America." In *The Market Revolution in America: Social and Religious Expressions,* edited by Melvyn Stokes and Stephen Conway, 259–81. Charlottesville: University Press of Virginia, 1996.

Hughes, Robert. *Nothing If Not Critical: Selected Essays on Art and Artists.* New York: Penguin Books, 1990.

Hundley, Norris. *Water and the West: The Colorado River Compact and the Politics of Water in the American West.* Berkeley: University of California Press, 1975.

Hurst, David. *Skull Wars: Kennewick, Archaeology, and the Battle for Native American Identity.* New York: Basic Books, 2000.

Hyde, Anne Farrar. *An American Vision: Far Western Landscape and National Culture, 1820–1920.* New York: New York University Press, 1990.

Jackson, Carlton. *Zane Grey.* Boston: Twayne, 1989.

Jacobson, Michael F. *Marketing Madness: A Survival Guide for a Consumer Society.* Boulder, Colo.: Westview, 1995.

Jakle, John A. "Touring by Automobile in 1932: The American West as Stereotype." *Annals of Tourism Research* 8, no. 4 (1981): 534–49.

Janetski, Joel C. "150 Years of Utah Archaeology." *Utah Historical Quarterly* 65 (1997): 100–33.

Jett, Stephen C. "The Great Race to Discover Rainbow Natural Bridge." *Kiva* 58, no. 1 (1992): 3–66.

———. *Tourism in the Navajo Country: Resources and Planning.* Window Rock, Ariz.: Navajo Tribe, 1966.

Johnson, Christopher G. "The Significance of Rainbow Bridge: From Prehistory to the Present." M.A. thesis, Northern Arizona University, 1996.

Judd, Neil M. "Byron Cummings, Archeologist and Explorer." *Science* 120, no. 3115 (1954), 407–408.

———. "The Discovery of Rainbow Bridge." In *The Discovery of Rainbow Bridge, the Natural Bridges of Utah, and the Discovery of Betatakin.* Tucson, Ariz.: Cummings Publication Council, 1959.

———. *Men Met along the Trail: Adventures in Archaeology.* Norman: University of Oklahoma Press, 1968.

———. "Pioneering in Southwestern Archeology." In *For the Dean: Essays in Honor of Byron Cummings on His Eighty-Ninth Birthday, September 20, 1950,* edited by Erik K. Reed and Dale S. King, 11–27. Tucson, Ariz.: Hohokam Museum Association, 1950.

Kant, Candace C. *Zane Grey's Arizona.* Flagstaff, Ariz.: Northland Press, 1984.

Kasson, John F. *Houdini, Tarzan, and the Perfect Man: The White Male Body and the Challenge of Modernity in America.* New York: Hill and Yang, 2001.

Kasson, Joy S. *Buffalo Bill's Wild West: Celebrity, Memory, and Popular History.* New York: Hill and Wang, 2000.

Kay, Jane Holtz. *Asphalt Nation: How the Automobile Took Over America and How We Can Take It Back.* New York: Crown, 1997.

Kehoe, Alice Beck. "Contextualizing Archaeology." In *Tracing Archeology's Past: The Historiography of Archaeology,* edited by Andrew L. Christenson, 97–106. Carbondale: Southern Illinois University Press, 1989.

———. *The Land of Prehistory: A Critical History of American Archaeology.* New York: Routledge, 1991.

Keller, Robert H., and Michael F. Turek. *American Indians and National Parks.* Tucson: University of Arizona Press, 1998.

Kelley, Klara Bonsack, and Harris Francis. *Navajo Sacred Places.* Bloomington: Indiana University Press, 1994.

Kelly, Charles. "Chief Hoskaninni." *Utah Historical Quarterly* 21 (1953): 219–26.

———. "Review: Land of Room Enough and Time Enough." *Utah Historical Quarterly* 2, no. 2 (1954): 175.

Kelly, Isabel T. *Southern Paiute Ethnography,* Anthropological Papers 69. Salt Lake City: University of Utah Press, 1965.

Kennedy, David M. *Freedom from Fear: The American People in Depression and War, 1929–1945.* New York: Oxford University Press, 1999.

Kerr, Walter A. "Byron Cummings, Classical Scholar and Father of University Athletics." *Utah Historical Quarterly* 23, no. 2 (1955): 145–50.

Klein, Kerwin Lee. *Frontiers of the Historical Imagination: Narrating the European Conquest of Native America, 1890–1990.* Berkeley: University of California Press, 1997.

Kluckhohn, Clyde. *Beyond the Rainbow.* Boston: Christopher Publishing House, 1933.

———. *To the Foot of the Rainbow: A Tale of Twenty-Five Hundred Miles of Wandering on Horseback through the Southwest Enchanted Land.* New York: Century Co., 1927.

Kluckhohn, Clyde, and Dorothea Leighton. *The Navaho.* Cambridge, Mass.: Harvard University Press, 1974.

Knipmeyer, James. "Did Prospectors See Rainbow Bridge before 1909?" *Utah Historical Quarterly* 77, no. 2 (2009): 166–89.

Kolodny, Annette. *The Land Before Her: Fantasy and Experience of the American Frontiers 1630–1860.* Chapel Hill: University of North Carolina Press, 1984.

———. *The Lay of the Land: Metaphor as Experience and History in American Life and Letters.* Chapel Hill: University of North Carolina Press, 1975.

Kroes, Rob. "American Empire and Cultural Imperialism." In *The Ambiguous Legacy: U.S. Foreign Policy in the American Century,* edited by Michael J. Hogan, 500–20. New York: Cambridge University Press, 1991.

Lamphere, Louise. "Symbolic Elements in Navajo Ritual." *Southwestern Journal of Anthropology* 25 (1975): 279–305.

Lasch, Christopher. *The Culture of Narcissism: American Life in the Age of Diminishing Expectations.* New York: W. W. Norton, 1978.

———. *The True and Only Heaven: Progress and Its Critics.* New York: W. W. Norton, 1991.

Lasky, Jesse L., Jr. *Whatever Happened to Hollywood?* New York: Funk and Wagnalls, 1973.

Leach, William. *Land of Desire: Merchants, Power, and the Rise of a New American Culture.* New York: Pantheon, 1993.

Lears, T.J. Jackson. *No Place of Grace: Antimodernism and the Transformation of American Culture 1880–1920.* New York: Pantheon Books, 1981.

Lee, John D. *A Mormon Chronicle: The Diaries of John D. Lee, 1848–1876.* Edited by Juanita Brooks and Robert G. Cleland. San Marino, Calif.: Huntington Library, 1955.

Lee, Ronald Freeman. "The Antiquities Act of 1906." *Journal of the Southwest* 42, no. 2 (2000): 197–269.

Lefebvre, Henri. *The Production of Space.* Translated by Donald Nicholson-Smith. Oxford: Blackwell, 1991.

Levy, Bill. *John Ford: A Bio-Bibliography.* Bio-Bibliographies in the Performing Arts. No. 78. Westport, Conn.: Greenwood, 1998.

Levy, Jarrold E. *In the Beginning: The Navajo Genesis.* Berkeley: University of California Press, 1998.

Linford, Laurance D. *Navajo Places: History, Legend, Landscape.* Salt Lake City: University of Utah Press, 2000.

Liu, Tessie P. "Race and Gender in the Politics of Group Formation: A Comment on Notions of Multiculturalism." *Frontiers: A Journal of Women's Studies* 12, no. 2 (1992): 155–65.

Louter, David B. "Windshield Wilderness: The Automobile and the Meaning of National Parks in Washington State." Ph.D. diss., University of Washington, 2000.

Luckert, Karl. *Navajo Mountain and Rainbow Bridge Religion.* Flagstaff: Northern Arizona University, 1977.

MacCannell, Dean. *The Tourist: A New Theory of the Leisure Class.* Berkeley: University of California Press, 1989.

Madsen, Steven K. *Exploring Desert Stone: John N. Macomb's 1859 Expedition to the Canyonlands of the Colorado.* Logan: Utah State University Press, 2010.

Massey, Doreen B. *Space, Place and Gender.* Minneapolis: University of Minnesota Press, 1994.

May, Stephen J. *Maverick Heart: The Further Adventures of Zane Grey.* Athens: Ohio University Press, 2000.

McBride, Joseph. *Searching for John Ford: A Life.* New York: St. Martin's Press, 2001.

McClintock, Anne. *Imperial Leather: Race, Gender, and Sexuality in the Colonial Contest.* New York: Routledge, 1995.

McNitt, Frank. *Richard Wetherill: Anasazi.* Albuquerque: University of New Mexico Press, 1957.

McPherson, Robert S. *A History of San Juan County.* Salt Lake City: Utah State Historical Society, San Juan County Commission, 1995.

———. "Naalyéhé Bá-Hooghan—House of Merchandise: The Navajo Trading Post as an Institution of Cultural Change, 1900–1930." In *American Nations: Encounters in Indian Country, 1850 to the Present,* edited by Frederick E. Hoxie, 64–93. New York: Routledge, 2001.

———. *Navajo Land, Navajo Culture: The Utah Experience in the Twentieth Century.* Norman: University of Oklahoma Press, 2001.

———. *The Northern Navajo Frontier, 1860–1900: Expansion through Adversity.* Albuquerque: University of New Mexico, 1988.

———. *Sacred Land Sacred View: Navajo Perceptions of the Four Corners Area.* Provo, Utah: Brigham Young University, 1992.

Meskell, Lynn. "Archaeology Matters." Introduction to *Archaeology Under Fire: Nationalism, Politics, and Heritage in the Eastern Mediterranean and Middle East,* edited by Lynn Meskell. London: Routledge, 1998.

Messaris, Paul. *Visual Persuasion: The Role of Images in Advertising.* Thousand Oaks, Calif.: Sage, 1997.

Miller, Perry. *Nature's Nation.* Cambridge, Mass.: Harvard University Press, 1967.

Mitchell, Lee Clark. *Westerns: Making the Man in Fiction and Film.* Chicago: University of Chicago Press, 1996.

———. *Witnesses to a Vanishing America: The Nineteenth-Century Response.* Princeton, N.J.: Princeton University Press, 1981.

Moon, Samuel. *Tall Sheep: Harry Goulding, Monument Valley Trader.* Norman: University of Oklahoma Press, 1992.

Mullin, Molly H. *Culture in the Marketplace: Gender, Art, and Value in the American Southwest.* Durham, N.C.: Duke University Press, 2001.

Nash, Gerald D. *The American West in the Twentieth Century: A Short History of an Urban Oasis.* Albuquerque: University of New Mexico Press, 1973.

Nash, Roderick. *Wilderness and the American Mind.* New Haven, Conn.: Yale University Press, 1967.

Neumann, Mark. "The Commercial Canyon: Culturally Constructing the 'Other' in the Theater of the West." In *Discovered Country: Tourism and Survival in the American West,* edited by Scott Norris, 196–209. Albuquerque, N.M.: Stone Ladder Press, 1999.

———. *On the Rim: Looking for the Grand Canyon.* Minneapolis: University of Minnesota Press, 1999.

Nicholas, Liza. "1–800–Sundance: Identity, Nature, and Play in the West." In *Imagining the Big Open: Nature, Identity, and Play in the New West,* edited by Liza Nicholas, Elaine Bapis, and Thomas J. Harvey, 259–71. Salt Lake City: University of Utah Press, 2003.

———. *Becoming Western: Stories of Culture and Identity in the Cowboy State.* Lincoln: University of Nebraska Press, 2006.

Nichols, Dudley, and John Ford. *Stagecoach.* New York: Simon and Schuster, 1971.

Nichols, Tad. *Glen Canyon: Images of a Lost World.* Santa Fe: Museum of New Mexico, 1999.

Nicholson, Marjorie Hope. *Mountain Gloom and Mountain Glory: The Development of the Aesthetics of the Infinite.* New York: W. W. Norton, 1959.

Nordenskiöld, Gustaf. *The Cliff Dwellers of the Mesa Verde, Southwestern Colorado; Their Pottery and Implements.* Translated by D. Lloyd Morgan. Stockholm: P.A. Norstedt and söner, 1895.

Nugent, Frank S. *The Searchers, Revised and Final Screenplay.* Los Angeles: C. V. Whitney Pictures, 1956.

O'Neill, Colleen. *Working the Navajo Way: Labor and Culture in the Twentieth Century.* Lawrence: University Press of Kansas, 2005.

Padget, Martin. "Travel, Exoticism, and the Writing of Region: Charles Fletcher Lummis and the 'Creation' of the Southwest." *Journal of the Southwest* 37, no. 3 (1995): 421–49.

Parsons, Talcott, and Evon Z. Vogt. "Clyde Kay Maben Kluckhohn 1905–1960." *American Anthropologist* 64 (1962): 140–61.

Patterson, Thomas C. *Toward a Social History of Archaeology in the United States.* Fort Worth, Tex.: Harcourt Brace College Publishers, 1995.

Pauly, Thomas H. *Zane Grey: His Life, His Adventures, His Women.* Urbana: University of Illinois Press, 2005.

Pearson, Byron E. *Still the River Runs: Congress, the Sierra Club, and the Fight to Save the Grand Canyon.* Tucson: University of Arizona Press, 2002.

Pells, Richard H. *Radical Visions and American Dreams: Cultural and Social Thought in the Depression Years.* New York: Harper and Row, 1973.

Pfeiffer, Charles G. *The Surprise Valleys of Zane Grey.* Columbia, S.C.: self-published, 1990.

Pinxten, Rik, Ingrid vanDooren, and Frank Harvey. *The Anthropology of Space: Exploration into the Natural Philosophy and Semantics of the Navajo.* Philadelphia: University of Pennsylvania Press, 1983.

Pomeroy, Earl. *In Search of the Golden West: The Tourist in Western America.* New York: Alfred A. Knopf, 1957.

Porter, Eliot, and David Brower. *The Place No One Knew: Glen Canyon on the Colorado.* San Francisco: Peregrine Smith Books, 1968.

Pratt, Mary Louise. *Imperial Eyes: Travel Writing and Transculturation.* New York: Routledge, Chapman, and Hall, 1992.

Price, Jennifer. *Flight Maps: Adventures in Nature in Modern America.* New York: Basic Books, 1999.

Prudden, T. Mitchell. "The Prehistoric Ruins of the San Juan Watershed in Utah, Arizona, Colorado, and New Mexico." *American Anthropologist,* n.s., 5, no. 2 (1903): 224–88.

Reisner, Marc. *Cadillac Desert: The American West and Its Disappearing Water.* New York: Viking, 1986.

Richardson, Elmo R. "Federal Park Policy in Utah: The Escalante National Monument Controversy of 1935–1940." *Utah Historical Quarterly* 33, no. 2 (1965): 109–33.

Richardson, Gladwell. *Navajo Trader.* Tucson: University of Arizona Press, 1986.

Rider, Rowland W., and Deirdre Murray Paulsen. *The Roll Away Saloon.* Logan: Utah State University Press, 1985.

Riley, Michael J. "Trapped in the History of Film: Racial Conflict and Allure in *The Vanishing American.*" In *Hollywood's Indian: The Portrayal of the Native American in Films,* edited by Peter C. Rollins and John E. O'Connor, 58–72. Lexington: University Press of Kentucky, 1998.

Robbins, L. H. "His Many Readers." In *Zane Grey, the Man and His Work,* 51–54. New York: Harper and Brothers, 1928.

Rome, Adam. *Bulldozer in the Countryside: Suburban Sprawl and the Rise of American Environmentalism.* New York: Cambridge University Press, 2001.

Roosevelt, Nicholas, and James E. Babbitt. "Across the Painted Desert: Nicholas Roosevelt in Northern Arizona, 1913." *Journal of Arizona History* 28, no. 3 (1987): 261–82.

Roosevelt, Theodore. *A Book-Lover's Holiday in the Open.* New York: Scribner's Sons, 1922.

Rosaldo, Renato. "Imperialist Nostalgia." *Representations,* no. 26 (1989): 107–22.

Rose, Gillian. *Feminism and Geography: The Limits of Geographical Knowledge.* Cambridge, Mass.: Polity Press, 1993.

Rothman, Hal K. *Devil's Bargains: Tourism in the Twentieth-Century American West.* Lawrence: University Press of Kansas, 1998.

———. *The Greening of a Nation? Environmentalism in the United States since 1945.* Fort Worth, Tex.: Harcourt Brace College Publishers, 1998.

———. "Ruins, Reputations, and Regulation: Byron Cummings, William B. Douglass, John Wetherill, and the Summer of 1909." *Journal of the Southwest* 35, no. 3 (1993): 318–40.

Rotundo, E. Anthony. *American Manhood: Transformations in Masculinity from the Revolution to the Modern Era.* New York: Basic Books, 1993.

Runte, Alfred. *National Parks: The American Experience.* 3rd ed. Lincoln: University of Nebraska Press, 1997.

Rydell, Robert. *All the World's a Fair: Visions of Empire at the American International Expositions, 1876–1916.* Chicago: University of Chicago Press, 1984.

Said, Edward. *Culture and Imperialism.* New York: Vintage, 1993.

———. "Invention, Memory, and Place." *Critical Inquiry* 26, no. 2 (2000): 175–92.

———. *Orientalism.* New York: Vintage, 1978.

Sale, Kirkpatrick. *The Green Revolution: The American Environmental Movement, 1962–1992.* New York: Hill and Wang, 1993.

Sanders, Jeffrey Mark. "Tribal and National Parks on American Indian Lands." Ph.D. diss., University of Arizona, 1989.

Sandweiss, Martha A. *Print the Legend: Photography and the American West.* New Haven, Conn.: Yale University Press, 2002.

Sayle, W. D. *A Trip to the Rainbow Arch.* Santa Fe, N.M.: Rydal Press, 1999.

Schaafsma, Curtis F. *Apaches De Navajo: Seventeenth-Century Navajos in the Chama Valley of New Mexico.* Salt Lake City: University of Utah Press, 2002.

Schama, Simon. *Landscape and Memory.* New York: Alfred A. Knopf, 1995.

Schumpeter, Joseph. *Capitalism, Socialism, and Democracy.* New York: Harper and Row, 1942.

Scott, Kenneth W. "The Heritage of the Desert: Zane Grey Discovers the West." *Markham Review* 2, no. 2 (1970): 10–14.

Sears, John F. *Sacred Places: American Tourist Attractions in the Nineteenth Century.* New York: Oxford University Press, 1989.

Sellers, Charles. *The Market Revolution: Jacksonian America, 1815–1846.* New York: Oxford University Press, 1991.

Shaffer, Marguerite S. *See America First: Tourism and National Identity, 1880–1940.* Washington, D.C.: Smithsonian Institution Press, 2001.

Shaw, Megan, and Rick Prelinger. "Freeway Landscapes and Timescapes." In *Signs of Life in the U.S.A.: Readings on Popular Culture for Writers,* edited by Sonia Maasik, 790–96. Boston: Bedford/St. Martin's, 2000.

Shepard, Paul, Jr. "The Cross Valley Syndrome." *Landscape* 10, no. 3 (1961): 4–8.

Shepardson, Mary, and Blowden Hammon. *The Navajo Mountain Community.* Berkeley: University of California Press, 1970.

Silberman, Neil Asher. *Between Past and Present: Archaeology, Ideology, and Nationalism in the Modern Middle East.* New York: Henry Holt, 1989.

———. "Promised Lands and Chosen Peoples: The Politics and Poetics of Archaeological Narrative." In *Nationalism, Politics, and the Practice of Archaeology,* edited by P. L. Kohl and C. Fawcett, 249–62. Cambridge, U.K.: Cambridge University Press, 1995.

Simmon, Scott. *The Invention of the Western Film: A Cultural History of the Genre's First Half-Century.* Cambridge, U.K.: Cambridge University Press, 2003.

Singal, Daniel Joseph. "Towards a Definition of Modernism." *American Quarterly* 39 (1987): 7–26.

Slotkin, Richard. *Gunfighter Nation: The Myth of the Frontier in Twentieth-Century America.* Norman: University of Oklahoma Press, 1993.

———. *Regeneration through Violence: The Mythology of the American Frontier, 1600–1860.* Hanover, N.H.: Wesleyan University Press, 1973.

Smith, Henry Nash. *Virgin Land: The American West as Symbol and Myth.* 1978 ed. Cambridge, Mass.: Harvard University Press, 1978.

Snead, James E. "Lessons from the Ages: Archaeology and the Construction of Cultural Identity in the American Southwest " *Journal of the Southwest* 44, no. 1 (2002): 17–34.

———. *Ruins and Rivals: The Making of Southwest Archaeology.* Tucson: University of Arizona Press, 2001.

Soja, Edward W. *Postmodern Geographies: The Reassertion of Space in Critical Social Theory.* London: Verso, 1989.

———. *Thirdspace: Journeys to Los Angeles and Other Real-and-Imagined Places.* Cambridge, Mass.: Blackwell, 1996.

Spence, Mark David. *Dispossessing the Wilderness: Indian Removal and the Making of the National Parks.* New York: Oxford University Press, 1999.

Sproul, David Kent. "A Bridge between Cultures: An Administrative History of Rainbow Bridge National Monument." Washington, D.C.: Department of the Interior, 2001.

Steen, Charlie R. "The Natural Bridges of White Canyon: A Diary of H. L. A. Culmer, 1905." *Utah Historical Quarterly* 40, no. 1 (1972): 55–87.

Stegner, Wallace. "The Marks of Human Passage." In *This Is Dinosaur: Echo Park Country and Its Magic Rivers,* edited by Wallace Stegner, 3–17. New York: Knopf, 1955.

Strong, Douglas H. *Dreamers and Defenders: American Conservationists.* Lincoln: University of Nebraska Press, 1971.

Sutter, Paul S. *Driven Wild: How the Fight against Automobiles Launched the Modern Wilderness Movement.* Seattle: University of Washington Press, 2002.

Swanson, Frederick H. *David Rust: A Life in the Canyons.* Salt Lake City: University of Utah Press, 2008.

Tanner, Clara Lee. "Byron Cummings, 1860–1954." *Kiva* 20, no. 1 (1954): 1–20.

Tatum, Stephen. "The Problem of the 'Popular' in the New Western History." *Arizona Quarterly* 53, no. 2 (1997): 153–90.

Tavernier, Bertrand. "Notes of a Press Attache: John Ford in Paris, 1966." *Film Comment* 30, no. 4 (1994): 66–75.

Thomas, Jeffery Allen. "Promoting the Southwest: Edgar L. Hewett, Anthropology, Archeology, and the Santa Fe Style." Ph.D. diss., Texas Tech University, 1999.

Thompson, Mark. *American Character: The Curious Life of Charles Fletcher Lummis and the Rediscovery of the Southwest.* New York: Arcade, 2001.

Thompson, Raymond Harris. "Edgar Lee Hewett and the Political Process." *Journal of the Southwest* 42, no. 2 (2000): 272–318.

Timmerman, Carolyn. "From G-R-A-Y TO G-R-E-Y." Special feature no. 4, www.zanegreysws.org.

Tompkins, Jane. *West of Everything: The Inner Life of Westerns.* New York: Oxford University Press, 1992.

Torgovnick, Marianna. *Gone Primitive: Savage Intellects, Modern Lives.* Chicago: University of Chicago Press, 1990.

Towner, Ronald H., ed. *The Archaeology of Navajo Origins.* Salt Lake City: University of Utah Press, 1996.

———. *Defending the Dinétah: Pueblitos in the Ancestral Homeland.* Salt Lake City: University of Utah Press, 2003.

Towner, Ronald H., and Jeffrey S. Dean. "Questions and Problems in Pre–Fort Sumner Navajo Archaeology." In *Archaeological Concepts of Navajo Origins,* edited by Ronald H. Towner, 3–18. Salt Lake City: University of Utah Press, 1996.

Trachtenberg, Alan. *The Incorporation of America: Culture and Society in the Gilded Age.* New York: Hill and Wang, 1982.

Trigger, Bruce G. *A History of Archaeological Thought.* Cambridge, U.K.: Cambridge University Press, 1989.

———. "Romanticism, Nationalism, and Archaeology." In *Nationalism, Politics and the Practice of Archaeology,* edited by P. L. Kohl. Cambridge, U.K.: Cambridge University Press, 1995.

Tuan, Yi-fu. *Topophilia: A Study of Environmental Perception, Attitudes, and Values.* Englewood Cliffs, N.J.: Prentice Hall, 1974.

Turgeon, Laurier. "The Tale of the Kettle: Odyssey of an Intercultural Object." *Ethnohistory* 44, no. 1 (1997): 1–29.

Turner, Frederick Jackson. *The Frontier in American History.* 2nd printing. Tucson: University of Arizona Press, 1992.

Tuska, Jon. *The Filming of the West.* New York: Doubleday, 1976.

————. "The Filming of the West." *Western Review* 4 (May 1991).

Twitchell, James. *Twenty Ads That Shook the World: The Century's Most Groundbreaking Advertising and How It Changed Us All.* New York: Three Rivers Press, 2000.

Van Valkenburgh, Richard. *Dine Bikeyah.* Window Rock, Ariz.: U.S. Department of the Interior, 1940.

Virilio, Paul. *The Lost Dimension.* Translated by Daniel Moshenberg. New York: Semiotext, 1991.

Walters, Harry. *A New Perspective on Navajo Prehistory.* Navajo Community College Publication. Shiprock, N.M., n.d.

Watson, Editha L. *Navajo Sacred Places.* Window Rock, Ariz.: Navajo Tribal Museum, 1964.

Weigle, Marta. "Southwest Lures: Innocents Detoured, Incensed Determined." *Journal of the Southwest* 32 (1990): 499–540.

Weigle, Marta, and Barbara A. Babcock. *The Great Southwest of the Fred Harvey Company and the Santa Fe Railway.* Phoenix, Ariz.: Heard Museum, 1996.

Wetherill, Benjamin Alfred. *The Wetherills of the Mesa Verde.* Lincoln: University of Nebraska Press, 1977.

Wetherill, John. "Notes on the Discovery of Betatakin." In *The Discovery of Rainbow Bridge, the Natural Bridges of Utah, and the Discovery of Betatakin,* 44–45. Tucson, Ariz.: Cummings Publication Council, 1959.

Wetherill, Louisa Wade. "Creation of Burro." *Kiva* 12, no. 2 (1947): 26–28.

————. "Some Navajo Recipes." *Kiva* 12, no. 1 (1946): 5–6.

————. "The Woman Whose Nose Was Cut Off Twelve Times or the Woman Who Controls the Weather." *Kiva* 12, no. 2 (1947): 25–26.

Wetherill, Louisa Wade, and Harvey Leake. *Wolfkiller: Wisdom from a Nineteenth-Century Navajo Shepherd.* Salt Lake City, Utah: Gibbs Smith, 2007.

Wheeler, Joseph Lawrence. "Zane Grey's Impact on American Life and Letters." Ph.D. diss., George Peabody College for Teachers, 1975.

White, Richard. "American Environmental History: The Development of a New Historical Field." *Pacific Historical Review* 54 (1985): 297–335.

————. "'Are You an Environmentalist, or Do You Work for a Living?' Work and Nature." In *Uncommon Ground: Toward Reinventing Nature,* edited by William Cronon, 171–85. New York: W. W. Norton, 1995.

————. "Frederick Jackson Turner and Buffalo Bill." In *The Frontier in American Culture,* edited by James R. Grossman, 6–65. Berkeley: University of California Press, 1994.

————. *The Organic Machine.* New York: Hill and Wang, 1995.

Wiebe, Robert H. *The Search for Order: 1877–1920.* New York: Hill and Wang, 1984.

Willey, Gordon R. *Portraits in American Archaeology: Remembrances of Some Distinguished Americanists.* Albuquerque: University of New Mexico Press, 1988.

Williams, Raymond. *The Country and the City.* London: Hogarth Press, 1973.

————. "Ideas of Nature." In *Problems in Materialism in Culture: Selected Essays,* 67–85. London: NLB, 1980.

————. "Metropolitan Perceptions and the Emergence of Modernism." In *The Politics of Modernism,* 37–48. London: Verso, 1989.

————. *Problems in Materialism and Culture: Selected Essays.* London: NLB, 1980.

Wills, Garry. *John Wayne's America: The Politics of Celebrity.* New York: Simon and Schuster, 1997.

Wilson, Alan. *Navajo Place Names: An Observer's Guide.* Guilford, Conn.: Jeffrey Norton, 1995.

Wilson, Chris. *The Myth of Santa Fe: Creating a Modern Regional Tradition.* Albuquerque: University of New Mexico Press, 1997.

Worster, Donald. *A River Running West: The Life of John Wesley Powell.* New York: Oxford University Press, 2001.

Wrobel, David M. *The End of American Exceptionalism: Frontier Anxiety from the Old West to the New Deal.* Lawrence: University Press of Kansas, 1993.

Wyman, Leland C. *Blessingway.* Tucson: University of Arizona Press, 1970.

————. *Navajo Beautyway: Its Uses, Mythology, Songs, and Geographical Setting.* New York: Pantheon, 1957.

————. *The Sandpaintings of the Kayenta Navajo.* Albuquerque: University of New Mexico Press, 1952.

————. *The Windways of the Navaho.* Colorado Springs, Colo.: Taylor Museum, 1962.

Wyman, Leland C., and Stewart K. Harris. *The Ethnobotany of the Kayenta Navajo: An Analysis of the John and Louisa Wetherill Collection.* Albuquerque: University of New Mexico Press, 1951.

Young, Stewart M. "Statement of Stuart M. Young concerning the Discovery of Rainbow Bridge." In *The Discovery of Rainbow Bridge, the Natural Bridges of Utah, and the Discovery of Betatakin,* 14. Tucson, Ariz.: Cummings Publication Council, 1959.

Zolotow, Maurice. *Shooting Star: A Biography of John Wayne.* New York: Simon and Schuster, 1974.

FILMS

Adventure Bound! Detroit and Chicago, Ford Motor Co., ca. 1933.

Cheyenne Autumn, directed by John Ford, Warner Bros., 1964.

December 7th, directed by John Ford and Gregg Toland, U.S. Navy Department, 1943.

Fort Apache, directed by John Ford, Argosy Pictures, 1948.

Let the River Run, directed by Lili Schad, Glen Canyon Institute, 1997.

My Darling Clementine, directed by John Ford, Twentieth Century Fox, 1946.

The Searchers, directed by John Ford, C.V. Whitney, 1956.

Sergeant Rutledge, directed by John Ford, Warner Bros., 1960.

She Wore a Yellow Ribbon, directed by John Ford, Argosy Pictures, RKO Radio Pictures, 1949.

Stagecoach, directed by John Ford, United Artists, 1939.

The Vanishing American, directed by George B. Seitz, Paramount Pictures, 1925.

Index